D0235270

THE
PAUL HAMLYN
LIBRARY

DONATED BY
THE PAUL HAMLYN
FOUNDATION
TO THE
BRITISH MUSEUM

WITHDRAWN

opened December 2000

CARTHAGE

By the same author

THE NORTH AFRICAN PROVINCES FROM
DIOCLETIAN TO THE VANDAL CONQUEST

CARTHAGE

REVISED EDITION

B. H. Warmington

 *Robert Hale & Company, Publishers*
London

Copyright © B. H. Warmington, 1960 and 1969
First published in Great Britain 1960
Second edition (revised and reset) 1969

SBN 7091 0953 9

Robert Hale & Company
63 Old Brompton Road
London S.W.7

939.73
WAR

PRINTED IN GREAT BRITAIN BY
EBENEZER BAYLIS AND SON, LTD.
THE TRINITY PRESS, WORCESTER, AND LONDON

Contents

Illustrations

MAPS

ACKNOWLEDGEMENTS

Radio Times Hulton Picture Library: 1; Aerofototeca, Ministero de Pubblica Istruzione, Italy: 2; Professors V. Tusa and S. Moscati and the Istituto di Studi del Vicino Oriente, Università di Roma: 3, 4, 12, 13, 16, 17, 30, 31a, 31b; Musée du Bardo, Tunis: 5, 6a, 9, 11, 15, 21, 22, 23, 24, 26, 27, 28a, 29; *L'art à Carthage*, by Max-Pol Fouchet, Editions George Fall, Paris, 1962: 6b, 8, 10; Janet March-Penney: 7; Villa Giulia, Rome: 14; *Carthaginian Gold and Electrum Coins*, by G. K. Jenkins and R. B. Lewis, Royal Numismatic Society, 1963: 18, 20; Service des Antiquites du Maroc: 25; *Essays in Roman Coinage presented to Harold Mattingly*, ed. R. A. G. Carson, Oxford University Press, 1956: 19; *The Phoenicians*, by D. B. Harden, Thames and Hudson, 1962: 32.

Preface

It is many years since a book about ancient Carthage appeared in this country, in spite of the fact that Carthage played a major part in the history of Rome and of the Greek colonies in Sicily. I hope that this attempt to give an account of Carthaginian history and civilization and to describe its position in the ancient Mediterranean world will do something to fill the gap.

The difficulty which faces anyone who tries to write such an account is that he must rely largely on the information provided by the Greek and Roman enemies of Carthage, since nothing survives of the Carthaginians' own literature. It is true that there were several Greek writers who described the history of the wars of Carthage with Rome from a standpoint favourable to the former, but their works are lost, and what we know of them has to be deduced from later writers who used them as a source. Essentially the Carthaginians are portrayed for us by Greeks—for whom they were a people who disputed possession of Sicily—and by Romans—for whom they were the rivals in a struggle for mastery of the western Mediterranean—and it is not surprising that the picture is an extremely hostile one. The task is to separate the truth from the fiction, the legitimate criticism from the tendentious, without indulging in unjustified sentiment in favour of a state which suffered such a cruel end. There is the further point that Carthaginian history is only recorded when it impinges on the history of Rome or of the Greeks in Sicily. However, the information which can be gathered from ancient authors about the general history, institutions, religion, and trade of the Carthaginians can be augmented by the results of the archaeological work which has been done in North Africa over the past fifty years, and especially since 1946. There can be no doubt that as a result of the discoveries and analyses of material which have been made

9

lately, the archaeology of Carthage is entering a new and important phase.

I have sought to combine these two sources of information, while admittedly concentrating on the literary material, which must be the basis of all historical writing. It must be said that in some places the narrative of events is presented as if the facts were certain, which is very far from being the case; almost every important aspect of Carthaginian history has been the subject of several different interpretations by modern scholars. But a discussion of all the problems would have required an apparatus of footnotes and qualifications which would have been out of keeping with the purpose of the book, designed as it is for those who have an interest in the history of antiquity but not a specialized knowledge. Some of the variant interpretations have been briefly mentioned where it seemed essential, and may be found worked out in detail in the books mentioned in the bibliography.

I wish to express my thanks to the Trustees of the Colston Research Fund and to the University of Bristol for financial help towards a visit to Tunisia, and also to the President and officials of the Institut National d'Archéologie et Arts, Tunis, and the Conservateur of the Musée Alaoui, Le Bardo, Tunis, for their assistance.

Bristol   B.H.W.
October 1958

Preface to the Second Edition

Some important archaeological work has been done on Phoenician and Carthaginian sites since the first edition of this book. I have taken the opportunity of a fully revised edition both to rewrite and expand the passages (chiefly in chapters 1, 2 and 6) where new material has made this desirable, and to increase substantially the number of illustrations. This edition also incorporates the minor revisions and the references to the sources which were included in the Pelican edition (1964). An additional bibliography with references to a number of recent publications, primarily of archaeological excavations, has been added.

Bristol   B.H.W.
December 1968

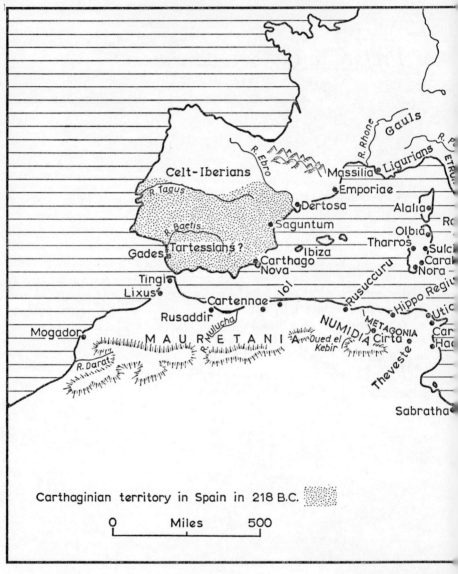

Celt-Iberians

R. Tagus

R. Baetis

Tartessians?

Gades

Tingi

Lixus

Mogador

R. Darat

Rusaddir

R. Mulucha

MAURETANIA

Cartennae

Iol

R. Ebro

Massilia

Emporiae

Dertosa

Saguntum

Ibiza

Carthago
Nova

Rusuccuru

Gauls

Ligurians

R. Rhone

R. P...

ETRU...

Alalia

Olbia

Tharros

R...

Sulc...

Cara...

Nora

Hippo Regi...

*Oued el
Kebir*

NUMIDIA

Cirta

METAGONIA

Uti...

Car...

Ha...

Theveste

Sabratha

Carthaginian territory in Spain in 218 B.C.

0   Miles   500

Cannae

MACEDONIA

eapolis

LUCANIA Tarentum

EPIRUS

LYDIA

Lipara

Panormus

Syracuse

Sparta

Athens

Miletus

RHODES

Salamis

CYPRUS

Al Mina

Ugarit

Aradus

etum

Malta

Paphos

Berytus

Sidon

Tyre

CRETE

Oea

Cyrene

Jerusalem

Ascalon

Lepcis Magna

Alexandria

Garamantes

Arae Philaenorum

Memphis

Eilath

CARTHAGE

I

The Phoenicians and
the Western Mediterranean

THE origin of Carthage is to be found in the cities of Phoenicia on the coasts of Lebanon and Syria, a thousand miles to the east, and its history is that of the only successful expansion of people from the Near East into the western Mediterranean before the conquest of North Africa by the Arabs in the century of Mohammed. The Phoenicians were a people about whom there was a great deal of highly speculative writing in the last century, when because of their reputation for far-flung trading activities, and the difficulties of identifying their manufactures, 'Phoenician influence' was seen in the most unlikely contexts. There are still very serious gaps in our knowledge of Phoenician archaeology, and it is unfortunate that we know more about the Bronze Age in Phoenicia, before about 1200, than we do about the later period in which the Phoenicians sent their traders and colonists to the western Mediterranean. What we do know tends to reduce somewhat their supposed influence in the Mediterranean world, while leaving untouched some real achievements the more impressive because they were accomplished by a very small population.

The Phoenicians[1] inhabited a strip of coast between the sea and the mountains of Lebanon and Galilee. The most thickly settled portion of their territory, between the River Eleutheros in the north and Mt Carmel in the south, was not more than 130 miles in length, but within this narrow stretch of land were five cities of importance; from south to north these were Akko, Tyre, Sidon, Berytus and Byblos. Akko was not as strong as the other cities and alternated for some time between Phoenician and Israelite control, after the latter entered the area about the twelfth century. North of the Eleutheros valley there were some isolated Phoenician settlements, in particular those of Aradus and Ugarit, but none to the north of Mt Kasios.

The coastal fringe of Phoenicia, though narrow, was fertile and well watered, but there is no doubt that it was very early in their history that the Phoenicians turned to trading. They were well situated on the caravan route running north from Egypt into Asia Minor, and were at the end of another coming out of Mesopotamia. They even possessed primary products which they could sell or turn into manufactures; the cedar of Mt Lebanon and other wood was much in demand, particularly in Egypt; fine sand from the shore went into Phoenician glass which had a wide distribution in the east, and from the shell fish murex was made a purple dye which was even more famous.

The language of the Phoenicians was one of the north-west Semitic group, and very close to Hebrew. Their evolution as a separate people is by no means clear; there were traditions that they had migrated at an early period from the shores of the Red Sea or the Persian Gulf, but these cannot be considered trustworthy. Their own name for their land as a whole was Canaan, but they were also called Sidonians, presumably after the city of Sidon. Sidonians appear in Homer, and in the Old Testament, a king of Tyre is called 'king of the Sidonians'. Our name Phoenicians comes from the usual Greek name for the people, and is found in Homer; the generally accepted explanation is that it derives from a Greek word meaning 'purple' and that the Greeks named the people after one of their distinctive products, purple-dyed cloth.[2]

Each Phoenician community early developed into a city ruled by its own king and independent of its neighbours, but for the first thousand years and more of their history they were intimately bound to Egypt. From very early times the Egyptians had had to obtain wood from outside their country for their larger ships, and the most suitable source was Phoenicia. As a result, Byblos—which was nearest to the forests— was the most important city in the earliest period, and the amount of

Egyptian influence in its art and life was considerable. There is no doubt that for long periods the Phoenician cities were vassal states of Egypt. Between 1700 and 1500 there was a decline in Egyptian power, but it was restored by the Pharaoh Thutmose III (*c.* 1505–1447), who brought the whole coast of the Levant as far as Antioch, and much of the interior, under his control. For more than a century Egyptian rule over this area was much firmer than ever before, and substantial tributes were exacted from the subject states. However, the trading cities of Phoenicia profited economically from their inclusion in this very substantial empire and from the greater security now established. They had contacts outside the Egyptian Empire also, in Cyprus, Crete, and Mesopotamia.

In the fourteenth century, the power of Egypt declined again under unwarlike rulers, pressure from the Hittite Empire in Asia Minor, and the difficulty of maintaining control over the diverse and vigorous peoples of the area, constantly increased by nomadic invaders from the Syrian and Arabian deserts. A temporary revival under Rameses II (*c.* 1292–1225) was of little avail, since vast changes were afoot throughout the entire Middle East. The capital of the Hittite Empire, Boghaz-koy in Anatolia, was destroyed by barbarian invaders, and this led to the collapse of Hittite rule in Asia Minor. Then opened a generation of disorder and disaster, in which the existing Bronze Age civilizations were almost all swept away. There was a movement of barbarian peoples, referred to in the Egyptian records as the Sea Peoples, similar in many ways to that of the Germanic tribes at the end of the Roman Empire. The origins of these earlier peoples is still uncertain, in spite of many hypotheses about their obscure tribal names in the Egyptian records. Some arrived on the Levant coast by sea, others travelled by land; one group has certainly been identified, the people we know as Philistines, who settled down after their wanderings in the south of Palestine. In the early years of the twelfth century, the Sea Peoples made destructive raids through Syria and Palestine as far as Egypt itself, and a vast number of ancient centres of civilization were destroyed. In Phoenicia, Ugarit was taken, and Aradus; Sidon seems to have escaped with relatively little damage. Berytus may have been destroyed, as it is not heard of again for centuries, and Byblos ceased to be the most powerful of the cities. Other important cities destroyed included Aleppo and Charchemish in the interior, and Alalakh, a Syrian port.[3]

Although the invaders were driven away from Egypt, they had broken for ever her rule over the various states of Palestine and southern

Syria, and the disorder cannot but have been injurious to the Phoenicians. In addition, their kinsmen the Canaanites of the interior were being gradually driven from their strongholds by the Israelites. The whole movement, which briefly anticipated the similar events in Greece in which the Mycenean civilization was destroyed, brought to an end the Bronze Age and ushered in a new age, that of iron, in which, while copper and bronze continued to be used as common metals, iron appeared by their side in sufficient quantities to introduce notable changes in weapons and agriculture.

In one sense the changed situation was to the advantage of those who had survived the destruction of the actual raids, since they were now freed from the domination of an imperial power. This independence is shown most clearly in the Egyptian record known as the report of Wen Ammon.[4] This official was sent in the middle of the eleventh century to try to obtain some cedar wood at Byblos. He was robbed at Dor, nearly killed on Cyprus, and had the greatest difficulty in getting an interview with the king of Byblos. It is often assumed that the Phoenician cities at once went ahead and rapidly became as prosperous as before, but it is as well to be cautious about this.

For various reasons, most of the archaeological evidence about Phoenician civilization concerns the Bronze Age, and there is very little to show what conditions were like in the first centuries of the Iron Age. On the other hand it is clear that the Philistines, in their five main cities between Gaza and Joppa, were one of the most vigorous powers on the Levant coast and effectively hindered commercial contacts between Egypt and the north. It was against them that the alliance between the Phoenicians and the Israelites was formed, in the tenth century. In the interior, the Old Testament records some of the intermittent conflicts which went on in these centuries between the Israelites and their neighbours—Moabites, Ammonites, Canaanites, Philistines, Midianites—while excavations have shown that Bethel, a few miles north of Jerusalem, was sacked four times during the twelfth and eleventh centuries.

It is true that the damage to the general material standards of civilization in the east at this time was not so great as it was in Greece, where a real 'Dark Age' followed the destruction of Mycenae; the merits of Phoenician civilization in the tenth century may be seen in the large and finely-constructed buildings erected under their guidance in Palestine.

The Phoenician city which first became prominent in the new situation in the Levant was not Sidon or Berytus, but Tyre.[5] This city was on a rocky island separated from the mainland by a few hundred yards of sea, and must have depended on its ships from earliest times, since the island itself had no spring water. A tradition of Phoenician origin said that the people of Sidon, defeated by the king of Ascalon, sailed away and founded Tyre at a date which the Greeks worked out as one year before the sack of Troy, by our reckoning 1194. Another dated the earliest king of Tyre to about the same period. This cannot be the real date of the foundation of Tyre, which was certainly much older, but the traditions probably recorded a decisive stage in the development of the city; we might surmise that Sidon was so severely injured in the raids of the Sea Peoples and in the time of anarchy which followed them that a number of its people emigrated to Tyre, which was strengthened by the increase in her population—it is noteworthy that Ascalon, mentioned as a victor over Sidon, was a city of the Philistines.

What we know of the history of Tyre and the rest of Phoenicia before the eighth century comes mostly from the Old Testament and from Assyrian records. The best-known circumstance is the alliance between Hiram of Tyre (*c.* 969–936) and King Solomon, and there were close relations between Tyre and the Israelites for the next two centuries. It is probable that Tyre exercised some sort of control over almost all the cities of Phoenicia from the time of Hiram to the seventh century; there was a common system of weights and measures, and it is impossible as yet to distinguish between the products of the different cities. The prosperity of Phoenicia increased rather than diminished with the establishment of the Assyrian Empire in the Levant between 746 and 728 under Tiglath Pilesar III; even before this date Tyre had on occasion paid a tribute of wool, metal, and cedar wood to the more vigorous Assyrian rulers.[6]

It is true that the Assyrian Empire was by far the cruellest and most destructive of the ancient imperial states of the East, but its advantage from the Tyrian point of view was that it brought some sort of order into the *Kleinstaaterei* of Syria, and increased Tyre's importance as a market for products brought from all over the Middle East by caravan. Tyrian rulers were not always loyal to Assyria, whose tribute was very heavy; as their predecessors had done in the time of Egyptian greatness in the second millennium B.C., they tried to assert full independence at the slightest sign of weakness, but when menaced by the threat of retribution, backed up by overwhelming force, paid the amount demanded rather than risk total destruction, which was so often the fate of those who resisted Assyria to the end.

Tyre was preserved on several occasions by her almost impregnable position on her island and the ability of her sailors. This happened shortly before 700, when she withstood a siege of five years—though in such a context a siege can hardly have been too rigorous—and came to reasonable terms after the flight of the king who had led the revolt. It was at this point that the prophet Isaiah described Tyre as 'the crowning city, whose merchants are princes, whose traffickers are the honourable of the earth'.[7]

A similar result was reached after a more famous and certainly more destructive siege by Nebuchadnezzar, ruler of the Babylonian Empire which succeeded the Assyrian. This siege traditionally lasted from 586 to 573, and is the subject of remarkable chapters by Ezekiel, who enthusiastically but erroneously foretold the destruction of the city: 'it shall be a place for the spreading of nets in the midst of the sea . . . all the princes of the sea . . . shall take up a lamentation for thee and say to thee, How art thou destroyed that wast inhabited of seafaring men, the renowned city which wast strong in the sea'.[8]

He goes on to give a picture of the brilliance of Tyre as a market for commodities from all over the known world. Her own ships were made of cypress from Mt Hermon, their masts of cedar from Lebanon, and the oars of oak from Bashan; sail-cloth came from Egypt. Precious metals were imported from Tarshish, while Greeks and men of Pontus brought slaves and articles of brass; precious stones came from Syria, and agricultural products from Judaea. There is also mention of various Arabian states, and Mesopotamia as far as Assur. It is clear from this list that Tyre was a great exchange market for a considerable area of the East, and that at least as much of her wealth came from this source as from the trading enterprises of her own merchants; most of the movement of goods by land was not in her hands but in those of the Aramaeans of Syria.

It was from Tyre, so the universal tradition of antiquity held,[9] that the Phoenician colonies to the west set out, and there is no reason to doubt this, though it is certain that people from other Phoenician cities, including those which had been established on Cyprus, took part. Various motives for the movement have been alleged. One Roman source[10] specified surplus of population, social discord and the ambition of the leaders, but this looks as though it is a mere deduction from the better documented movement of Greek colonists, in which all these factors were present. In recent times it has been suggested that pressure from the Assyrians forced some Phoenicians to find new homes overseas, but there is little to show that Assyrian overlordship was exacting till the end of the eighth century at the earliest. Over-population was a factor likely to have played some part; it is known that Tyre imported food from an early date, though she was better able to pay for it than Greek cities faced with the same problem.

However, it is clear that the great majority of Phoenician settlements in the west were not founded with a view to the exploitation of a fertile hinterland. Their classic situation was an off-shore island or a peninsula with landing places on either side, suitable for use in almost all winds. In other words, the colonists looked to the sea rather than the land. In the case of Carthage, we know that it was several centuries before the colony acquired much territory, and though the growth of its population was certainly slow to start with, it could hardly have fed all its inhabitants. It is of course certain that some Phoenician settlers engaged in farming; recent discoveries in southern Sardinia reveal an unexpected density of settlement at an early date which seems to presuppose effective use of the land. But the majority of Phoenician colonies remained small places for a long time, in comparison with a number of successful Greek colonies, and there can be no doubt that their main purpose to start with was to provide safe anchorage and supplies for the merchants of Tyre on their Mediterranean voyages.

This brings us to the key to the motives of the Phoenicians in the west. The most sought after raw material in antiquity was metal, in particular gold, silver, copper and tin. Phoenicia was lacking in mineral resources and her merchants began to seek it in the west as the sources in the east became known and exploited. A particular objective was Spain, which had been one of the sources of silver and tin for the Mediterranean since prehistoric times, though the total amount exported was probably small. At some date this led the Phoenicians beyond the Straits of Gibraltar—a considerable achievement in the tiny merchant ships of the time—to an area on the Atlantic coast of Spain called by the Greeks Tartessos. This name was apparently applied to three different things by the Greeks; first a kingdom covering roughly south-west Andulusia, occupied in Roman times by a tribe called the Turdetani, a name connected in some way with Tartessos; second a river, undoubtedly the Guadalquivir, which was said to have its source in mountains of silver; third a trading post.[11]

The clearest account of Phoenician aims here comes from Diodorus Siculus,[12] writing in the time of Augustus, but following Timaeus, a Sicilian Greek writer of the third century.

> The land of the Iberians (i.e. southern Spain) contains more numerous and more productive silver mines than any other . . . the natives were ignorant of its use till the Phoenicians on their trading voyages acquired

silver in exchange for a small quantity of merchandise; carrying this to Greece, Asia, and other countries, they gained great wealth. Their power also increased through this commerce, carried on for a long time, and they were able to send out numerous colonies to Sicily and the neighbouring islands, to Africa, Sardinia, and Spain itself.

One of these Spanish colonies was Cadiz, the Roman Gades, and the silver mines were located in the Sierra Morena. The Phoenician name Gadir, from which Gades derived seems to mean 'a port', and in antiquity it was, like Tyre, an island separated by a narrow arm of the sea from the mainland; it was thus an ideal situation for a trading post.[13] The nature of the trade shows why it was so attractive to the Phoenicians and to the Greeks, and it can be compared with similar trade in the age of discovery in late Renaissance times. In both there is the same characteristic—the exchange, by people of relatively advanced culture, of manufactured goods of little value for precious metals. Diodorus (or Timaeus) was incorrect in saying that the Tartessians had no knowledge of the use of silver; in fact they participated in the search for tin. They are said to have traded up the Atlantic coast for it as far as islands off the coast of Brittany, or at any rate Galicia, and they knew Britain and Ireland. There is sufficient evidence for trading connexions between Spain and the British Isles in prehistoric times for this to be true.

An unexpected source provides us with some information which is probably to do with Tartessos. This is the Old Testament, and the passages concerned are those which are translated in our version's 'ships of Tarshish'. Tarshish is taken by some (though not all) scholars to be the Hebrew form of the name, which would be almost identical in Phoenician, and which was Hellenized as Tartessos; there seems in fact to have been an alternative form Tarseia, which is somewhat closer to Tarshish. Some of the texts refer to the days of Hiram and Solomon; one of the best known states that Solomon had 'ships of Tarshish', and that they came every three years bringing gold, silver, ivory and monkeys. Solomon's ships sailed from Eilath down the Red Sea and it is fairly clear from this and other texts that the phrase 'ships of Tarshish' was a technical term meaning a kind of ship capable of making long voyages, such as that from Phoenicia to Spain, rather like our 'East Indiaman'. Ezekiel, describing the wealth of Tyre and the presence there of merchants from all nations, mentions silver, iron, tin, and lead as traded by Tarshish.[14]

In the conditions of navigation in antiquity, the long routes from Phoenicia to Spain needed many points for its protection. This was not so much because of danger from ships of competing states, in particular the Greeks, but because of the general practice of anchoring each night and the slow sailing of early ships. It has been estimated that there was probably an anchorage used by Phoenicians every thirty miles along the North African coast. Whether or not this is so, it is certain that there were far more places known to and used by Phoenician mariners than later grew to permanent colonies. The growth of the latter no doubt depended on a number of factors—the safety of their harbours, and the nature of the hinterland and general strategic position. It is significant that three of the most important, all of which have early Phoenician material, Carthage, Utica, and Motya, are all well placed on the narrows leading from the eastern to the western Mediterranean, and dominate both routes, that along the North African coast and that by way of Sicily, Sardinia and the Balearic Islands.

The colonizing movement of the Phoenicians, like that of the Greeks, was made easy by the fact that almost all the peoples of the western Mediterranean were at the time in a lower state of civilization and weaker militarily than those of the east. This was the more important for the Phoenicians because they do not appear to have had the man-power to found really large colonies in a hostile environment, and many of their anchorages must have been effectively at the mercy of the native inhabitants. It is probable that they first used the North African coast as the most direct route, even though in general it was forbidding and inhospitable, with abrupt cliffs and dunes and a paucity of good harbours. The interior was equally unprepossessing; it was difficult to penetrate except by the few rivers, as the mountains run parallel to the coast for long distances. North Africa was notorious in antiquity for its abundance of wild animals, including many now extinct in the area—elephants, lions, panthers, bears, and hyenas.[15] Only limited areas along the coast were suitable for cultivation, so it is not surprising that the largest of these, northern Tunisia, was the site of almost all the Phoenician settlements in Africa which grew to any size. The climate of the region in ancient times does not seem to have differed greatly from what it is today, the fact that some areas now barren were under cultivation in Roman times being due to better utilization of the available water than has been attempted until the last few decades. In the immediate vicinity of the coast the rainfall was and is adequate for the successful growing of all sorts of fruit trees, while inland in the valleys of the Medjerda and the Miliana there was intensive growing of cereal crops. Then as now the summers were dry and hot, the winters mild with intermittent and sometimes torrential rain; the danger came when the rain failed, particularly in the spring.

When the Phoenicians first visited North Africa, the native inhabitants were more backward in material civilization than almost all others of the western Mediterranean. This was in great measure due to the fact that Africa north of the Sahara is in effect a vast island, and as a result its inhabitants in an earlier period of history were very much cut off from the movements of peoples and the consequent spread of techniques in the east and north of the Mediterranean. The Sahara was a barrier to the south, and other deserts—and the immense distance—reduced contacts between North Africa and the Nile valley to a minimum. The Mediterranean was certainly not impassable, but the North African coasts had little or nothing to attract migrant peoples.

One language, from which derive the modern Berber dialects,[16] was spoken throughout the region; this was probably due to the length of time it had been inhabited by the same people, rather than to imposition by conquest. Yet the difficulties of communication imposed by the mountain ranges and the few rivers prevented the formation of a unified state, and even in Roman times the unity of North Africa was only maintained with great difficulty. Lack of minerals also kept the inhabitants from any great material advances, and when the Phoenicians arrived they were still in the Stone Age. Some had adopted a sedentary life, particularly in Tunisia, but the majority were still semi-nomadic pastoralists, living in small clans or tribes. Later, under the impulse of the higher civilization of the immigrants, some of the tribes coalesced to form relatively large states, but these were still confined to fairly well marked geographical regions.

The site of Carthage[17] conformed to the general pattern of Phoenician colonies but also was well situated for expansion into the fertile land of the surrounding coastal areas and the interior when—a long time after the foundation—this became desirable. It was near the end of a peninsula projecting eastwards into the Mediterranean, the actual end of the peninsula being Cape Carthage, now capped by the village of Sidi bou Said. The peninsula was joined to the mainland by an isthmus between two and three miles wide at its narrowest point; this isthmus was bounded on the south by the Lake of Tunis (El Bahira) and on the north by the Sebka er Riana, which in antiquity was a gulf of the sea. Both north-west and south-west of Cape Carthage there are stretches of sandy beach and behind them fairly gentle slopes rising to about 200 feet at the summit of the hill of St Louis. This hill, less than a mile from the sea, was undoubtedly the earliest citadel of Carthage, called Byrsa.

Most of the beaches were exposed to winds from the north and east, the exception being the little bay of El Kram which, protected by a small headland from the east, faces south. It can hardly be doubted that it was at this sheltered spot that the Phoenician traders first anchored and the earliest colonists disembarked. It was inland from this bay that the artificial harbour of Carthage was built, and less than one hundred yards to the west was the recently discovered sacred enclosure called the 'Sanctuary of Tanit' which was dedicated at an early date, perhaps by the first settlers. Tradition connected Byrsa with the earliest days of the settlement, and no doubt the colonists quickly seized on this defensible point within easy reach of the bay, since the whole of the peninsula could not have been defended until the population had reached a considerable size.

Such was the setting of the city which outstripped in wealth and power all those of Phoenicia itself, and which retained its ancestral language and culture long after these had disappeared in the east. The date of its foundation, and of that of other Phoenician colonies in the west, has long been the subject of controversy because of an apparent contradiction between the information we find in Greek and Roman authors, and the discoveries of archaeologists. The Greeks believed that the Phoenicians entered the western Mediterranean long before they themselves did—and the earliest Greek colony in the west, Cumae on the bay of Naples, was founded about 750. On the other hand, in spite of the many important excavations in the last decade, Phoenician material for which a case for a date earlier than about 800 can be made out is negligible in quantity.

The date almost universally accepted in antiquity[18] for the foundation of Carthage was thirty-eight years before the first Olympiad, i.e. 814. This date, and much of the tradition about the circumstances of the foundation, was first publicized in the Greek world by Timaeus; his own works have not survived, but they were used by many later writers whose books we possess. As a Sicilian he certainly had the opportunity of finding out the Carthaginians' own version of the foundation of their city. But it was believed that Carthage was a late-comer among the Phoenician colonies; various authors, probably ultimately dependent on Timaeus, dated Phoenician voyages to the west, and some settlements, to the period immediately after the Trojan War; specific dates were given for Gades (1110), Lixus on the coast of Morocco (earlier than Gades) and Utica, near Carthage (1101).[19]

These last dates look legendary. One of the difficulties is that even for their own history the Greeks had no very certain chronological knowledge for the period before the middle of the eighth century, and had to reckon by inexact methods such as generations to calculate early dates. Fixed points which they used, such as the sack of Troy (traditionally 1194) and the first Olympiad (776) have an air of exactitude which is certainly deceptive; consequently, caution has to be used in dealing with dates for non-Greek history which the Greeks fitted into their own chronological system, with the added possibility of error in their use of foreign traditions.

Greek authors, many of them intelligent and critical men, but inevitably lacking the apparatus of modern historical scholarship for testing the truth of their data, were not reliable when dealing with the past of non-Greek peoples. For example, they were very interested in the Assyrians, with whom they coupled the Babylonians. There are many references to them in Greek writers from the time of Herodotus (late fifth century) onwards; yet a comparison of our information derived from classical sources with that obtained by modern archaeologists shows how little grasp the Greeks had of early Oriental history. Queen Semiramis and King Sardanapalus can just be identified with historical rulers of Assyria, but for the rest are figures of romantic legend. Between 281 and 262 a priest of Baal from Babylon called Berossos[20] wrote a history of Babylon which was little more than a chronicle of kings and their wars. He certainly used native Babylonian records yet is accurate only for the period after 746. In any case, Greeks preferred to read the romantic fantasies about the 'mysterious East' put out by Ctesias, an earlier historian. The conclusion is that it is not possible to put much faith in Greek accounts of the history of non-Greek peoples.

One reason why the Greeks attributed a venerable antiquity to the Phoenician colonies is that in the poems of Homer, the Phoenician appear in a western Mediterranean setting, though not as colonists. Many Greeks regarded these poems as historical, and it was natural for them to conclude that the period immediately after the Trojan War saw some Phoenician settlements. But there was more to it than this; all ancient states liked to project their history as far into the past as possible and Greeks and Carthaginians were no exception. Claims of historical priority had some propaganda value; they were used in disputes among the Greeks themselves, and when there seemed to be a chance that they could drive the Phoenicians from Sicily in the sixth century, it was claimed that the island had once belonged to Heracles, and thus a war to regain it would be one of reconquest of land once Greek.[21] The admission by the Greeks that the Phoenicians preceded them in the west must therefore in itself be regarded as good evidence.

Turning to the archaeological evidence, nothing has so far been discovered in the western Mediterranean to confirm the early dates attributed to Utica, Gades, and Lixus. One small statuette of possible Phoenician origin and apparently early date, found in the sea off Selinus, is all that can be advanced in support. On the other hand, the number of sites producing Phoenician material of the eighth century has grown substantially in recent times; they include precisely these three supposedly very early settlements. Even if we assume a period of a generation or so in which sites were visited before being settled, this still leaves a gap of nearly three centuries between the traditional dates and those attested by archaeological evidence. It seems most unlikely that this gap will be filled. Obviously argument from the mere absence of evidence is not fully satisfactory, but the more Phoenician sites are discovered, and none earlier than the eighth century, the more it may be found convincing.

In the case of Carthage, we have archaeological evidence that gives a date within two generations of the traditional one, if not closer still. On the basis of finds at Carthage and Utica, a convincing attempt has been made to establish a chronological series for Carthaginian pottery.[22] Since pottery is the most important single item in fixing early chronology the significance of the work is obvious. The Carthaginian material is dated basically by its association with Greek and Egyptian imported objects; most come from graves at Carthage which by and large were beyond the reach and interest of the Roman soldiers when they destroyed the city, and were undisturbed by the building of the later Roman colony.

Important material also comes from the so-called Sanctuary of Tanit, which was almost certainly in the area of earliest occupation, near the harbour, and in which were buried the urns containing the bones of sacrificial victims. In the course of centuries the lower levels were overlaid by the deposits of later generations; since there seems to have been no temple on the site, it too escaped the attentions of the Romans in spite of their professed horror at the human sacrifices performed there. On several grounds the sanctuary is held to belong to the earliest days of Phoenician settlement and consequently the lowest levels of the utmost importance.

The sanctuary was discovered in 1922, but since the last war a French archaeologist, P. Cintas, has discovered on the bedrock at the lowest level a small chamber cut in the rock containing a remarkable group of pottery objects. The most extraordinary feature is that nine of the thirteen objects are Greek, constituting a collection unique at any date in Carthage. It would be difficult to date any of them to earlier than

725, though another vase found near but not in the chamber is perhaps slightly earlier. The group has the character of a dedicatory deposit, in which case it ought to date the sanctuary itself; but why it should contain these Greek objects, none of which is in any way remarkable, is a mystery.

The earliest datable imported object from the rest of the sanctuary is from about 650, but there is Carthaginian pottery earlier than this and in fact earlier than any found in the graves; and Cintas believes that some of these are contemporary with the traditional date of the foundation, which he accepts; he recognizes, however, that there are difficulties in relating the 'foundation deposit' to the rest of the sanctuary, and in the absence of Greek objects to confirm the date of the earliest Carthaginian pottery. A study of Egyptian objects such as amulets, scarabs, beads, and so on found in quantity in the early tombs has produced somewhat similar results, though in this case there is nothing which can be dated earlier than the seventh century.

Little can be deduced from the tales about the foundation of Carthage told in many ancient sources—all important cities had 'foundation myths', most of them highly implausible. The most popular about Carthage told of a dynastic quarrel at Tyre. Elissa, sister of King Pygmalion, married her uncle Acherbas, a priest of Melkart and wealthy member of the royal house. He was killed on the orders of Pygmalion, who coveted his fortune, but Elissa escaped, accompanied by a number of Tyrians opposed to the king. She sailed to Cyprus where the high priest of Astarte joined her on condition that the high priesthood of this deity in any new colony should be hereditary in his family; eighty virgins who had been destined for ritual prostitution were also taken, to ensure the continuation of the colony. In Africa, good relations were soon established with the native population, to whom a rent was paid for the land occupied by the settlement; subsequently, however, Elissa committed suicide rather than marry a native chieftain. There can be no doubt that this story, which had several embellishments which need not be repeated here, was constructed in a Greek Sicilian environment with some knowledge of Carthaginian institutions and nomenclature. It is possible that the reference to Cyprus is significant; there is much evidence at Carthage and other western Phoenician sites of the importance of Cyprus, on which there were both Phoenicians and Greek cities, in the trading contacts of the eighth and seventh centuries.

At some stage the name Dido was associated with Elissa and became standard, though Elissa represents a genuine Phoenician name whereas

Dido apparently does not. There were several different versions of the story of Dido, until Virgil effectively swept them away with his tale of the love of Aeneas. It may be noted that Virgil, probably following an earlier Roman poet Naevius, put the story centuries earlier than the accepted foundation date in order that it might be introduced into the saga of Aeneas fleeing from the sack of Troy on his way to Italy and thus to confront in romantic fashion the founders of the two cities who later disputed the mastery of the Mediterranean. The variants of the tradition, its highly romantic character and ruthless disregard for chronology and probability indicate well enough the facility with which classical antiquity constructed or altered legends to take the place of exact knowledge of the distant past.

Utica, some thirty miles north-west of Carthage, has also been the scene of recent discoveries; two groups of graves have been excavated. Imported objects from the middle or late seventh centuries have been found, with some local attempts at imitation. Phoenician pottery from the site goes a good deal further back than this, however, though there is not yet sufficient to provide a full chronological series. The material from Utica is considered by Cintas to be more archaic in character than that of Carthage, and he sees in this confirmation of the earlier foundation of Utica; none of it, however, is to be dated earlier than the eighth century. Characteristic of Carthage and Utica in their early stages was the use of a fine burnished red pottery which has been identified on a number of other sites in the western Mediterranean, and appears to be imported directly from Phoenicia.

On general grounds, it could be supposed that the Phoenicians visited the southern coast of Sicily as early as they did the North African coast. Towards the end of the fifth century, the Greek historian Thucydides wrote that at one time there were Phoenician settlements all round the island, but that they withdrew to Motya, Panormus, and Solus, in the west of the island, when Greek colonists began to arrive.[23] This assertion by the greatest of Greek historians has sometimes been taken at its face value, though it is difficult to see where he obtained such an important piece of information not referred to by any other ancient writer. Several Greek colonies have been excavated down to their earliest levels, and not one has produced anything Phoenician of a date prior to the arrival of the Greeks; in some, earlier native Sicilian remains have been found. The statement of Thucydides was no doubt his own argument to explain why there were no Phoenician settlements in the east of Sicily, since he believed like everyone else that they had preceded the Greeks into Sicilian waters. In fact, the geographical

limitation of the area of Phoenician settlement in Sicily has recently
been used as an argument in favour of the thesis that the Phoenicians
only became interested in Sicily after the Greeks had settled the rest of
the island. This is unlikely—there were good sites on the south of the
island closer to Africa than Motya still unoccupied by the Greeks when
Motya was settled. Motya and Panormus (Solus was a later foundation
of sixth-century date) seem to have been chosen to provide anchorages
on the route to Italian waters and to Sardinia.

Motya was first excavated after the First World War and is the
object of intensive research at the present time.[24] The site was an off-
shore island in an almost landlocked lagoon. A causeway to the mainland (still in use) was built in the sixth century. Present evidence goes
to show that the settlement was in existence towards the end of the
eighth century, and the colonists appear to have lived for some time
side by side with a native Sicilian community. There is a good deal of
imported pottery and some evidence that there were colonists from
northern Syria as well as from Phoenicia proper. Little is known about
Panormus because it is covered by the later city, but in view of its
known importance in the sixth century, there can be little doubt that
it was established much earlier, perhaps in the same period as Motya.

Malta and Gozo are mentioned in literary sources as Phoenician
settlements,[25] and this is confirmed by numerous, if sporadic finds. In
view of the importance of the islands on the route to the west, it is
notable that we hear nothing of a Greek interest in the island in early
times, a fact which no doubt testifies to early occupation by the
Phoenicians. The early name of Gozo was Gaulos, and this may be
connected with the fact that a characteristic type of Phoenician merchant ship was called a *gaulos*. Tombs of the eighth century have been
found in the region of Rabat on Malta.

The most important discoveries in Phoenician and Carthaginian
archaeology in recent times have been made in Sardinia.[26] The Phoenicians seem to have been first attracted to the island in their search for
copper. The mines in Sardinia appear to have been much more inten-
sively exploited after the arrival of the Phoenicians; furthermore, the
culture of the settlers influenced the native culture, which had long been
relatively isolated from the main currents of development in the
Mediterranean, at an early date. Settlements in Sardinia were likewise
of importance in protecting the route to Spain. Indeed, one legend said
that Nora was not only the earliest Phoenician colony in Sardinia but
was actually founded from Spain, and this may be a memory of a close
connexion. A famous inscription in Phoenician letters was found at

Harbours of Carthage (view taken in 1925)

Air photo of lagoon and island of Motya

Nora and this has been dated to the ninth century by comparison with inscriptions known to be of that date from Phoenicia itself. It may however be later than this in view of known conservative tendencies in letter forms outside Phoenicia. Other archaeological evidence is of the eighth century, and Sulcis and Tharros have yielded material of the same date; slightly later material has been found at Calaris and Bythia. All these sites, like Motya, have a good deal of imported pottery of oriental origin, testifying to the wide variety of Phoenician connexions.

All the Sardinian sites are in the south and west of the island, showing clearly the direction of their interests. Furthermore, recent excavation has shown that the Phoenician settlement was much denser, at least by the sixth century, than was previously suspected. A few miles inland from Sulcis a substantial fortress was built *c.* 600 on Monte Sirai after the destruction of an existing *nuraghe* (native Sardinian fort). This is the earliest known example of Phoenician military building in the west. Its purpose was no doubt to defend the area of Sulcis on the landward side. There is evidence of an intensive settlement along the coast from Sulcis to Bythia.

Our knowledge of the early Phoenician period on the Spanish coasts has been slowly increasing in recent years. The site of Phoenician Gades lies under the modern city and no intensive excavation has been possible. A substantial number of tombs have been found over the years, producing material of the seventh century. No trace has yet been found of the temples of Baal Hammon and of Melkart known from literature, the latter being particularly famous in antiquity.[27] Recently an important cemetery has been scientifically excavated at San Cristobal near Almunecar, the ancient Sexi, already known as a Phoenician colony.[28] The tombs contained the characteristic red pottery imported from Phoenicia, and some Corinthian pottery of early seventh-century date; another cemetery at Torre del Mar has produced similar material. Isolated finds of similar character have been made in several other places in southern Spain. However, little is known of the density and character of the settlements. It is possible that an area like that in southern Sardinia may be discovered, but at present it looks as though early Phoenician settlement in Spain was not thick on the ground.

The settlement on Ibiza was said to have come directly from Carthage, not from Phoenicia, and was dated to 654 by our reckoning. The original settlement was on the Isla Plana, and a seventh-century date has been confirmed by archaeological finds. It is probable that the settlement on Ibiza served primarily as a station on the route from Sardinia to Spain.

Lastly may be mentioned three sites in Morocco known to be early Phoenician settlements. An important cemetery has been found on the little island of Siga (Rachgoun);[29] the tombs have provided material of seventh-century date, including weapons, a relative rarity in Phoenician graves; it may be supposed that this site at least had some military significance. Important discoveries at Lixus have been made, but are at present unpublished. However, it appears that the tradition of its importance is true to this extent, that it was a settlement of some size, as it were a sister-city to Gades. The earliest material so far discovered is of the seventh century, as at Gades, in both cases much later than the traditional dates.

The third is the island of Mogador, of a very different character.[30] This site is over 600 miles from Gades, and several hundred south of the later Roman frontier in Morocco, and by far the most distant Phoenician site known. There is no sign of a permanent settlement as at Lixus and Siga, but rather the debris of seasonal habitation. We must imagine the sailors living in temporary huts or even in the boats, in extremely squalid conditions. Yet they had with them not only Phoenician but also Greek pottery of the seventh and sixth centuries. It is by no means clear what the original function of Mogador, and for that matter of Lixus, was. It is tempting to connect these sites with the gold acquired in West Africa, to which we have references of a later date, and Mogador looks precisely like the sort of bartering place described in our sources (see below pp. 69). Yet neither place is anywhere near identifiable sources of West African gold.

The number of settlements throughout the western Mediterranean of eighth- and seventh-century date is impressive testimony of the vigour of Phoenician expansion at that time. It has become clear that though the great majority of sites were chosen for their place on the trade routes to the west, and that the exploitation of a fertile hinterland was secondary and late in being undertaken, many of the colonies must have been largely self-supporting at a fairly early date. This is not to say that they rivalled a number of Greek colonies in size. Their relationship with Tyre and the other Phoenician cities who took part in the movement is obscure. It is generally considered that they were not intended to become self-governing communities within a short space of time, as were the Greek colonies, and this is probably the case. Nevertheless, the realities of their situation, their distance from Phoenicia, and the slow decline of the power and influence of their homeland made independent local developments inevitable in the end. Archaeological evidence indicates increasing differences in cult practices and artistic preferences between the settlements in Sicily, Sardinia and Spain. There is, however, no indication that there was ever a breach between the colonies and Phoenicia; even when Carthage was fully independent, she continued to pay out of sentiment the tribute which in early days had been obligatory.

2

Early Contacts with the Greeks

IT was inevitable that the entrance of the Carthaginians into more adequately recorded history should take place in Sicily, as the island became an important field for Greek colonization in the eighth century. The traditional dates of the foundation of the Greek colonies are more acceptable than those attributed to the Phoenician; in fact the whole chronology of early Greek pottery, with all its implications, largely rests on the reliability of the Sicilian dates. The foundation of these cities was contemporary with the revival of Greek civilization after the 'Dark Age' of four centuries which had followed the destruction of the Mycenaean Empire, and in fact began one of the most important movements of people in antiquity.

From the late eighth century to the end of the third a large part of the external history of the Greeks consists in a ceaseless flow of emigrants to practically every part of the Mediterranean, first as merchant adventurers and colonists, then as mercenaries, and finally as settlers in Asia in the wake of Alexander the Great. It is sometimes difficult to realize, when one thinks of the inglorious showing of the later Greeks when they encountered the Romans, that one of their chief characteristics in their early days was a dynamic energy. Starting with a material and demographic equipment well below that of several contemporary peoples, they not only developed a civilization which was artistically, intellectually, and morally superior to that of their predecessors; they were also technically and militarily more efficient.

Greek colonization was a more complex movement than the Phoenician. There were two main forces at work in bringing it about, the first of which, in order of time, was trade. Thucydides[1] knew that in early Greece the state of all communities was one of great poverty, which he said was due to the fact that they did not trade. In this he was certainly correct. No one will dispute that the volume of trade throughout antiquity was small, and at some periods largely without social and political consequences. However, at certain specific points a negligible volume of trade was of the greatest significance in elevating material standards just sufficiently to stimulate the growth of societies very different from the peasant communities which had preceded them. This came about through the direct acquisition of new materials and products, through the spread of techniques in the meeting-places of different peoples, and through social changes produced inside the communities concerned. The Greeks, being divided into a number of small independent communities, were particularly open to the effects of even a limited amount of trade because these were more immediately visible.

In the eighth century, the intermittent contacts between Greece and Asia were transformed into regular economic exchanges. The citizens, or at least the nobility, of certain states in the south of Greece and in Ionia acquired desires and needs for foreign goods which could only be satisfied by piracy or trade. Barter must have been the rule; but the exportable surplus of goods produced by these states was at first extremely small. Hence there was a great incentive to undertake voyages to parts of the Mediterranean from where at least the desired raw materials could be obtained more cheaply; this led to the discovery of areas where the inhabitants were few or weak and which, even if they had no mineral wealth or similar attraction, could provide a field for colonization.

This brought into play the second impulse in point of time, though undoubtedly the first in importance, the over-population of some Greek states. It was the force of this in Greek colonization which as far as can be seen distinguished it from the Phoenician. It is possible that some cities attempted to solve the problem of feeding a growing population by importing food, but the scale of the colonizing movement shows that this had only a limited success. It is true that in many cases the overpopulation was artificial, the real cause of poverty and famine being the concentration of land in the hands of the aristocracies which ruled in the Greek cities at this time; however, where traders had marked the way, colonists followed, especially to Sicily and southern Italy, where they founded cities which outgrew the founding communities and made this part of the Mediterranean proverbial for wealth and luxury. With very few exceptions, the colonies were originally designed or soon grew to be cities whose chief wealth was in their fertile land, a very different picture from the present economic state of the area.

Among the Greek states participating in the movement[2] to the west were the Dorian Crete, Rhodes, Corinth, and Argos, and the Ionian Eretria, Chalcis, and Naxos; there appears to have been little rivalry or jealousy among them, in spite of the fact that Corinth obtained a commanding position in the trade between Greece and the west in the seventh century. To mention just a few of the foundations, the earliest was Cumae (c. 750) on the bay of Naples, through which the copper ore of Etruria and Campania was obtained. More specifically agricultural was Naxos (734), which itself soon planted offshoots at Catane and Leontini. Zancle (later better known as Messana) and Rhegium were founded at about the same time, on either side of the Straits of Messina; the foundation date of the most important of all, Syracuse, was 733. By c. 700 further sites had been occupied in Sicily and southern Italy, of which the chief were Sybaris—whose wealth is still remembered in our epithet for decadent luxury—and Tarentum.

Besides the leading motive for their existence, a further peculiarity of the Greek colonies distinguished them from the Phoenician and had its effect in later history. From the very first, the colonies, though officially sponsored by the founding cities and sent out with considerable religious solemnity, were independent states, bound to their founders only by the ties of sentiment and religion. Thus there was no question of a Greek 'empire' in the west, but simply a substantial increase in the number of independent Greek states, every one of which developed its own particular institutions and way of life and manifested the common Greek ideal of autonomy.

We have no historical record of hostility between the Greeks and Phoenicians in the west before the beginning of the sixth century, though presumably there were incidents sufficient to give the latter the bad name they have in the *Odyssey*. In that poem, which probably attained the form in which we have it between 750 and 650, the Phoenicians are referred to quite often, and this is noteworthy since the poem is much concerned with the western parts of Greece. The Phoenicians, it seems, had an evil reputation. In the guise of traders they kidnapped children and sold them into slavery; if they behaved honourably to a stranger, it was cause for comment; they were 'famous for their ships, greedy men' and other epithets referred to them as crafty and deceitful. On the face of it this hostile, as it were 'anti-semitic', attitude should date to a period of rivalry or competition between Greek and Phoenician in the west, which could have occurred at any time from the early eighth century onwards, though it must be said that we have no other information of open hostility till the sixth century. No doubt the Phoenicians were guilty of all the things they were accused of, nor should we assume that at this early date Greek traders were more honourable. In any case a prejudice of class as well as of race was involved. The aristocratic audience of the poems would identify themselves with the Greek heroes, for whom it was laudable to get wealthy by piratical raids but not by trade; when the Phoenicians did rob, they did it ingloriously, by stealth; one of the most humiliating insults was to be taken for a merchant.[3]

However, at this early date the distinction between piracy and trade was one of might rather than right. The lack of a tradition of early conflict, and the position of the two groups of colonies on the map, have led some to think that there was some agreement about recognized 'spheres of influence'. This is most unlikely. Apart from anything else, there was the practical consideration that every Greek state with the need or desire to send out a colony would have had to agree. Also, a notion such as a 'sphere of influence' in a recognized diplomatic sense did not exist till much later in antiquity, if even then. The geographical distribution and the lack of conflict result from the motives and circumstances of the foundations.

The Greeks discovered the fertile lands of eastern Sicily and southern Italy through voyages to Etruria, and were the more inclined to concentrate their attention on them because they were so close to Greece itself. The Phoenicians, whose colonies were concerned with trade and its protection, continued with their voyages to the west, for a long time without rivals. Nearly all Phoenician colonies imported Greek products throughout the seventh century and later. However, in the last quarter of that century, the vigour of the Greeks and the now powerful Siceliots (as the Greeks in Sicily were called) began to impinge upon one Phoenician interest after another. In 631 a colony was founded at Cyrene by Dorian Greeks from Thera. This was the first Greek venture on the North African coast; previously the area of Cyrenaica had been inhabited by Libyan tribes under intermittent Egyptian control. From their earliest days both Carthage and Utica had had trading relations with Egypt, as had their founder, and the new city of Cyrene between Egypt and Carthage, whether one sailed along the African shore or by way of Crete was a possible source of interruption to this trade and an unwelcome sign of Greek interest in Africa. Again, only just before the foundation of Cyrene, there had occurred the voyage of Colaeus to Tartessos, followed by the enterprising merchants from Phocaea.

According to Herodotus,[4] Colaeus was a merchant of Samos and was the first Greek to visit Tartessus, being driven there by accident in a storm. He made a greater profit on his cargo than any other Greek merchant known. The Phocaeans who followed him were traditionally the best sailors in this early period and we are told that they made their voyages in fifty-oared warships, not merchant ships. After founding Massilia shortly before 600, Phocaea traded actively down the east coast of Spain and established several small stations including one, Mainake, in the area of Malaga, which was close to the Phoenician settlement of Sexi and must have been in or near the territory of the Tartessians. The Phocaeans were welcomed by the native population, perhaps because they brought an element of competition from which they could profit. However, Herodotus' statement that the king of the Tartessians, Arganthonios, was king for eighty years and lived to be 120 makes it clear that by the time Herodotus wrote, Greek knowledge of southern Spain had degenerated into legend. This was because, as will be described later, the Phoenicians were able to exclude the Greeks in the late sixth century.

In Sicily the north and south coasts (the latter very inhospitable) had not been the object of attention by the Greeks after the foundation of Gela in 688. Some time after the middle of the century a colony composed chiefly of people from Zankle was founded on the north coast at Himera. This was well placed for trade with Spain and as a port of call for ships sailing between Carthage and Etruria or Campania. Shortly after this, in 628, Sicilian Megara founded Selinus on the south coast. This site had no natural advantages and no proper harbour, yet Selinus flourished,[5] and it is clear that this was in part due to trade with Carthage, to which it was the nearest Greek city. These colonies, though late, were among the earliest in Sicily to use coinage (before 550), and must have got their silver from Spain or Campania. There is nothing to show that they had been founded as a step towards the Hellenization of all Sicily, but the Phoenicians might be justifiably alarmed, as both were founded by already existing colonies and testified to their vigour. Solus, the third of the colonies ascribed to the Phoenicians in Sicily, probably dates from this period, as an outpost of Panormus designed to prevent the expansion westwards of Himera.

In 580 and the following years an attempt was made by the Greeks to drive the Phoenicians entirely from Sicily. It is probable that the wealth to be gained by increased trade with Spain was a principal motive; if the Phoenicians could have been excluded from the island, the voyages of the Greeks to the west would have increased, just as those of the Phoenicians would have declined. Further, the position of the Phoenicians in Sardinia would have become almost untenable, as their communications with Africa could have been cut, and this island also would have become open to the Greeks. The leaders of the move seem to have been the Selinuntines, who by their proximity to the Phoenician colonies knew as well as any what would be gained. They were probably behind the establishment by Rhodians and others of the colony at Acragas in 580; this site was a few miles from the sea, but of such natural strength that within a century it rivalled Syracuse and was in effect an advance guard of the Sicilian Greeks against the Phoenicians. At about the same time, a certain Pentathlos of Cnidos led a force of Rhodians and Cnidans to Lilybaeum, the extreme western point of Sicily. This was a threat of destruction to the Phoenician settlements, as Lilybaeum dominated the sea-lane to Motya. They had as allies a native tribe called the Elymians, their neighbours in the west of the island, themselves under attack from Selinus.

This reconstruction[6] of events is from very brief and unsatisfactory sources, but it is at any rate certain that the Phoenicians were faced with an attempt to drive them out from the island. This attempt they defeated; the Elymians overcame Pentathlos when he was helping Selinus in an attack on their capital Segesta; and later, Elymians and Phoenicians together destroyed the settlement at Lilybaeum. The survivors did no good to the Greek cause by their settlement on Lipara[7]; from there they engaged in piracy against Etruscan ships sailing to the Greek ports on the Straits of Messina. At this period the Etruscans appear not to have had a powerful fleet, and it was the piracy of the Liparans which led them to form an alliance with the Phoenicians against the Greeks.

It was after the expedition of Pentathlos and probably as a result of it that Carthage began to assume the leadership of the Phoenicians in the west, 200 and more years after her foundation. It must be said that prior to the middle of the sixth century there is no indication in the archaeological finds at Carthage that the city was outstripping the other Phoenician settlements in the west. There is certainly a substantial amount of Greek and Phoenician imported pottery, and an abundance of small objects such as jewellery, rings and seals imported from Egypt which indicate some wealth. But such articles are found in most of the western colonies and were part of the cargoes brought in Phoenician ships to be traded with the Tartessians and others. The importance for Phoenicia of this grew in the seventh century as the Phoenician trader gradually disappeared from the Aegean where he had previously been so common; the latter development was due to the rapid growth of the Greeks' own commerce and the superiority of their products.

There is a possibility that Carthage was intended to be the leader of the western Phoenicians from the first. Its name in Phoenician, Karthadasht, meant 'new city', which might imply priority of status as well as origin. However, the occasion for the emergence of Carthage was probably the inability of the mother city to protect her colonies any longer. Tyre had participated in the revolt against Nebuchadnezzar which led to the destruction of Jerusalem in 586. The next year the Babylonians began a siege of Tyre which by tradition lasted thirteen years. Tyre was saved by her insular position and her fleet, but in the end had to recognize Babylonian supremacy. The siege apparently weakened the city, and there was internal unrest later in the sixth century which led at one stage to the overthrow of the monarchy and the establishment of an aristocratic republic.[8]

This is not to say that there was any breaking of ties with Phoenicia, nor can we identify any point at which the Carthaginians clearly considered themselves to be independent. Even if they were not at this stage notably richer and more powerful than the other Phoenician settlements, their geographical position must have made them aware of their vital position in the Phoenician world in the west. Their intervention in Sicily in the sixth century was the first indication of what was to be a cardinal point in Carthaginian policy for over three centuries—the determination to retain a foothold in the island. It was their conviction that if western Sicily were lost to the Greeks, the latter would dominate the western Mediterranean, isolate the Sardinian colonies and reduce Carthage and the rest to a limited existence in Africa. Thus, all attempts by the Greeks and later the Romans to take western Sicily were resisted to the last.

The details of the first operations of Carthage in Sicily are not known but we hear of victories over the Greeks, presumably in the years following the death of Pentathlos. The Carthaginian leader is called Malchus in our sources[9] but this is perhaps a misunderstanding of the Phoenician word for king, *melek*. At this stage, if not before, Motya was equipped with a substantial defensive wall, and some time between 575 and 525 a causeway was built linking the island to the mainland. This facilitated both the movement of troops and more peaceful contacts, in particular with the neighbouring Elymians.[10] The Carthaginian position was strengthened by the fact that Selinus accepted as final the check to Greek hopes in the west of Sicily, and changed her policy. There is no doubt that her prosperity and unwarlike appearance in the sixth century were due not only to her trade but also to her friendship with Carthage. Himera and Acragas, however, remained hostile. This is not to say that we must envisage constant war between the Greeks and Phoenicians: some trade at any rate was carried on; Greek imports continued to enter Carthage and Utica, Carthaginian Sardinia and Ibiza, and at Motya there were Greek residents before the end of the sixth century. The Elymians, in spite of their alliance with the Phoenicians, were far more receptive of Greek culture than the other native inhabitants of Sicily; Segesta, their chief city, became so hellenized that in the fifth century its citizens had the right of intermarriage with those of Selinus, a privilege given to non-Greeks with great rarity.[11]

However, when the position of the Phoenicians and their allies in Sicily had been secured as far as possible, Malchus went to Sardinia, presumably with the same objective, but suffered a heavy defeat at the hands of the native population. There seems to be evidence of this setback in damage to the fort at Monte Sirai, but it is clear that it was only temporary.[12] In the course of the sixth century, the fort was rebuilt and strengthened, and there is other evidence that in Sardinia as well as Sicily, the Carthaginians were able to consolidate the position of the Phoenician settlements. However, they were very far from dominating the whole island at this stage, and during the century Sardinia was regarded by the Greeks as a possible area for colonization.

In particular, the Phocaeans of Massilia had an interest in it[13]; they had already founded a colony at Alalia in Corsica in 560; twenty years later, at the time of the conquest of Asia Minor by the Persians, a proposal was made that all the Ionian Greeks should emigrate to Sardinia to escape from non-Greek rule. This was too drastic for most of the Ionians, but the energetic Phocaeans had decided to emigrate whatever the rest of the Ionians did. Some half of their people left to join their fellows at Alalia, and engaged in more or less continuous piracy against Carthaginian and Etruscan shipping.[14]

Shortly after the arrival of the second group of colonists, the

Carthaginians and Etruscans formed an alliance to put down the nest of pirates. The Etruscans were the most advanced people in the west in the eighth century; it was believed by Greeks and Romans that they had emigrated to Italy from Asia Minor, and though there are some difficulties involved in accepting this view, there is no doubt that there was a dominant non Indo-European element among them which differentiated them from the rest of the Italian peoples. In the eighth century they evolved as city states, rather like the Greeks and Phoenicians, and were in close contact with both cultures; Phoenician material from the early seventh century onwards has frequently been found in Etruria, though it never rivalled Greek imports in quantity. The alliance between the Carthaginians and the Etruscans, which is attested for both the sixth and fifth centuries, was formed to check the expansion of all the Greeks in the west, though the Phocaean venture appears to have been the occasion for it. Each contributed fifty ships to a fleet, which met the Phocaeans somewhere off Sardinia. The latter only had sixty ships, and though they drove the Carthaginians and Etruscans from the place of battle, their own loss of forty ships was so heavy that they had to leave Alalia.[15]

The effect of this withdrawal was considerable. Corsica passed to the Etruscans, and the Phoenicians in Sardinia were no longer directly threatened. More than this, the power of the Phocaeans in the west was so weakened that within a very short time they—and naturally all other Greeks—were excluded from Tartessus and the rest of southern Spain. The monopoly which the Carthaginians henceforth enjoyed in this area is reflected in the ignorance of the Greeks during the succeeding centuries about the area of the Straits of Gibraltar. The Phocaeans were left with a limited though important sphere of activity along the Catalan and southern French coasts.

The alliance between Carthage and the Etruscans—or at least their coastal cities—was a lasting one. It is true that the Etruscans had a passion for Greek imported objects of many kinds which was unparalleled in the western Mediterranean, and Greek artisans had settled there at an early date; but since most of their cities were inland and those on the coast only had relatively few warships before the end of the sixth century, they were forced into the alliance by the activities of the Phocaeans, Liparans, and others. They were not hostile to all Greek states; for example, they had agreements with Sybaris, the most powerful Greek colony in south Italy until its destruction by a rival in 510. Imports from Greece were unloaded at Sybaris and transported across the isthmus to Laos, where they were picked up by Etruscan ships. This enabled the Etruscans to avoid the pirates of Lipara and the interference of Zancle and Rhegium, who doubtless exacted a toll from ships passing through the Straits of Messina. The fact is that piractical attacks on Carthaginian and Etruscan ships were made by a minority of Greek states and were a disservice in the long run to the cause of the western Greeks.

The close ties between Carthage and Etruscan cities were graphically illustrated by a discovery made in 1964 at Pyrgi, the harbour town of Caere. Three gold tablets, one inscribed in Phoenician, the other two in Etruscan, were found in the excavation of ancient temples. They recorded the dedication of a holy place to Astarte by Thefarie Velianas, of Caere. The tablets are of fifth-century date, and most philologists date them to between 500 and 480. There is some evidence that Caere was the most important Etruscan city at this period, and it remained prosperous for some time to come. It is probable that there were political overtones in the dedication by an Etruscan ruler of a shrine of one of the most popular Phoenician deities, which would no doubt be used by visiting Carthaginian sailors and merchants. The Etruscans had suffered some setbacks in Italy during the generation after Alalia, and were no doubt anxious to retain the best possible relationship with Carthage.[16]

The role of protector of the Phoenicians of the west was a heavy burden on Carthage, as the reform of the army during the sixth century shows. We are told that after the defeat of 'Malchus' in Sardinia, he and his army were sentenced to exile; this may perhaps be interpreted as an order to remain in Sardinia as colonists. The troops mutinied and forced their way back into Carthage, though Malchus was subsequently executed. There then came to the fore as the most powerful family in Carthage, the Magonids, so called after the first to become prominent, Mago.[17] He was a successful general and responsible for the change in the army.

Up to this date, as the mutiny in Sardinia shows, the army had consisted of a citizen levy, like that in any other ancient city state; from the time of Mago, it largely consisted of contingents drawn from subject states and of mercenaries, though the generals were Carthaginian.[18] The reason for the reform was that the population of Carthage was too small to provide for the defence of so widely scattered an empire. The numbers of inhabitants of ancient states even in the best recorded periods are very uncertain, so no estimate of Carthage's population at this early date can be more than hypothetical; but it can hardly have reached six figures. It was cheaper to use the revenues of the state to hire mercenaries than to withdraw a large number of citizens from the trading activities which provided so great a part of its wealth.

It is not the case that Carthaginians entirely disappeared from the army, as they are recorded as forming a part of various expeditions to Sicily in the fifth and fourth centuries; but it does not seem that they were numerous.[19] Their last appearance in a Carthaginian army outside Africa itself was in 311.[20] Shortly before this, in 339, we hear for the first time of a body called by our Greek sources the 'Sacred Band'; this was an *élite* corps of Carthaginian citizens, not more than 3,000 strong, and trained to fight as heavily armed infantry like Greek hoplites.[21] It is possible that it owes its development to similar institutions in the Greek world in the fourth century, for instance at Thebes.

Of all non-Carthaginian peoples who served in her army, the Libyans of Tunisia had the biggest share. Those who fought in Sicily in 480,[22] at which date we get our first glimpse of the various contingents, were presumably mercenaries, as at that time Carthage had no dependent territory, but subsequently it is probable that Libyan communities were obliged to provide recruits. In the third century Libyans are again found as mercenaries, and it is possible that by this date it had been found preferable to exact a tribute from them, with which volunteers could be hired.[23] Libyans were particularly suitable for use as light infantry; they could tolerate the heat of the sun better than most, and their own tradition of fighting was one of ambushes and swift raids; yet they were often used as front-line troops as well, and were a particularly effective part of Hannibal's army when he invaded Italy.[24]

As mercenaries, or more usually under treaties of alliance, Numidian and Mauretanian cavalry from more distant parts of North Africa formed an essential part of all Carthaginian expeditions, and in Roman times these peoples still provided some of the most effective horsemen in the western Mediterranean. Their value was fully recognized by Hannibal, who had over 6,000 at his disposal, and who suffered his only defeat when they were no longer available.[25]

We find Spanish[26] mercenaries in the service of Carthage from 480 till the Hannibalic war; during the time of Carthaginian domination in Spain (237–210) many were enrolled compulsorily but were paid as mercenaries. Most of the Spanish soldiers were Iberians or Celtiberians from the hills. Both these peoples were very backward in their way of life and had no unit of society larger than the clan; endemic clan wars and raids accustomed them to a life of fighting, and they would serve any master. Like the Libyans, whom in many ways they resembled, they were ideally suited for light infantry and for use in guerrilla warfare, for which the Spaniards have always been famous. They were also at home as cavalry, again lightly armed. The only technique in which they had outstripped their neighbours was in the manufacture of a special type of short sword equally suitable for thrusting and cutting.[27] During the second Punic War this sword was adopted by the Roman army as a standard weapon.

Balearic[28] islanders are found on occasion in the armies of Carthage, and became notorious both for their prowess as slingers and for their savage way of life; they were paid in women rather than in gold or silver.

Gauls appear first in 340, but were most used during Hannibal's invasion of Italy. They were famous for the impetuosity of their assault and for fighting without armour, but except in the hands of Hannibal were unreliable, especially when hard pressed.[29] Also during the fourth century Carthage made use of Campanians.[30] These hardy Italians were different from the types of mercenary so far mentioned, as they came from an area long influenced by Etruscan and Greek culture, yet they had the worst possible reputation for treachery and barbarism; they were only employed by Greeks and Carthaginians because their efficiency was out of all proportion to their small numbers, and in this as in other ways they may be compared to the Normans in the eleventh and twelfth centuries.

Lastly, mention may be made of the Greeks,[31] whose military reputation remained undimmed till the end of the third century. It is not often possible to say whether those in the service of Carthage came from Sicily or Greece. Perhaps in the fourth century Siceliots predominated, but in the third we hear of two distinguished officers from Greece, one of whom played a large part in saving Carthage during the first Punic War.

The disadvantages of the system for Carthage have generally been exaggerated. We hear of mercenary desertions, but these do not seem to have been the direct cause of many Carthaginian defeats; the only really serious disaster[32] was the revolt of the mercenaries in 241 after the end of the first war against Rome, when Carthage found it difficult to pay them off. Reflection will show that if Carthage had relied on her citizen troops, she might not have survived till the Roman period at all; her population was simply not large enough to stand more than one or two serious defeats, much less the enormous losses suffered by a whole series of mercenary expeditions, since a substantial part of the fleet was almost certainly manned by citizens.

Carthage was the first city state to attempt to rule an empire, and was able to maintain her rule for three centuries. The next attempt, that of Athens in the fifth century, in which the entire military burden was borne by the Athenian citizens, lasted less than a third of that time. This is not to say that through the use of mercenaries Carthage was able to pursue a more expansive policy; like all states whose wealth depends on trade, she knew well enough the losses caused by war, and was certainly one of the least warlike states of the Mediterranean. It is true that she maintained her trading monopolies by the simple process of sinking ships of other states who ventured inside her preserves, but this was apparently not regarded as warlike action by the victims' governments. In fact many states no doubt had treaties with Carthage, similar to those signed with Rome, which recognized Carthaginian monopolies.[33]

From the beginning of the fourth century other states, especially in the Greek world, began to use mercenaries, though not to the same extent as Carthage. Ultimately Rome was able to defeat Carthage, largely because of her greater resources in manpower, but she would have won much sooner if Carthage had had to rely on her own citizen body. Mercenaries made up in experience what they lacked in patriotic *élan*, and not a few Carthaginian generals from families in which there was a military tradition were successful in overcoming the difficulties involved in the tactical handling of heterogeneous armies. The resistance of Carthage to Rome was far more prolonged than that of the Hellenistic monarchies, with their larger resources and impressive military traditions inherited from Alexander himself. It is not sufficient to condemn the reliance on mercenaries as inglorious and typical of a greedy merchant state desirous of waging war on the cheap, without admitting that it served the needs of Carthage in preserving her limited manpower.

Mago was succeeded in Sardinia towards the end of the sixth century by his elder son Hasdrubal, who met his death in the island.[34] By this date, however, Carthaginian control of the coast of Sardinia was assured, though some tribes still maintained their independence in the hills in the interior. Throughout this time there was apparently no major conflict with the Greeks in Sicily, and the acquiescence of the latter in the status quo was shown in their indifference to the venture of the Spartan prince Dorieus.[35] About the year 514, this man, younger brother of Cleomenes, one of the kings of Sparta, received permission to lead a number of Spartans on a colonial expedition. As it was a principle of Spartan policy not to allow her citizens to emigrate, it is a fair assumption that some serious dynastic quarrel made the project acceptable. Dorieus sailed to the mouth of the river Kinyps on the coast

Tophet at Motya

Stele from Motya

of Tripolitania. It is probable that the Carthaginians had not yet founded any of the stations which later existed in this region, but they certainly regarded as threatening this settlement in an area monopolized by them, particularly as it was assisted by the Greeks of Cyrenaica. Only a few years before there had been a momentary threat to Carthage from this direction.[36] In 525 the Persian king Cambyses had conquered Egypt and Cyrenaica and planned to attack Carthage. He was prevented from carrying out this plan by the Phoenicians who provided the bulk of the Persian fleet; although they were subjects of the Persians, they refused to sail against their own foundation. It was true that Dorieus could have had nothing to do with any later Persian project in North Africa, but the Carthaginians were doubtless alarmed by a considerable amount of talk amongst the Greeks of the merits of the Gulf of Gabes as a field for settlement.

Within three years, with the help of some Libyan tribes, the Carthaginians drove out Dorieus and the settlers. The enterprising prince was not discouraged, and after recruiting more men in Greece he ventured right into the Carthaginian area of Sicily, attempting to settle near Eryx, a city of the Elymians. But he probably had no more than a thousand men, and none of the Siceliot cities provided any help; a force of Carthaginians, Sicilian Phoenicians and Elymians overwhelmed the colony and Dorieus was killed.

In the next generation, however, there were profound changes in the internal politics of the Siceliots and in the external affairs of the Greeks as a whole, both of which reacted on Carthage. The Siceliots had in some ways lagged behind in the social and political developments of the rest of the Greek world. This was partly because they were not in contact with advanced civilizations, as were the Greeks in Asia, partly because of the very success of the colonial movement in lessening economic distress and social unrest. By the end of the sixth century a number of important states in Greece and Asia Minor had passed through a political evolution in which landowning aristocracies were overthrown by dictators who rose to power through popular resentments, only to be overthrown in their turn by more or less democratic régimes; but in Sicily most states were still aristocratically governed. Now, however, these were challenged by the growth of new classes and interests and by the influx of ideas from the rest of the Greek world, particularly through refugees from Ionia after the failure of the revolt against the Persians (499–494).

Once the political scene changed in Sicily, it changed with a vengeance, and the Siceliot cities became notorious for the violence and

4

instability of their politics. This was partly due to the particular ruthlessness of some of the earliest Siceliot 'tyrants'. This word is conven-
tionally used by historians to represent the Greek word *turannos*; it
meant an autocrat who obtained and preserved his position by violence,
or at any rate by unconstitutional means, generally having some popular
support because of grievances against aristocratic régimes. The moral
censure implied in the word today was already present in the time of
Plato, and was due to the resentments of aristocrats, the criticism by
philosophers of the deleterious effect of absolute power on personal
character, and the many examples of thoroughly vicious tyrants who
justified the philosophers' strictures. Greek tyrants obviously resembled
certain popular dictators of modern times; the conventional term is,
however, used throughout this book.[37]

One of the earliest Siceliot tyrants was Hippocrates of Gela, who
came to power in 498. While in Greece itself most tyrants had devoted
at least some attention to the social and economic problems which had
brought about their rise, Hippocrates was the first of a long series of
aggressive and destructive Siceliots with large schemes of conquest and
personal aggrandizement and a ruthless disregard for their subjects.
After conquering several of the colonies in north-eastern Sicily, he was
succeeded in 491 by one of his officers named Gelon.

In the next few years, this tyrant was engaged in a war with Carthage
of which hardly anything is known.[38] It was described as a war to
avenge Dorieus; and thus Gelon was the originator of a popular motif of
Siceliot tyrants, namely patriotic war of Greeks against Carthaginians.
Although on many occasions the Carthaginians were represented as
a threat to Hellenism, analysis will show that on most occasions it
was one Siceliot tyrant or another who was the aggressor. Gelon
planned a campaign to 'liberate' the area of Carthaginian settlement
round the Gulf of Gabes, but this was never put into effect because of
the lack of support from other Greeks and Gelon's lack of a fleet. The
plan is noteworthy as it shows that some Greeks were still interested in
settling the North African coast. The situation of Carthaginian Sicily
became more difficult when Gelon made an alliance with another
tyrant, Theron of Acragas, without whose help, indeed, no effective
military operations against the Carthaginians in the west of Sicily
would have been possible.

The decisive moment in the growth of Gelon's power came in 485.
In this year the aristocrats of Syracuse, who had been overthrown in a
democratic revolution a few years earlier, appealed to Gelon for help.
He took over the city without a blow being struck, and then gave the

clearest proof of his ability; he saw that the position of Syracuse with its magnificent harbour and easy access to Greece made it the natural leader of Greek Sicily, and moved his seat of government there. Regardless of the feelings of the inhabitants, he forcibly removed to Syracuse, in order to increase its population, all the citizens of Camarina, half those of Gela, and the wealthier inhabitants of Sicilian Euboea and Megara. In this ruthless way Gelon made himself master of most of Greek Sicily and a substantial army and navy.

The record and personality of Hippocrates and Gelon made it obvious to the Carthaginians that sooner or later they would be the object of a major attack. However, they were by no means without friends in Sicily as the rulers of several Greek cities observed the aggressive progress of Gelon. Selinus remained as before an ally of Carthage; Terillos, the tyrant of Himera, was a guest friend of Hamilcar, the leader of the Magonids since the death of his brother Hasdrubal in Sardinia.[39] Moreover Anaxilas, the tyrant of Rhegium, who also controlled Messana, sought a connexion with the Carthaginians through a marriage alliance with Terillos. This group of states suffered a serious blow in 483 when Terillos was driven from his city by Theron of Acragas. Terillos appealed to Carthage, and was supported by his son-in-law Anaxilas, who handed over his children as hostages to Hamilcar to demonstrate his loyalty. It is clear that Carthage took some time responding to the appeal (unless our date for the expulsion of Terillos is wrong), since the expedition she sent to Sicily did not leave till 480.

The situation was complicated by events in the East which ought to have improved the chances of Carthaginian success. Xerxes, the king of Persia, was pressing on with his plans to add Greece to the Persian Empire, and in 481 some of the Greek states sent an embassy to Gelon asking for help. Herodotus[40] gives an amusing though doubtless inexact account of the arguments used by the embassy and the answer of Gelon. It was clear that Gelon, faced with the threat of a major war in Sicily, could not think of sending any help to Greece (whose subjugation by the vastly superior Persian forces must in any case have seemed inevitable); on the other hand he could not expect any help from Greece.

This raises the question whether the Persian attack on Greece and the Carthaginian intervention in Sicily were deliberately timed to coincide. Herodotus tells us[41] that Gelon's victory occurred on the same day as that of the Athenian fleet over the Persians at Salamis. Other historians agreed with this synchronism, but it is noteworthy that Herodotus regarded it as a coincidence, as also did Aristotle much later.[42] Another group of authors declared that there was an understanding between

Persia and Carthage, even an embassy to arrange the details.[43] On the whole the view of Herodotus ought to be accepted, with this proviso; the Carthaginians could easily have got to know of the Persian plans—since a large part of the Persian fleet was drawn from the cities of Phoenicia—and then without any formal understanding timed their intervention in Sicily accordingly; this might account for the delay in taking up the cause of Terillos. It is hardly to be thought that the quarrel of a distant and minor power like Carthage could have had any influence on the Persian plans.

The Carthaginians knew well enough that their attempt to restore their ally would be resisted not only by the tyrant of Acragas but by Gelon also. They therefore put a major effort into enrolling an army, and its composition (the first of which we have any details) shows that the reform of Mago was by now fully effective; in addition to some Carthaginians there were Libyans, Iberians, Sardinians, and Corsicans. The fantastic figure of 300,000 is given as its strength in our Greek sources. Most ancient writers were notoriously inexact when giving the numbers of non-Greek armies, partly through the ignorance or prejudice which refers to 'barbarian hordes', partly through a desire to exalt Greek victories. It may be doubted whether in fact the force amounted to more than 30,000, though it is pretty certain it outnumbered that of Gelon. The number of troop transports given—3,000—is also to be rejected, but the figure of 200 warships is more likely, at least as representing the Carthaginian potential. Gelon is said to have had the same number, and his fleet was the largest in the Greek world after that of Athens.[44]

The general entrusted with this army, the largest Carthage had yet enrolled, was Hamilcar the Magonid. It is not known whether he had instructions to do more than restore Terillos and defeat any opposition; if we may judge from later Carthaginian practice, he was given a good deal of freedom of action, but the view that he was leading a Carthaginian attempt to subdue the whole of Sicily is pure supposition, unsupported by worthwhile evidence. It derives mainly from its association with the campaign of Xerxes, which certainly had the aim of conquering Greece, but Carthage's objective was limited to the support of Greek states hostile to Syracuse, in order that the whole of Greek Sicily should not fall under one ruler. This appeared essential, because the history of the previous generation had shown that Greeks and Siceliots were still thinking of expansion in the west.

Hamilcar's fleet sailed without hindrance into the harbour of Panormus. He was assisted by the fact that with Selinus an ally of Carthage the Siceliots had no suitable base on the south coast of the island from which to intercept his fleet as it made its way to Sicily by the shortest route; yet the inactivity of Gelon's fleet compares unfavourably with the dash of the Athenians against greater odds. From Panormus Hamilcar marched to Himera, where he pitched camp to the west of the city, while his fleet was beached at the mouth of the river where the harbour was. He was met by Gelon, who had come out with about 24,000 foot-soldiers and 2,000 horse and encamped to the south of Himera.

The battle which followed was no set piece but a triumph for Gelon's opportunism. He intercepted a message from Hamilcar to Selinus summoning the cavalry contingent the city had agreed to supply. He sent his Syracusan cavalry to keep the rendezvous at the Carthaginian ships; the force guarding them was deceived, and they broke in among the ships and set them on fire. Hamilcar was present, and he was cut down as he was carrying out a sacrifice. This at any rate was one version of his death, though Herodotus reports a Carthaginian account to the effect that having spent the day in a vain attempt to obtain favourable omens for the battle, he finally threw himself into the sacrificial fire in an attempt to appease the apparently hostile deities. The cavalry squadron and the Himerans then attacked the Carthaginian camp. Its defenders, no doubt shaken by the unexpected disaster, put up little resistance, and as the ships were almost all destroyed, those who were not killed were taken prisoner, having no means of escape.

The loss of the ships was far more serious for Carthage than the destruction of her mercenary army, and it was clear that the attempt to restore Terillos had to be given up, even if this meant abandoning her other Siceliot friends. Gelon judged it prudent not to be led on to adventurous schemes because of one victory, and when the Carthaginians asked for peace, they obtained it on moderate terms. They had to pay an indemnity of 2,000 talents (over fifty tons of silver) and for the construction of two temples, in which were recorded the terms of the treaty.[45]

The sixth and early fifth century saw Carthage achieve full independence of her founder, apparently without friction, and a leading position among the states of the western Mediterranean. The narrative will have demonstrated that it was the expansive vigour of the Greek movement of colonization that brought about the recorded conflicts. A legitimate concentration on the intellectual achievements of Athens in the fifth century can make us forget this extraordinary movement, in which a large number of Greek states of no particular significance joined and in which it appeared that there was no area on the Mediterranean or Black

Sea coasts which might not have a colony planted on it. Carthage was clearly hard pressed at times to hold on to the sphere of activity which the Phoenicians of the west had won for themselves.

Further, it is to be noted that the conflicts with the Greeks were not commercial wars; in fact even the struggles with the Phocaeans, though the Carthaginian victory ended in re-establishing the monopoly in the Spanish silver and tin, was hardly a commercial war in the sense in which this term is used of wars in seventeenth-century Europe. No Greek state of this period—or before the Hellenistic Age—was concerned to promote the interests of its producers and merchants, to the extent of going to war. It is therefore incorrect to talk of Carthaginian and Greek competition in trade in the western Mediterranean as a leading motive in the wars, and this is true of those of the fourth century also. The Carthaginians' insistence on maintaining control of the route to Spain may be compared with the interest of the Athenians in the fifth and fourth centuries in the route to the Black Sea, from which they obtained supplies of corn for their large urban population. The exploitation of the metal production of Spain was as integral a part of Carthaginian existence as if the mines had been located a few miles from the city itself.

3

Carthaginian Expansion in Africa

ELON'S victory at Himera opened the
greatest period of Greek civilization in Sicily;
but just as the magnitude of the victory itself
has been exaggerated because of parallel events in Greece, and because
of the flourishing state of Greek Sicily in the following half century,
so the very different aspect of Carthage in the same period has led
some to see in the result of Himera a catastrophe for her.

The number of Carthaginians lost in the army was probably not
large, though there was a contingent of citizens providing a stiffening
to the mercenary force. The destruction of the latter doubtless had a
bad effect on the prestige of Carthage among the tribes from which
soldiers were hired, but so far as we know there was never any difficulty
in getting mercenary soldiers in the succeeding centuries.

The loss of the ships—and their rowers—was more serious, since the
empire could only be held together if Carthaginian seapower was
sufficient to deter her enemies from attacking it. Yet it was believed
by the Greeks in the years after Himera that Carthage would certainly

return to Sicily in force[1]; this means either that Carthage still had a respectable fleet in being or that a new one was constructed with great speed. No doubt the Carthaginians were as yet incapable of the tremendous efforts which they made in the war with Rome in the third century, in which entire fleets were built within a few months, but the Athenians had built a fleet of about 250 oared warships in two or three years in the previous decade, and the resources of Carthage were sufficient for a similar programme. Lastly, there is the significant inactivity of the Siceliots during the rest of the fifth century. There may have been conflicts with the Carthaginians in Sicily, but these amounted to no more than frontier skirmishes, which did not involve the whole power of Carthage or the leading Siceliot cities. If the battle of Himera was a catastrophe for Carthage, the Siceliots were remiss in not following it up, and it was not as though Gelon's personal power rested on the existence of a threat to Greek Sicily which he would be reluctant wholly to remove. There was probably a lack of confidence among the Syracusans in the ability of their fleet to defeat that of Carthage, and without this it was almost impossible to drive them from Sicily.

It is true that in the Aegean the Athenians were showing what a profit could be gained from their naval superiority over the Persians—in effect, the Phoenicians. At Himera, however, the only thing that had been demonstrated was that the heavily-armed Greek cavalry and hoplites (the Greek infantry soldiers) were superior to a motley army of non-Greek mercenaries. If Gelon and his advisers compared their success with those of their fellow Greeks against the Persians, it would have been with the battle of Plataea in 479. This land battle was less sensational than the naval battle of Salamis—though without a Greek victory on land Salamis would have been in vain—but in it was demonstrated, as at Himera, the superiority of the Greek hoplite and in particular of Spartans—Dorians, like the Syracusans.[2] For these reasons, the Carthaginians cannot have thought, at any rate after a few years, that their very existence was threatened by the defeat at Himera alone. In a more general sense, the impulses which had led to the Greek colonization no longer had their old power, and this made for a more settled state of affairs in the West.

The significance of Himera for Carthage lay in the fact that it came at a time of growing isolation. Her Etruscan allies were under pressure in Italy, and traditionally in 510–509 lost their hold on the plain of Latium, in which the most important community was Rome. This loss meant that the Etruscan ruling class in Campania was cut off from its homeland except by sea, and its position became worse when it

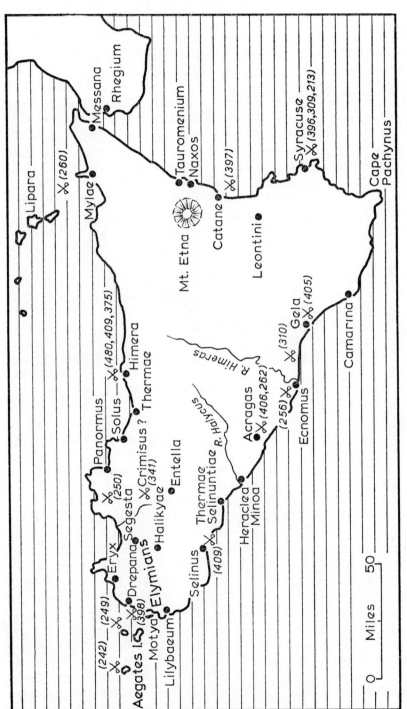

SICILY

Lipara

Rhegium
Messana
Mylae ✗ (260)

Tauromenium
Naxos
✗ (1397)
Catane
Mt. Etna
Leontini

Syracuse ✗ (396,309,213)

Cape Pachynus

Panormus
Solus ✗ (480,409,375)
Himera
Thermae
✗Crimisus ? (341)
Entella

R. Himeras

Gela ✗ (405)
✗ (310)

Camarina

Acragas ✗ (406,262)
✗ (256)
Ecnomus

Eryx ✗ (250)
Segesta
Drepana
Halikyae
Elymians
Motya ✗ (398)
Aegates I.
(242) ✗
(249) ✗

Thermae
Selinuntiae R. Halycus

Heraclea Minoa

Selinus ✗ (409)

Lilybaeum

0 Miles 50

suffered a severe defeat in the bay of Naples in 474 at the hands of Gelon's ships, which went to assist the tyrant of Cumae, Aristodemos. After this Etruscan power in Campania declined.

Also important in the isolation of Carthage were continued Greek successes in the eastern Mediterranean following the defeat of the Persian invasion. The Athenians formed a league comprising most of the islands and coastal cities of the Aegean, from which area they sought to exclude the Persians and their dependants; this included the Phoenicians, who provided the bulk of the Persian fleet. The Phoenicians suffered heavy losses in a naval battle with the Athenians in 468, and in 459 the coast of Phoenicia itself was raided[3]; even Cyprus came under Athenian control, though only for a brief period. Thus Carthage could not expect any assistance from the eastern Mediterranean, and this profitable market for the primary products she acquired was closed.

The defeat at Himera and the isolation from Phoenicia had very important consequences for Carthage. In the first place, there appear to have been considerable economic difficulties, resulting from the loss of the fleet and the payment of the idemnity. Archaeologically, these difficulties may be seen in a decline in imports from the Greek world, and also from Egypt and Etruria.[4] In general, the finds in graves of the fifth century tend to show that the material life of the Carthaginians was now poor and austere. On the other hand, since this apparent material poverty lasted most of the century, long after the immediate effects of Himera must have worn off, and when the benefits of expansion in Africa must have been felt, it is possible that a deliberate effort was made to restrict trade with, at least, the Greek world.

One factor which probably inhibited trade in any case was the lack of a Carthaginian coinage. By the beginning of the fifth century most Greek states of any importance had their own coinage, and even the Phoenicians, much of whose trade was still with peoples among whom barter was the rule, began to coin about 450. Carthage, however, did not coin till the early fourth century,[5] and then, it seems, chiefly to pay the mercenaries in the more frequent wars which she was then engaged in. Oddly enough, both Motya and Panormus had their own coinage, but our archaeological evidence shows that there was no diminution in Greek contacts with these places which clearly still enjoyed some economic independence. The lack of coinage naturally had no effect on trade with the more backward peoples of the western Mediterranean and North Africa where barter sufficed.

There was a good economic reason for ceasing to import Greek and other foreign goods. All these must have been paid for largely in raw materials and particularly gold and silver, since the Carthaginians manufactured little of any attraction to the Greeks. It is true that there was little appreciation at this period of the disadvantages of an unsatisfactory balance of trade; the primary concern of states was the security of their essential imports rather than the discovery of a satisfactory way of paying for them, and even Athens, the most commercially minded of Greek states, regularly paid with silver from her own mines for corn imported from south Russia. But at Carthage such a wastage would have been more immediately felt since she needed a substantial reserve of precious metal in case large armies had to be raised from mercenaries; other states had no such pressing need for a large balance of gold and silver.

A deliberate attempt to cut a state off from the broad current of Mediterranean development was not unique nor entirely impracticable. In the previous century the Spartans had sought with considerable success to isolate themselves from the rapid social and economic changes in progress in the Greek world; among other things they had prevented as far as possible contacts between their own people and other Greeks, refused to coin in gold and silver and prohibited their own citizens from owning these precious metals. Later, in the third century, there was a strong current of opinion at Rome against anything Greek, on the ground that it was injurious to Roman character; in this case social pressure rather than legislation was used in the vain effort to stop the influx of alien ideas.

Isolation from Phoenicia and a feeling of being under pressure from the Greek world were probably sufficient to limit the effect of Greek civilization on Carthage at this stage. In fact, in the latter part of the fifth century there was more Greek influence in Phoenicia than in North Africa.[6]

There was an important change in Carthaginian religion in the fifth century which must be connected in some way with the relative isolation of Carthage. The position of primacy among the deities of Carthage held by the supreme god Baal Hammon went, at least as far as popular worship was concerned, to the goddess Tanit.[7] It has been held that this was due to native Libyan influences, which would have been increasingly felt as Carthage acquired extensive territory in North Africa. However this may be, the cult had no place in the traditional Phoenician pantheon, and it became characteristic not only of Carthage herself but also of most Phoenician settlements in the west which she came increasingly to dominate; it does not appear, however, to have been popular in Spain.[8]

Territorial expansion in North Africa was the positive side of the superficially narrow and restricted life of the Carthaginians in the fifth century. In fact, expansion could only have been achieved with considerable effort, and it would seem that whatever the material standard of life of the individual Carthaginian, the power of the city recovered fairly rapidly from Himera. The acquisition of a substantial territory in Africa assured the city of an adequate supply of food and made possible a larger population. Nor did the policy in any sense mean a withdrawal from the sea; by making herself mistress of the entire coast of North Africa from Cyrenaica to the Straits of Gibraltar and beyond, she consolidated her hold on the trade in metals with Spain and West Africa.

It does not appear that the new policy was initiated by any alteration in the type of government[9]; the Magonid family continued to play the leading role in the city, in spite of the disaster of Himera, until at least the middle of the fifth century, when their dominance came to an end, though the family by no means disappeared from Carthaginian history; it was most probably Hanno the son of Hamilcar who died at Himera who was responsible both for conquests in the interior of Africa and for a famous voyage down the west coast of Africa. His achievement was loosely described by Dio Chrysostom[10] in the first century A.D. as 'transforming the Carthaginians from Tyrians into Africans; thanks to him they lived in Africa rather than Phoenicia, became very wealthy, acquired many markets, ports, and ships, and ruled on land and sea'. Naturally it was an exaggeration to attribute the settlement in Africa to Hanno, but the sense is that his conquests, coupled with the separation from Phoenicia, made the Carthaginians a great power in Africa and the West.

The amount of land conquered before the end of the fifth century is not known, but it must have included the whole of the Cap Bon peninsula, and a considerable area to the south-west of Carthage. Our earliest exact information comes from an account of the invasion of Africa by Agathocles in 310[11]; in this, there is mention of a town subject to Carthage named Tocai, almost certainly the Roman Thugga, modern Dougga. This town lies seventy-five miles south-west of Carthage in the most natural direction of expansion after the acquisition of the Cap Bon peninsula. The area watered by the Oued Medjerda and the Oued Siliana and their tributaries was the scene of particularly dense settlement in Roman times, and there was strong Carthaginian influence resulting from the earlier conquest. In 247, Theveste (Tebessa)[12] was captured by the Carthaginians, and the implication is that up to that date it had been independent; on the other hand, Sicca (Le Kef), mentioned as being in Carthaginian territory in 241, had probably long been subject.[13] It was near the western limit of the empire in the interior, because Madauros (Mdaourouch) was outside it.[14] No doubt there were variations in the amount of territory controlled at different times.

The inhabitants of the conquered lands seem generally to have been permitted to remain, and were not enslaved *en masse*, but there must have been a considerable amount of movement of the native population in the Cap Bon peninsula, where many Carthaginians had estates.[15] There was probably a distinction drawn between the land nearest to the city, and including Cap Bon, which counted as city land, and that to the south-west in the Medjerda valley, the inhabitants of which were subjects of Carthage and obliged to provide troops and pay tribute. The name 'Libyan' came to be restricted to these subjects, though originally it had extended to all the native non-Negro inhabitants of North Africa.[16] In addition, there were tribes of Numidians in the more distant parts of Tunisia and Algeria who were at times brought under Carthaginian control.[17] Greek writers regularly use the word *polis*, city, to describe Libyan and Numidian communities; what is implied, however, is that those of the tribes who were not nomadic but sedentary did not live dispersed throughout the countryside but in compact settlements.[18] The primary consideration was the water supply, another was defence. Most of the native settlements were on hill tops, and many were strengthened with fortifications.[19]

The stages by which Carthage got control of the entire coast of North Africa from Cyrenaica to the Atlantic are little known, because clear dating for specific acquisitions is scarcely ever to be had. Some may be as early as the sixth century, others as late as the fourth, but by the time Carthage resumed close contacts with the Greek world, shortly before 400, she possessed almost as much territory in Africa as she was ever to have.[20] In extent this empire was larger than that of Athens in the Aegean, but the two were alike in that they were empires controlled by city states, and their origins were similar. Most of the allies (really subjects) of Athens had initially surrendered some of their autonomy to Athens in return for protection against the Persians. Similarly the Carthaginians had started on the road to empire by protecting other Phoenician colonies against their enemies; this is certain for Sicily and Sardinia, and probable for Spain, though in Africa the original Phoenician colonies were presumably brought under control without any such excuse. Athens, however, did not send out colonies except to control recalcitrant subjects, nor did she win a land empire.

The Carthaginian colonies were numerous, but like those of the Phoenicians were mostly small; this is shown by the Greek word *emporia*—markets—used of many of them in our sources.[21] We must envisage small settlements of at most a few hundred people, at places to which native tribes brought their goods to trade, which could serve as anchorages and watering places; the most favoured sites were those which always appealed to the Phoenicians—offshore islands, headlands, and estuaries. Only a few grew to a size at which they could properly be called cities, even by ancient standards. This is understandable, since the citizen population of Carthage itself is unlikely, in spite of its growth, to have reached more than 200,000 in the fifth century.[22] There is a possibility that there was further emigration from Phoenicia during the century which may have contributed to the expansion, and much of the coast was very sparsely populated, so a substantial military force was not required. The term Libyphoenicians[23]—people of Phoenician race living in Africa—was used by the Greeks of the inhabitants of these colonies, and at a later date of natives who had been so influenced by the higher culture that they could be regarded as Phoenicians.

The eastern limit of the Carthaginian Empire was at the place called in Latin Arae Philaenorum (Altars of the Philaeni) on the Gulf of Sidra. Legend told of two heroic Carthaginians called Philaenus who were buried there, but the name probably describes some natural feature of the landscape. It was the boundary between the Carthaginians and the Greeks of Cyrenaica, as it was later between the Roman provinces of Tripolitania and Cyrenaica.[24] Settlements along the Tripolitanian coast were few, though it is likely that it was slightly more favourable to cultivation in antiquity than it is today. At Charax Carthage had a market where wine was exchanged for a valuable medicinal herb called silphium smuggled out of Cyrenaica, where the Greek colonies tried to monopolize its export.[25]

The principal settlement of the region was Lepcis, in Roman times Lepcis Magna. The earliest imported object found at this site is a Greek cup of the early fifth century; and while Carthage was doubtless interested in the area, and her ships regularly sailed to it before this date, it is probable that no permanent settlement was made till after the expedition of Dorieus—whose colony was only twelve miles to the east—had shown that there was a danger of the Greeks getting a foothold in this part of North Africa. Traces of the port at the mouth of the Wadi Lebda have been found, but little else of the pre-Roman period. It must have become one of the most prosperous Carthaginian colonies, because it is found as the administrative centre of the district on the Gulf of Gabes as far as Thaenae called by the Greeks Emporia. This district paid a tribute to Carthage which in the second century amounted to a talent a day.²⁶

We must not envisage anything in Carthaginian Lepcis as remotely resembling the grandiose Roman remains on the site, but the earlier civilization was so deeply entrenched that in spite of an admixture of Libyan elements we still find its language and institutions in use in the second century A.D.²⁷ Its wealth and that of its neighbours Oea and Sabratha came not so much from fishing and agriculture as from trade with the interior. This part of Tripolitania was or became the terminus of the shortest caravan route across the Sahara linking the Mediterranean with the middle and upper Niger. It was the starting point of Roman exploration to Cydamus and beyond, and so probably of a Carthaginian named Mago who claimed to have crossed the desert three times without taking a drink on the way. Such trade must have consisted in objects of little bulk and considerable value, and the chief Carthaginian demand seems to have been for precious stones, carbuncles, emeralds, and chalcedony. The tribesmen who brought them, the Garamantes of Roman times, doubtless accepted the usual consumer goods of Carthaginian commerce—cheap ornaments, beads, pottery, wine, and food. No date is known for the origin of Oea, and the tradition that it was founded jointly by Sicilians and Africans is most improbable.²⁸

Discoveries at Sabratha indicate that there was a period of seasonal occupation late in the fifth century, after which a small permanent settlement was built with houses of mud brick on stone foundations. Agriculture, and particularly the cultivation of the olive, was not neglected, and the prosperity of this part of Tripolitania in Roman times had its origin in the work of the Carthaginian colonists.²⁹

There was a settlement and port called Zouchis, or Zoucharis in Greek, which was well known for its salted fish and purple dye production.³⁰ In Roman times, pictures of marine life, sometimes fishing scenes, sometimes still-life representations of fish of many kinds, occur frequently in the magnificent mosaics of North Africa, and it is clear that fish was a very important article of food along these coasts throughout antiquity. The purple-dye industry shows the Carthaginians in Africa carrying on one of the crafts for which the Phoenicians had been famous for centuries. Near by was the island of Meninx,³¹ well cultivated in the fourth century. This island was the home of the Lotus Eaters in classical mythology, no doubt because of the reputation of its exceptionally good climate. It must have been a dependency of Carthage though there is no evidence that there were colonists on it.

The same is true of the mainland towns Gigthis and Tacapae[32]; both were substantial places in Roman times, and neo-Punic (the later form of the Carthaginian language, as it developed after the Roman conquest) was spoken there. North of the Gulf of Gabes the control of Carthage was more secure; the boundary of the city's inland possessions reached the east coast of Tunisia at Thaenae.[33] Further north was Acholla, supposed to have been founded by colonists from Phoenician Malta. Like several of its neighbours, it was a place of some size in the second century and joined the Roman side in Carthage's final struggle.[34] The same is true of Thapsus, which was certainly in existence in the middle of the fourth century.[35] Leptis Minor was so called in Roman times, to distinguish it from Lepcis in Tripolitania, which was also often spelt Leptis. It was reckoned as an original Phoenician foundation, but is first mentioned in a historical circumstance in the third century; it is known to have had very strong fortifications.[36]

The largest city on the east coast of Tunisia was Hadrumetum[37]; like Leptis, it was said to be a Phoenician foundation. A sanctuary and graves of the sixth century have been found, and like Carthage it had, at least at a later date, an artificial harbour. Some distance to the north lay the place called by the Greeks Neapolis, its Phoenician name being unknown. A Carthaginian station existed here in the late fifth century, and by the end of the fourth century it was a strong town from which a road ran to Carthage across the base of the peninsula of Cap Bon. Thus ships arriving from the east, and prevented for any reason from rounding the cape, could put in at Neapolis and have their cargoes transported to Carthage by land.[38]

At Dar Essafi[39] almost at the end of Cap Bon, was a Carthaginian town which was never occupied after its desertion, apparently in the years immediately following the Roman conquest in 146. Preliminary excavations on this promising site show that the town was built in the fifth century, though tombs found in the same neighbourhood are of the sixth and indicate some earlier occupation. It stretched along the cliff for over 500 yards, and had a depth of over 100 yards. The houses were well built, the walls in some cases being extremely thick, over six feet, and designed to carry several stories or a heavy rounded roof of brick; in the later period there was substantial Hellenistic influence. A characteristic pink cement, polished smooth, sometimes containing in its make-up small fragments of white marble, was used for floors, and walls were covered with a purple-coloured stucco. A notable feature

Stele from Carthage, in the form of
'Sign of Tanit', sixth or fifth century

Stelae from Carthage with 'Sign of Tanit'; (top) fourth or third century (bottom) third century.

was the attention to hygiene; there were baths and lavatories and well-constructed sewers and drains.

On the west side of the Cap Bon peninsula, there were no Carthaginian settlements, though naturally the whole bay was controlled from an early date; the quarries at Sidi Daoud were worked throughout the history of Carthage. West of Carthage, the coastline has altered considerably since ancient times, as a result of changes in the course of the River Bagradas (Oued Medjerda) and the amount of silt brought down from the fertile plains through which it flows in its middle and lower course.

As a result, the site of Utica, which was a port in Carthaginian and Roman times, is now over seven miles from the sea. Excavations during the last ten years have been chiefly concerned with the Phoenician cemeteries, which were less damaged by later Roman building than the city itself. The earliest graves so far discovered date from the late or possibly middle eighth century B.C., and present features similar to but not identical with those of Carthage itself. The initial settlement was apparently made on a small island separated from the mainland peninsula by a narrow and shallow creek, or a tributary of the Medjerda; the cemeteries were on both sides of this water-course, which must have served as the harbour. The city soon extended to the mainland, and because of its traditional priority, which there seems no good reason to doubt, it always had a special position amongst the dependants of Carthage. Utica is named beside Carthage in the second treaty with Rome (348), and in spite of her defection in the Mercenary War appears again as nominally equal with Carthage in the treaty between Hannibal and Philip of Macedon (215). She does not appear in the first treaty with Rome (508), which perhaps means she was then fully independent and not even bound in an alliance.[40]

Beyond the headland of Cape Farina the coast of North Africa stretches away to the west as far as the Straits of Gibraltar. Along it there were numerous markets and anchorages, some first used by the Phoenicians, others after the rise of Carthage. These places were generally to be found roughly thirty miles apart, this representing the distance which could be sailed in a day by small coasting vessels. In general the coast was too inhospitable to attract many colonists, and it is clear that few if any of the settlements reached anything like the prosperity of those on the east coast of Tunisia. One of the more important was Hippo Acra, known to Romans as Hippo Diarrhytus (Bizerta) whose natural advantages as a port must have been utilized at an early date; it was certainly in existence by the middle of the fourth century.[41] The

5

other Hippo, later called Hippo Regius, was a port of some size in Roman times and was probably of Carthaginian origin.

The area on either side of Cape Metagonion (Cap Bougaron) seems to have been in a special category within the Carthaginian Empire. At any rate, Greek geographers and historians used the term Metagonia to cover the coast to the east and west of the cape probably as far as Thabraca and the River Ampsaga (Oued el Kebir) respectively.[42] These were the boundaries of the later Roman province of Numidia, which were apparently based on this earlier division. The population of the interior was entirely Numidian, but there were several Carthaginian stations on the coast. In addition to Hippo, Thapsus was a port in the fourth century,[43] Rusicade is a name of Phoenician origin borne by a Roman town, while Carthaginian objects of the fourth and third centuries have been found in Chullu.[44] In the interior, Cirta was an important Numidian stronghold; in the third century it was greatly influenced by Carthaginian civilization.

Between the Oued el Kebir and Algiers there were apparently no substantial towns, but in Roman times there were a number of places whose names betray their origin, e.g. Rusazu, Rusippisu, Rusuccuru, Rusubiccari, Rusguniae, all of which contain the Phoenician element *rus* meaning 'cape'. Saldae was important enough to issue its own coins in the period after the fall of Carthage, and probably had a Phoenician element in its population.[45]

Excavations at Tipasa since the last war show that it was first visited by Carthaginians towards the end of the sixth century, but that only very limited settlement, perhaps even seasonal, existed before the third century. The early visitors seem to have been simple fishermen or traders. It is likely that exact excavation rather than haphazard finds would give a similar picture of many of the Carthaginian settlements in this region.[46] Iol was perhaps a place of some consequence; at any rate, in the time of Augustus it was chosen as the capital of Mauretania by Iuba, one of Rome's dependants. At Gunugu have been found tombs of the fourth and third centuries, while Cartennae, Portus Magnus, and Rusaddir all show Carthaginian influence of second-century date.[47] Rachgoun and Mersa Madakh, in the region of Oran, are the only places on the northern coast of Algeria to produce material from the period of Phoenician rather than Carthaginian expansion, but there can be little doubt that others will be found. Tingi (Tangier) is referred to in the fifth century, and it is certain that the Phoenicians had a station there as soon as they had conceived the aim of preventing the Greeks from getting through the Straits of Gibraltar to Tartessus.[48]

The question of colonies on the Atlantic coast of Morocco is connected with the voyages of exploration undertaken by the Carthaginians in the fifth century. Before considering these voyages, mention must be made of the notion which the Greeks and Romans—and no doubt the Carthaginians also—had about Africa and the question whether it could be circumnavigated. Greek opinion was divided about this; some held that it could not be circumnavigated,[49] for various not altogether satisfactory reasons, including the belief that there was a land mass attaching India to East Africa. Others[50] said that it could, but they were ignorant of the greatest obstacle of all, namely the vast size of the continent. Greek knowledge of the East African coast either through visits of their own people after 330, or from Arabian or Egyptian informants, hardly stretched beyond Somalia, and it was held by many that at about that point the coast turned westwards towards the Straits of Gibraltar.[51] There was no strong motive compelling any of the ancient peoples of the Mediterranean to attempt the circumnavigation as there was for the European powers of the Renaissance, when the desire for a route to the Far East free from interference was imperative. It is true that commodities were imported into the Mediterranean from East Africa or southern Arabia, and that these had to come by way of Egypt or the caravan cities of Arabia, but there is no evidence that the ancient attempts at circumnavigation were made in order to by-pass these expensive routes. Those who explored the area of the Red Sea and beyond were interested in getting to India more than anything else.

The first attempt was in fact a voyage from east to west made on the orders of one of the later kings of Egypt, but the sailors and ships were Phoenician. If references in the Old Testament[52] can be taken literally, when the Phoenicians and Israelites were allies in the time of Solomon, the former had sailed from Israelite territory near Eilath on the Gulf of Akaba down the Red Sea, and thus gained direct access to the markets of Arabia and Africa. This trade must have collapsed in the succeeding centuries when the Israelites lost their hold on the head of the gulf. It was in the seventh century that the Egyptians, who normally adopted a very exclusive attitude towards foreigners, allowed a number of Greeks and Phoenicians into the country, and it was the latter who made the voyage.

Herodotus[53] says that King Necho (*c.* 610–594) sent Phoenician mariners to sail down the Red Sea, circumnavigate Africa, and return through the Straits of Gibraltar. They took over two years on the journey, having twice halted to sow and reap a crop of wheat. This story has caused a great amount of comment from antiquity to the present day. Herodotus believed that the voyage had been successful, but some of his successors had the strongest doubts. It can be said that there is nothing inherently improbable in the account, and the project itself need not be doubted, even if its success is. Necho was a man of grandiose schemes, and is best known for his attempts to build a canal joining the Nile to the Red Sea so that ships could sail from the latter through to the Mediterranean. Work on this ancestor of the Suez Canal was interrupted before completion and a successful circum-navigation might have indicated whether or not it was necessary. If in fact the Phoenicians got round Africa, the length of the voyage and the primitive nature of the peoples encountered on the various coasts must have removed ideas about the possibility of using this route from the Red Sea to the Mediterranean.

It is obvious that the Phoenicians of the west must have known of the attempt of their fellows, especially if it was successful, and Herodotus in fact reports that the Carthaginians believed that Africa could be circumnavigated.[54] They must also have been aware of another attempt recorded by Herodotus.[55] This took place after the Persians had con-quered most of the east, including Phoenicia. Sometime between 485 and 465 a connexion of the Persian King Xerxes called Sataspes was condemned to death as a result of a court scandal; he was given the chance of a pardon if he sailed round Africa, leaving by the Straits of Gibraltar and returning up the Red Sea—in other words the opposite direction to the earlier attempt. Sataspes procured a ship and crew in Egypt (though we are not told that they were Egyptian and were perhaps Phoenician). It can hardly be supposed that he made his way into the Atlantic without procuring information or even pilots from the Carthaginians or other western Phoenicians who knew something of the Moroccan coast. Sataspes continued south for many months beyond Cape Spartel but eventually turned back, because 'however far he went there was always need to go still farther'. He also reported to Xerxes that at the most southerly point reached he had found the coast inhabited by pygmies who wore clothes made of palm leaves. These had abandoned their villages and made for the hills when he had landed. As to his failure to continue, he declared that the ship had been brought to a standstill and could make no headway. Xerxes was not convinced by this explanation and the unfortunate prince was impaled. It is impossible to say how far he sailed, except that it was clearly beyond the southern limit of the Sahara.

The voyage of Sataspes took place at a time when Carthaginian contacts with Persia were close because of the hostility of the two powers to the Greeks, but we know nothing of the motives which inspired Xerxes to order it. It is difficult to see what practical advantage could have been gained by the Persians, who had little interest in trade, and we may perhaps consider that the voyage was simply due to a desire of Xerxes to be the sponsor of a great feat of exploration. However, it approaches in time two voyages made by known Carthaginians which had eminently practical motives, one led by Hanno down the coast of Morocco, the other by Himilco northwards along the Atlantic coast of Spain and France.

We are told by the elder Pliny[56] that the two men were contemporaries and that their voyages were made at a time when the power of Carthage was at its height—the latter statement probably being designed to cover his own ignorance of the exact date. Reports of the voyages were known to Greeks of the fourth century, and though it seems unlikely that Herodotus, writing about 430, knew of Hanno's voyage, he had heard of Carthaginian trade on the coast of Morocco. The passage in which he describes this is reproduced because it indicates what must have been the basis of much Carthaginian wealth[57]:

> The Carthaginians also tell us about a part of Libya and its inhabitants beyond the Straits of Gibraltar. When they reach this country, they unload their goods and arrange them on the beach; they then return to their ships and send up a smoke signal. When the natives see the smoke, they come down to the sea and place on the shore a quantity of gold in exchange for the goods and then retire. The Carthaginians then come ashore again and examine the gold that has been left; if they think it represents the value of the goods, they collect it and sail away, if not they go back to the ships and wait until the natives have added sufficient gold to satisfy them. Neither side tricks the other; the Carthaginians never touch the gold until it equals in value what they have brought for sale, and the natives do not touch the goods until the gold has been taken away.

This is the earliest description of the method of dumb barter in trade with primitive peoples, which is known to have existed on the west coast of Africa in the Muslim middle ages (thirteenth century) and to have lasted till the nineteenth.[58] It is even possible that it was the Carthaginian desire for gold that first stimulated this sort of trade and the exploitation of the sources of gold in West African south of the Sahara. It goes without saying that the trade was immensely profitable to the Carthaginians, in spite of its risks; the gold provided by the natives must have been many times the value of the goods exchanged, except in their own eyes, and it cannot be doubted that exploitation of this source of gold, with similar methods of acquiring silver and tin in northern Europe, were the foundation of the Carthaginian Empire from the late fifth century onwards. The voyages of Hanno and Himilco were undertaken to ensure complete control of the two routes, and the general consensus sees in them two members of the Magonid family in the middle of the fifth century, at the time when they were leading Carthaginian expansion in North Africa.

A Greek version[59] of what was said to be Hanno's report has been preserved, and a full translation of this is given here, because with all its difficulties it probably does represent in some form a Carthaginian original and is thus the nearest we have to a specimen of Carthaginian 'literature'.

A report of the voyage of Hanno, king of the Carthaginians, to the parts of Africa beyond the Straits of Gibraltar, which he dedicated in the temple of Baal; the following is the text:

1. The Carthaginians decreed that Hanno should sail beyond the Straits of Gibraltar and found colonies of Libyphoenicians. He set sail with sixty fifty-oared ships, men and women to the number of 30,000, and food and other essentials.

2. After passing the Straits and sailing on for two days, we founded the first colony which we called Thymiaterion, near which is a large plain.

3. Then sailing westwards, we arrived at the place called Soloeis, a cape covered with trees.

4. After we had dedicated a sanctuary there to Poseidon, we turned and sailed east for half a day, after which we arrived at a lagoon not far from the sea, covered with thick, high reeds. Elephants and many other animals were there feeding.

5. We skirted this lagoon for a day, and then left [new?] colonists at Carian Fort, Gutta, Acra, Melitta, and Arambys.

6. From here we sailed to the Lixus, a great river which flows out of Libya. On its banks the Lixites, who are nomads, pasture their flocks. We remained for some time with this people, with whom we became friends.

7. Beyond them lived barbarous Ethiopians in a country full of savage beasts, crossed by mountain ranges, in which they say the Lixus rises. Around these mountains live a people of a peculiar aspect, the Troglodytes; the Lixites claim they can run faster than horses.

8. Taking interpreters from the Lixites, we sailed south along a desert coast for two days and then east for one day. There we found in a gulf a small island with a circumference of 5 stades [three quarters of a mile]; we called it Cerne and left colonists on it. From the distance we had sailed we calculated it was situated opposite to Carthage, for the sailing time from Carthage to the Straits of Gibraltar was the same as that from the Straits to Cerne.

9. From there, passing a large river, the Chretes, we came to a lagoon containing three islands larger than that of Cerne. Leaving them, we sailed for a day and reached the head of the lagoon which was dominated by very high mountains, inhabited by savages, who wore the skins of wild beasts and prevented us from landing by throwing stones at us.

10. From there we entered another deep wide river, full of hippotami and crocodiles; we then returned to Cerne.

11. Later we again sailed south from Cerne for twelve days along the coast, all of which was inhabited by Ethiopians, who ran away from us. Even the Lixites with us could not understand their language.

12. On the twelfth day we anchored under a high wooded mountain range, the trees on which were fragrant and of many different kinds.

13. We passed this mountain range in two days' sail, and arrived at an immense bay on either side of which was low-lying land. From here we saw at night fires flaring up on all sides at irregular intervals.

14. Taking on water, we sailed along the coast for five days until we reached a great gulf, which the interpreters said was called West Horn. In it was a large island, and in this island a marine lake itself containing an island. Landing on it we saw nothing but forest and at night many fires being kindled; we heard the noise of pipes, cymbals, and drums, and the shouts of a great crowd. We were seized with fear, and the interpreters advised us to leave the island.

15. We sailed away quickly and coasted along a region with a fragrant smell of burning timber, from which streams of fire plunged into the sea. We could not approach the land because of the heat.

16. We therefore sailed quickly on in some fear, and in four days' time we saw the land ablaze at night; in the middle of this area one fire towered above the others and appeared to touch the stars; this was the highest mountain which we saw and was called the Chariot of the Gods.

17. Following rivers of fire for three days we came to a gulf called the Southern Horn. In this gulf was an island like the one last mentioned, with a lake in which was another island. This was full of savages; by far the greater number were women with hairy bodies, called by our interpreters 'gorillas'. We gave chase to the men but could not catch any for they climbed up steep rocks and pelted us with stones. However we captured three women who bit and scratched their captors. We killed and flayed them and brought their skins back to Carthage. This was as far as we could sail owing to lack of provisions.

This report was the object of criticism[60] by some ancient writers including the elder Pliny, and in modern times a whole literature of scholarship has grown up around it. The account is incoherent and at times certainly incorrect, and attempts to identify the various places mentioned on the basis of the sailing directions and distances almost all fail. Some scholars resort to textual emendations, justified in some cases; but it is probable that what we have before us is a report deliberately edited so that the places could not be identified by the competitors of Carthage. From everything we know about Carthaginian practice, the resolute determination to keep all knowledge of and access to the western markets from the Greeks, it is incredible that they would have allowed the publication of an accurate description of the voyage for all to read. What we have is an official version of the real report made by Hanno which conceals or falsifies vital information while at the same time gratifying the pride of the Carthaginians in their achievements. The very purpose of the voyage, the consolidation of the route to the gold market, is not even mentioned.

It is notable that apart from this omission, the later parts of the report dealing with West Africa is in essentials more accurate than the earlier part dealing with the Moroccan coast, the reason being that it was unlikely that any Greeks who did get through the Straits of Gibraltar would dare to venture far south. The West African sections with their somewhat lurid descriptions of ferocious savages, drums in the night, and rivers of fire, were doubtless calculated to inspire alarm among the Greeks, but are consistent with reports of voyages in Renaissance times. In these circumstances, with only one or two sentences in the text providing undisputed information, a full commentary is a hazardous task, even if this were the place for one. Various attempts may be found in some of the works referred to in the bibliography. However, a brief mention will be made of some of the more important points and possible identifications. The figures in parentheses refer to the sections of the report.

It is generally said that either the number of the ships or of the passengers (1) is incorrect. If so, this is more likely to be the case with the latter figure, because none of the evidence we have about the other Carthaginian colonies leads to the conclusion that the colonies were of such a size, even when such a number was to be divided among seven places. The actual colonizing voyage cannot have lasted long, for the report glosses over the fact that almost all the colonies were sited within a short distance of the Straits; their purpose was at least partly to strengthen control of the Straits, though this stretch of coast was attractive to the Carthaginians for a more commercial reason, the wealth of fish. Of the seven colonies named, only two—Thymiaterion (on the River Sebou) and Cerne (Herne Island at the mouth of the Rio de Oro)—are subsequently mentioned in later writings, and consequently any identifications are most tenuous.

The report is deceptive about the River Lixus, and does not even mention the colony of Lixus itself; no doubt this was because it was the most important place on the Atlantic coast[61] and the key to trade further south. The River Lixus, whose present name is almost identical—Loukkos—is the first major river on the Atlantic coast sailing south, and lies well to the north of Cape Soloeis (Cap Santin) whereas the report puts it to the south. The interpreters whom Hanno drew from the Lixites were no doubt Phoenician settlers, not native people, and constitute evidence of a long period of contact between the colony and the tribes to the south. The river called Lixus by Hanno, with nomadic tribes along its banks, was apparently the Oued Draa, known in antiquity as the Darat. If the Greek word for 'left new colonists' in section 5 is used exactly, we have clear evidence of an intention to strengthen existing settlements, which were perhaps in a difficult position following the decline in Phoenician power in the century preceding Hanno's voyage. The only archaeological evidence so far for Phoenician and Carthaginian activity on the Atlantic coast, apart from Lixus, comes from Mogador, several hundred miles further south. The site itself, and the fact that it seems to have been seasonally visited rather than an actual settlement, seems to fit in very well with our account of the barter system. Yet it does not appear to be near the sources of gold. However, it is interesting to note that the place appears to have been no longer visited after the middle of the sixth century, for whatever reason, and cannot be identified with any of the places in Hanno's report.

Most commentators identify Cerne with Hern Island in the mouth of the Rio de Oro. It is mentioned by a number of ancient authors, though most of what they write is speculative and derived from uncertain sources. The identification rests on general grounds, such as the absence on the coast of any other place like that described, the similarity of the place names, and the admittedly very approximate equivalence of distance between it and the Straits and the Straits and Carthage. The geographer known as pseudo-Scylax,[62] writing about 338 B.C. has an interesting passage which has at any rate some substance in it, probably derived from a Carthaginian source.

One cannot sail beyond Cerne because of the shallows, mud, and seaweed, which is as wide as a man's hand but sharp enough to prick. At Cerne, Phoenicians [i.e. Carthaginians] carry on trade; when they arrive, they anchor their 'gauloi', as their merchant ships are called, and pitch tents on the island. After unloading their goods, they take it over to the mainland in small boats; there live Ethiopians [Negroes] with whom they trade. In exchange for their goods, the Phoenicians acquire the skins of deer, lions, and leopards, elephant hides, and tusks; the Ethiopians wear skins and drink from ivory cups, their women wear ivory necklaces, and even their horses have ivory decorations . . . The Phoenicians bring perfume, Egyptian stones [? faience], and Athenian pottery and jars.

The geographer was probably correctly informed about the goods traded by the Carthaginians, but was deceived about what they obtained in exchange, except for the ivory; at that period of North African history, the skins of the animals named could all be obtained much nearer Carthage, in Mauretania or even part of Numidia. The real purpose of the market at Cerne—the gold trade—was concealed. The description of pseudo-Scylax, with its reference to the merchants pitching their tents on the island, make it doubtful whether in fact Hanno really left colonists at such a distant point; or if he did, conditions probably became too difficult for a permanent settlement.

Hanno made two voyages from Cerne, the first a relatively short distance, the second much longer. The River Chretes and the river 'full of crocodiles and hippopotami' are probably the two arms of the Senegal; the latter was known as the Bambotum in Roman times. It may be noted that the paragraphs dealing with the final voyage from Cerne contain no sailing directions, and it could be argued that this is an indication of the fictitious nature of at any rate the last part of Hanno's report. However, the details have their own consistency, and it looks as if the voyage was one of reconnaissance along a stretch of coast rarely visited by the Lixites or other Carthaginians, and there was so little to attract future expeditions that there was no occasion to record more exact information.

The high wooded range (12) twelve days' sail from Cerne was Cape Verde, if the identification of Cerne is correct; twelve days' sail would be adequate for the distance of about 675 miles between the two places. Similarly, West Horn was Bissagos Bay. The 'region from which came streams of fire' was a grass fire, and the 'Chariot of the Gods' probably Mt Kakulima. On the basis of the description it has been said that Hanno saw a volcano, probably Mt Camerun, in eruption, but this seems to be altogether too far for him to have sailed, even if we dismiss the distances given as being corrupt. The 'gorillas' were not, of course, the anthropoid apes who were thus named by their modern discoverer, from the word in Hanno's report. There have been attempts[63] to connect the word with dialects spoken in the region in modern times, but this supposes an almost unparalleled stability in language over a period of more than 2,000 years, besides an accurate Greek rendering of a

Phoenician representation of a native word. What were said to be the skins of the captured, perhaps pygmies, were on view at Carthage at the time of its destruction.[64]

Such was the voyage of Hanno down the west coast of Africa. One of the remarkable things about it was the small effect it had in later times. After the fall of Carthage in 146, the historian Polybius sailed as far as the Bambotum beyond Cerne but discovered nothing worthwhile.[65] It looks as though the West African gold trade had come to an end at an earlier date than this, presumably after the defeat of Carthage in the war of 218–201. The success of the Carthaginians in keeping their competitors out of the western Mediterranean is particularly clear in the case of this area, and was effective even before the voyage of Hanno.

According to Pindar,[66] writing between 478 and 470, the Straits of Gibraltar were the limits of the accessible world. The 'Columns of Hercules', whether actual monuments or the natural features, by which name the Greeks called the Straits, were presumably so named because of the identification of the Phoenician Melkart with Hercules, and several of the myths associated with Hercules were located in those parts of the world from which the Greeks were excluded. At Lixus was located the kingdom of Antaeus, and at the same place Hercules won the golden apples from the Garden of Hesperides, a deed which according to one version brought about his apotheosis.

In the first century A.D. the higher criticism of the elder Pliny[67] reduced both fact and myth to a few words of ironic and sceptical description. For him Lixus was a Roman colony founded by the Emperor Claudius, about which the most unlikely reports were told by older authors, including the presence of the Garden of the Hersperides.

> There is an island in the river on which is an altar to Hercules, but nothing else besides a few olive trees of that gold-bearing grove we read about. People who wonder at the ridiculous fables put about by the Greeks concerning these topics and the river Lixus will be the less surprised when they consider that lately Roman writers have been responsible for equally absurd fictions, such as that Lixus was a vast city even larger than Carthage itself.

As for the report of Hanno, whom Pliny wrongly thought to have been ordered to circumnavigate Africa, 'many Greeks and Romans, on the basis of his report, tell of many other fabulous things and of many foundations of cities, of which in fact neither memory nor trace remain'. Pliny was over-critical, as recent discoveries at Lixus show, though naturally it was a small place compared with Carthage. Pliny was also ignorant of the fact that Mogador was again being visited in the century before he wrote by sailors from the Roman client state of Mauretania, though it seems that fish rather than gold was the objective.

The other trading voyage of which we know the leader's name was that of Himilco, who was said to be contemporary with Hanno, and if so was perhaps his brother. The report which he made was known in antiquity, but only a few scattered references have survived.[68] The object was to explore the Atlantic coast of Spain, Portugal, and France. Himilco reached the territory of the Oestrymnides (in northern Brittany) and described the calms which brought his ships to a halt, entangling weeds, extensive shallows, dense mists, and enormous sea-monsters. It is clear that like Hanno he lost no opportunity of deterring possible competitors from following his route, though all the details of his difficulties were within the limits of credence, even if exaggerated.

The economic purpose behind the voyage was to establish control over the trade in tin along the Atlantic coast of Europe. This trade was found interesting by several ancient writers, mainly no doubt because the Carthaginians allowed them to know very little about it; it has further been the object of some studies in modern times which can hardly be said to have advanced knowledge, because here again the Phoenician trader, leaving no visible trace behind, has left the field clear for romantic speculation.

The earliest Carthaginian (or Phoenician) voyages along these coasts followed the routes taken by the Tartessians, who traded with the Oestrymnians and knew of Ireland and Britain. The Tartessian trade is only mentioned by a late Roman writer, Avienus, but his source goes back to the fifth century B.C. at least; it was probably the latest phase in centuries of commerce of a rudimentary sort which had connected Spain and the British Isles as early as the Bronze Age[69]; if the Tartessians obtained tin from Britain, however, it was probably through the Oestrymnians. Naturally, any Phoenician voyage went from Gades, which at any rate after about 500 clearly had things its own way in the Atlantic. The last reference to Tartessus as a town in being is of about this date, but it may be doubted whether there ever was anything more than a trading post of the tribe, perhaps on the site of Gades itself, as the two are identified by some authors. One late authority talks of a war between the Phoenicians and the Tartessians, and it is obviously possible that the efforts of the immigrants to take a direct part in the Atlantic trade were resisted.

An important fact about Gades seems to emerge from the limited amount of archaeological evidence from the site; although no large scale excavation has been carried out there, tombs of the Phoenician period have been discovered at intervals for nearly a century, and none has produced articles of a date earlier than the fifth century. The implication is that up to the time of Carthaginian supremacy in the west, Gades was no more than a small trading post at which the Phoenicians picked up the silver which was obtained from the interior and the tin from the Atlantic coast. The great days of Gades only came with a substantial increase in the number of settlers under Carthaginian leadership and their direct participation in the Atlantic trade.[70]

There is no evidence that Himilco reached Britain, in particular Cornwall, in the search for tin; and in fact no Phoenician object has ever been discovered in Britain, so it must be regarded as highly problematical whether they ever got there. It is true that Cornish tin was exported to the continent in the first millennium B.C. Much of it reached the Mediterranean not by the Atlantic coast but across France to the Rhône valley and thence to Massilia.[71] What has led many to look for Phoenician trade in Britain is the number of references to the Cassiterides, a Greek word apparently meaning 'Tin Islands'. Herodotus had heard of them but knew nothing. Other writers placed them in the Atlantic 'opposite Spain' and said there were ten of them. The first person known to have brought tin from them (i.e. the first person from the Greek world) was called Midacritus, perhaps a Phocaean sailing in the years before the Carthaginian supremacy.

The most detailed information comes from Strabo, who wrote under Augustus but used much earlier material. He says that one of the ten islands was desert, but

> the rest are inhabited by people clothed in black cloaks and tunics that reach their feet, girdled at the breast, who walk about with staffs in their hands like the Furies in the Greek tragedies. They live off their herds and are mostly nomadic. Having mines of silver and lead, they exchange the metal and the hides for pottery, salt, and copper objects with visiting merchants. Formerly it was the Phoenicians [this includes Carthaginians] who had a monopoly of this commerce and kept the route a secret. When once some Romans followed a ship to discover the route, the captain deliberately sailed into a shoal and so destroyed his pursuers. He himself escaped on a piece of the wreckage and received compensation from the State. In the end the Romans learned all about this route; after Publius Crassus sailed there and saw the metal that was being dug from only a slight depth, he published the information for anyone who wished to trade over this part of the sea, though it is a wider stretch of water than that which separates Britain from the continent.[72]

The islands have often been identified with islands off Vigo, which have no tin, with the Scillies which have very little, or with Cornwall, the early sailors believing it to be a group of islands. In point of fact, it is impossible to identify them from Strabo's information or from that provided by other writers, and the most likely explanation is that they did not exist, that information about various real tin-producing areas was attributed to the 'Cassiterides' through ignorance. The Publius Crassus mentioned by Strabo was a governor of part of Spain *c*. 96 B.C., who conquered tribes on the Atlantic coast and opened up this tin-producing area for Roman exploitation. From about this time Spain was the chief source of tin for the Mediterranean, and after Caesar's conquest of the Veneti, a people in Brittany who had taken over the role of the Oestrymnians of earlier date as the chief agents of cross-channel trade, the Cornish tin trade ceased altogether. It is to be assumed, therefore, that the merchants of Gades, while having an interest through intermediate tribes in the Cornish tin traded down the Atlantic, also obtained the metal from north-west Spain. The trade in tin was probably less important than that in silver in making Gades such an important place in the Carthaginian period, and its prosperity continued under the Romans. Gades was the only Carthaginian dependency in the west besides Ibiza to issue coins[73] in the pre-Roman period, and according to Strabo its shipbuilders constructed more and better merchant vessels for use in both Mediterranean and Atlantic waters than any others.

Such was the empire built up in Africa by Carthage in the fifth century, which included territorial conquests and dependencies, colonies and trading posts, and the voyages, officially sponsored, to obtain a firm grip on the trade in metals in the west. Carthage was criticized in antiquity for harsh treatment of her subjects, and in particular for excessive demands for tribute.[74] It remains to be seen how much truth there was in this and how much it was a reflection of the popular view of the Carthaginians, two of whose principal vices were said to be greed and cruelty.

Like their contemporaries the Athenians and their successors the Romans, the Carthaginians left a great deal of the day-to-day running of affairs to their subjects themselves, keeping a centralized control limited to the amount considered necessary to ensure their dominant position and the regular payment of tribute. There were certainly different categories of subject communities, which reflected differences in the state of their civilization and in the origin of their dependent status. The most favoured were the old Phoenician settlements and the colonies of Carthage herself, the Libyphoenicians. Their relations with

Carthage were presumably governed by treaties in each case. If we may judge from evidence from Gades, Malta, and Tharros, all outside Africa but Phoenician or Carthaginian colonies, they had local officials and institutions similar to those of Carthage itself, but this does not mean that Carthage imposed uniformity.[75] The special place held by Utica among the dependants has been mentioned before. Polybius says that the Libyphoenicians had the same laws as the Carthaginians themselves; the implication is perhaps that they had the same civil rights and thus a status similar to that of the Latins in Roman history, with the right of becoming full citizens of Carthage if they went to live there.[76]

Carthage exacted dues on imports and exports at all these cities, and some at least seem to have paid direct taxes. On several occasions, troops were levied from Libyphoenician communities for campaigns when, it appears, Carthaginians themselves were not called upon.[77] It is remarkable that we are ill-informed about the manning of the Carthaginian fleet, but it would be strange if numbers of rowers were not drawn from the experienced sailors of the maritime cities. Lastly, it must be the case that Carthage controlled the foreign relations of the Libyphoenicians and increasingly in some measure their economic relations as well. In the first treaty with Rome (508–507) the Romans were allowed to trade in part of Africa and Sardinia if the business was carried out before an official, but in the second treaty of 348, they were excluded from the south of Spain, Sardinia and Africa except Carthage itself.[78] The position of the subject communities of various nationalities in Sicily was relatively favourable, no doubt because of the complex economic and political relations between them and the Greek cities outside the Carthaginian sphere. The Phoenician, Elymian, and Sican communities were allowed to live according to their own laws and institutions, and it is certain that Segesta, an Elymian city, was still an ally and a relatively free agent at least till the end of the fifth century.[79] On the other hand the cultural influence of the dominant power may be seen at Elymian Eryx where the chief magistrates came to be called by the Carthaginian term 'sufets'.[80] However, it is notable that the Phoenician and Elymian communities in Sicily had a privilege denied to the Libyphoenicians in that they issued coins throughout the fifth century. This must have been an inevitable concession in view of their position in an island where they were bound to have close contacts with the free Greek cities. In the fifth century Eryx and Segesta had coins similar to those of Greek cities, with legends in Greek, and the coins of Panormus, Motya, and Solus were also to all intents and purposes Greek, though the legends on some Motyan coins were Phoenician.

There was a whole series of coins imitating Greek models but with the
Phoenician letters ZIZ; the meaning of this is not known but it seems
to have some connexion with Panormus.[81]

The position became somewhat more complex when Carthage conquered some Greek cities in the island at the end of the fifth century.
The coinage of Selinus ceased with its destruction in 409 and was not
resumed even when the site was reoccupied; the coinage of Thermae,
the successor to Himera, also lasted only a short time. That of Segesta
also stopped at the end of the fifth century, and the coins of Eryx subsequently carried Phoenician legends. Solus continued to issue her own
coins with both Greek and Phoenician legends and there were coins of
Heraclea Minoa under its Phoenician name Rus Melkart.[82]

The evidence provided by coinage that the Sicilian cities were
allowed a considerable amount of freedom in economic matters is
strengthened by the permission granted in the Roman treaties for merchants to trade in Sicily on the same terms as merchants of other states.
It is not known what these conditions were, but at any rate there seems
to have been trade with a number of Greek and Italian communities.[83]
The later Greek subjects of Carthage had to pay a tribute, and the same
is probably true of the others in Sicily. It is supposed that it was a tenth
of the produce, since this amount was levied by the Romans when they
took over the island, and they are assumed to have followed existing
practice.[84] There were certainly Carthaginian garrisons in some of the
cities,[85] as there were in those on Sardinia. The latter island was of some
economic importance to Carthage, and we know that on several
occasions when Carthage was in difficulties about food because of
African revolts, supplies were brought in from Sardinia. To judge from
the Roman treaties, Carthage had imposed a monopoly of trade with the
island by the middle of the fourth century.[86]

The Libyans of the interior were certainly worse off than the
Libyphoenicians and the Sicilians, even though they were apparently
permitted to follow their ancestral way of life under their own chief-
tains, so long as this did not interfere with the requirements of Carthage.
We hear of Carthaginian citizens who held profitable offices among the
subjects.[87] Among these there must have been officials to supervise the
delivery of tribute and the enrolment of soldiers when these were
needed, and to maintain security.

During the First Punic War, the Libyans had to pay one half of their
crops in tribute[88]; since at the same time the taxes of the city-dwellers
were doubled, it is taken that the normal exaction from the Libyans
was a quarter, an extremely burdensome figure. The Libyans were also

Stele from Carthage, late form

Stelae from Ghorfa, Roman period

required to provide soldiers, and from the early fourth century onwards were the largest single element in the Carthaginian army. It is unlikely that they received payment except in booty, at any rate prior to the Punic Wars. The passage in which Polybius tells of the fifty per cent tax in the First Punic War goes on to tell how the Libyans took part in the destructive revolt of the mercenaries which followed it, being animated by a desperate hatred of Carthage through this and other oppressive actions[89] : 'the Carthaginians had admired and honoured not those governors who had treated the subjects with moderation and humanity, but those who had exacted the greatest amount of supplies and treated the inhabitants most ruthlessly; among these governors was Hanno [the Great].' In point of fact, a series of revolts took place among the Libyans from the fourth century onwards, and in respect of these subjects there seems no doubt that the criticisms levelled against Carthage were justified.

The failure of Carthage to bind her subjects to herself, as Rome did, by liberal treatment (admittedly backed by overwhelming power) has often been noted. It is true that to do this in Africa was a hard task, as the Libyans were far below the Carthaginians in material civilization and very different in their ways of thinking; there were no common social or religious institutions as there were in Italy. Nevertheless, the impression remains that the Carthaginians did far too little to move the Libyans out of the backward state in which they lived. In this they did themselves a disservice and showed that they did not possess that sense of the Greco-Roman world that life in a properly organized city was one of the essentials of civilization, and a thing to be encouraged by imperial states. This is not to deny that the beginnings of urbanization in the interior of North Africa were due to the Carthaginians; the more we know of Roman Africa the more we see that the Romans' success in promoting the development of towns and cities was most marked where Carthaginian influence had been strongest. In the plain of El Fahs, some fifty miles south-west of Carthage, a number of small Roman towns grew from settlements which may well have included a number of Carthaginians as well as native Libyans. However, it is clear that the population of Carthage was too small to allow for an active policy of land settlement in the interior even if it had been desired.

The position as regards the Libyphoenicians is perhaps more complex. Speaking in the most general way, the Phoenicians, though capable of a fanatical patriotism second to none in times of danger to their very existence, did not have that political outlook which animated the

6

Greeks and to a lesser extent the Italians, and made the achievement or preservation of full autonomy objectives worth a great deal of trouble and risk. Their way of life as merchants encouraged prudent realism about the facts of political power. Consequently, just as the Phoenicians in their homeland had acquiesced in the rule of a series of imperial states, so those in Africa accepted the rule of Carthage, perhaps the more easily because of the ties of blood and religion. It is true that as a result they were deprived of the possibilities open to the city states of other races of the Mediterranean because of the Carthaginian prohibition on their trade with anyone else; but we hear of no revolts until the last years of the existence of Carthage, when it appeared prudent to desert a ruler whose destruction seemed inevitable (the defection of Utica and Hippo in the mercenary war are isolated exceptions, due largely to pressure from the rebel forces). It must therefore be assumed that Carthaginian rule was tolerable to the Libyphoenicians, with one proviso. It is not necessarily the case that an absence of revolts can be taken as a sign of satisfaction with an imperial power; not so much the possession of overwhelming force, but the determination to use it with the utmost ruthlessness if necessary, is an inhibiting factor to which not enough attention is generally paid; such the Carthaginians had in full measure.

4

The Wars in Sicily
against Dionysius of Syracuse

FOR most of the fifth century[1] Greek and Phoenician lived peaceably side by side in Sicily in spite of various episodes which in later generations would have led to war between them. The power of the tyrants of Syracuse was more strongly entrenched than ever by Hiero, who in the characteristic policy of Sicilian tyrants continued the forcible transplanting of the population of places opposed to the tyranny. However, the Siceliots were not disposed to put up with autocracy indefinitely, and by the 460s most of the communities had governments of oligarchic or democratic complexion.

The next decade saw a movement in which Carthage might have intervened had not her policy of non-involvement outside Africa now been firmly established; between 459 and 450 there was a formidable grouping of the remaining independent native Sicilians against the Greeks, which was only defeated with some difficulty.

It was in the same decade that the expansive Athenian democracy turned its attention to the world of the western Greeks, with important long-term results. In 453, there had been a boundary conflict between Selinus and Segesta, in which the latter had had the worst of it; Carthage refrained from helping the city to which she had been previously allied, and apparently no objection was raised to her seeking support elsewhere. Segesta and a Sican city, Halicyae, made a treaty of friendship with Athens. No military obligations were undertaken, but the treaty was evidence of Athenian interest in the west, which was extended in 433 when she made an alliance with Rhegium and Leontini. In these alliances Athens was assuming the protection of Ionian against Dorian Greeks, of whom the chief representative in Sicily was Syracuse. During the Peloponnesian War which broke out in 431 between Athens and her enemies, led by Sparta, there were repercussions in Sicily, and in 427 Athens sent some help to the Ionian states against Syracuse. However, in 424 representatives of the Sicilian states met at Gela and agreed on peace terms which in effect excluded Athens from any *locus standi* in their disputes.[2]

The Carthaginians remained aloof from these events and were no doubt satisfied that the divisions amongst the Greek cities were to their advantage. The next episode, however, led ultimately to very different results. In 416, there was another conflict between Selinus and Segesta, the former being supported by Syracuse.[3] The Carthaginians again sent no help to the Elymian city, though this was certainly requested, and an appeal was sent to Athens. There had been a truce between Athens and Sparta for some time, and it seemed to many at Athens that intervention in Sicily was desirable, because if successful it would bring a number of states into her alliance and reduce to impotence the Spartans' chief friend in Sicily, Syracuse. It impinged upon the Carthaginians because there had been airy talk among the more exuberant Athenians of conquering Sicily and even the Carthaginian Empire.[4] Whether this hope was in the minds of the generals who led the Athenian expedition may be doubted. As far as Carthage was concerned, after the recall of Alcibiades, the chief sponsor of the expedition, she was invited by the general left in command to send help—some Etruscans offered it without being asked. We hear nothing of any response by the Carthaginians, and it must clearly have been negative; even if the Carthaginian government did not take seriously the talk of an attack on their empire, Athens was far too powerful a state to be assisted in a venture which if successful would make her still more formidable. It was wiser to leave her to undertake an attack on Syracuse without help, in the hope that both would be weakened in the process. In point of fact the Athenian expedition was entirely destroyed in 413, and it appeared that the power of Syracuse was likely to become as formidable as it had been under Gelon and Hiero.

It was in such circumstances that Carthage again received an appeal from Segesta.[5] In 410 there was a renewal of hostilities between this state and Selinus, and the Segestans feared that they would be entirely destroyed, as a punishment for bringing the Athenians into Sicily a few years before. They gave up the disputed lands, but the Selinuntines continued to press their attacks. The appeal was then sent to Carthage together with an offer to hand the city over as a dependent member of the empire. Various factors must have weighed with the Carthaginian senate as it debated whether to alter the policy of seventy years' standing. The moment was by no means as propitious for intervening in Sicily as several others which had occurred in the past, with the Syracusans flushed with success and liable to go to the help of Selinus if needed. However, the danger to the old Phoenician settlements if Segesta were destroyed would be great, as Selinus would then hold a stretch of land right across the west of Sicily. Further, the offer of the Segestans was attractive, and there is no doubt it marked a stage in the growth of Carthaginian supremacy in the west of Sicily. It is obvious from the connexions of Segesta with Athens that up to now she had been a free agent, allied to but not dependent upon Carthage, and the same may even be true of the Phoenician cities. It is only after this date that we read of the Carthaginian *epikrateia*, 'province',[6] in the island, to denote a territory all the inhabitants of which could be regarded as properly subject to Carthage.

Our source gives a personal reason as the one which finally decided the issue. The leading figure at Carthage was Hannibal[7] the son of Gisgo, and grandson of the Hamilcar who had died at Himera. Gisgo had been exiled with his brother Hanno when the Magonids' power was weakened in the middle of the fifth century,[8] and he had gone to live in Selinus; this does not appear to mean that relations between the two cities were bad at that date or in fact at any time in the middle and late fifth century before 410. Whether Hannibal went into exile with his father is not known, but he is credited with a burning hatred for the Greeks and a determination to avenge his grandfather's death. It is not now as easy as it used to be to dismiss such an irrational emotion as a determining factor in a state's policy.

The story has been rationalized to mean that the return of the Magonid family to power at Carthage signalled a return to an expansive policy overseas as opposed to a concentration on the development of the African conquests. In point of fact, however, it has been seen that it was a Magonid, Hanno,[9] who led the campaigns in Africa in the years following Himera, and it is to be doubted whether there was in fact a division in the Carthaginian aristocracy between those whose wealth was chiefly in land and those who were primarily concerned with commerce. What was important in Hannibal's case and led to his being entrusted with the command of the expedition was that he was a member of one of the very few families at Carthage which had a military tradition; this was of importance in view of the unwarlike nature of Carthaginian society and the wise refusal not to allow mercenaries to hold the supreme commands.

Before help was sent to Segesta, a last attempt at diplomacy was used. An embassy went to Selinus demanding a stop to the attacks on Segesta, but the party in the city in favour of acceding to this was overruled. Next, a joint embassy of Segestans and Carthaginians was sent to Syracuse, offering to submit the dispute to Syracusan arbitration. This reasonable proposal had behind it the sense that if the Selinuntines were intransigent, as was expected, the Syracusans would be reluctant to help them; this was precisely what happened, and Syracuse spent the first months of the war in an uneasy neutrality.[10]

The size and composition of the force proves that Carthage had had no intention of intervening in Sicily before the Segestan appeal; it always took a good year to put a large mercenary army into the field, and in 410 Hannibal took only 5,000 Libyans, to which were added 800 Campanians who had been in Sicily since the collapse of the Athenian expedition. With this force he drove back the Selinuntines into their own territory. During the winter, Syracuse was persuaded to take up her ally's cause, though with little practical effect, and in 409 the magnitude of the Carthaginian effort was seen. The exact numbers are not known, but the force probably outnumbered anything which was put against it, and perhaps reached 50,000; besides further contingents of Libyans, there were Iberian and even Greek mercenaries.

After landing near Motya, Hannibal at once struck across the western end of the island and besieged Selinus. Its inhabitants and the rest of the Siceliots were dismayed by the size of the Carthaginian army and its formidable siege engines, and by Hannibal's evident determination to take the city by storm rather than waste time in a long siege as was the common practice in Greek warfare. The city was fully invested, and six siege towers high enough to overtop the walls, with an equal number of battering rams, were brought up at different points. Hannibal had an advantage over Greek generals in a similar situation in that because of the nature of his army he could afford the heavy casualties involved in assault operations, which Greek generals at the head of citizen forces had to avoid. In addition, the Carthaginians had inherited from their Phoenician homeland the techniques of siege warfare which had been a feature of the ancient Assyrian Empire. The speed of his attack partly accounts for the failure of any Greek state to send assistance in time, though appeals had been made to Acragas and Gela in addition to Syracuse; but the scale of the Carthaginian attack, quite apart from its speed, was beyond what could immediately be met by citizen armies.

The sack of Selinus after nine days of repeated attacks was the first two episodes which confirmed (if they did not form) Hannibal's reputation as a hater of Greeks and that of the Carthaginians' for superstitious cruelty. The inevitable looting, rape, and massacre was followed by the mutilation of the dead, an action of particular horror to the Greeks, for which the Iberian contingents were responsible. 16,000 were killed, 5,000 were taken prisoner and enslaved. When an embassy from other Greek cities approached Hannibal with a view to ransoming the captives and obtaining an assurance that he would not destroy the temples, he voiced the common opinion of the time, particularly of the Semitic peoples, that the capture of the city was a sign of its desertion by its gods. Centuries later, in A.D. 70, when the Romans were sacking Jerusalem, it was said that a divine voice was heard in the temple saying 'let us depart'. In fact, it appears that the temples were looted but not destroyed; the walls of the city were slighted, but a few Selinuntines who had escaped to Acragas were later allowed to settle among the ruins as subjects of Carthage.[11] The capture of Selinus ensured the safety of Segesta and fulfilled the main purpose of the Carthaginians. The independent coinage of Segesta stopped at about this time, which shows that its absorption into the Carthaginian Empire was complete, while that of Panormus changed from the Greek to a Carthaginian style, because the new policy in Sicily was bound to bring about changes in the pattern of trade.[12]

Hannibal, whose position allowed him considerable freedom of action, now used his huge force for his own personal plan of vengeance, though obviously a reversal of the defeat of Himera would be gratifying to the pride of all Carthaginians. He was joined by many Sicels (native Sicilians) who welcomed the opportunity of striking a blow against the Greeks, and marched on Himera. This city had not been left entirely without help, for Hannibal's plans were known; some 4,000 Greeks, mostly Syracusans, had come to its aid under the leadership of Diocles, a prominent figure in the Syracusan democracy. This small force, however, shows how difficult it was for the Greek cities to mobilize their full strength unless they were visibly threatened. Adopting the same tactics as had proved successful at Selinus, Hannibal attacked the walls at once, this time by undermining; a breach was made, but the attackers were repelled. Next morning a combined force of Himerans and Syracusans made a desperate sally, but after an initial success they fell into disorder and a Carthaginian counterattack drove them back into the city with heavy losses.

At this point a fleet of twenty-five Syracusan warships which had been recalled from the Aegean, where they had been fighting on the Peloponnesian side, arrived at the city. Hannibal had been so confident of a quick success that he had made no disposition of his fleet to prevent help getting in by sea. The arrival of the ships could have strengthened the effectiveness of the defence, so he resorted to a trick and made as if to give up the assault and march directly on Syracuse.

As he expected, this produced alarm amongst the Syracusan contingent, and Diocles, anxious to get back to his city, persuaded the Himerans to abandon theirs. The unfortunate Himerans saw that the Syracusans would leave, whatever appeals were made to them, and that with the ships available they might at least escape with their lives. About half the population was put aboard the ships, to be disembarked at Messana, after which the remainder could be collected. Diocles and his men, accompanied by some Himerans, were able to escape by land, as no continuous line had been drawn around the city. The soldiers who had been left to defend it till the return of the ships were now hopelessly outnumbered; they were still holding out, however, when the ships came into view, but at the same moment the wall was breached by the Spanish contingent. While allowing his troops to plunder at will, Hannibal ordered as many prisoners to be taken as possible. The women and children were distributed as prizes amongst the soldiers; the male prisoners to the number of 3,000 were taken out to the spot where Hamilcar had died, and after being tortured, were killed as a sacrifice to his spirit. The city was razed to the ground, and was never reoccupied.

After the destruction of Himera, Hannibal returned to Carthage with his own and his city's aims fully achieved; the disbanding of the huge army shows clearly enough that Carthage had no thought of further conquest, in spite of the rapid successes which had been won.[13]

It is probable that the situation would have become stable again, as it had done after the earlier battle at Himera, if it had not been for internal changes at Syracuse. A politician named Hermocrates, who had inspired the defence of the city against the Athenians, had led the fleet to the Aegean in 412 to carry on operations against Athens on

Stele from Hadrumetum with relief of Baal Hammon,
fifth century

Stele showing priest or worshipper with sacrificial victim

Baal Hammon (Roman period)

Sanctuary at Monte Sirai (*detail of statue shown facing page 96*)

the Spartan side. Although he performed creditably enough, the easy victories which the Syracusans in their overconfidence had expected never came about, and the contingent was involved in the defeats suffered by the Spartans and their allies. Meanwhile Diocles, the chief political opponent of Hermocrates, gained the confidence of the Syracusans, and on the news of a defeat suffered by Hermocrates in 409 the Syracusan assembly vented its disappointment on him, forgetful of his services in the past, and passed a decree of banishment in his absence. New officers were sent out to the fleet, which was recalled because of the situation in Sicily.

Hermocrates made no attempt to rouse his men to his support—like most Greek sailors they were probably in favour of radical democracy —but obtained money from the Persians, with which he hired ships and mercenaries and sailed for Sicily. He arrived at Messana just about the time of the fall of Himera, and enrolling 1,000 refugees from that city, he tried to force his way into Syracuse. When this failed, he set himself up as ruler in the dismantled Selinus, which was not garrisoned by the Carthaginians when their army left Sicily; there he was joined by many other refugees and soon disposed of a force of 6,000 men. He carried out raids into the territory of Motya and Panormus, and defeated the troops who came out against him. These successes compared very favourably with the actions of Diocles at Himera, and opinion at Syracuse turned in favour of Hermocrates. He acquired further popularity by sending for burial in their homeland the bodies of the Syracusans who had fallen at Himera, which Diocles in his haste had left unburied, an act of omission regarded as deplorable. Finally, in 407, the supporters of Hermocrates in the city succeeded in procuring the banishment of Diocles, but failed to bring about the recall of Hermocrates; he made another attempt to return by force, but was killed in the fighting.[14]

Carthage decided to make the attacks of Hermocrates against her Sicilian dependencies the excuse for an attempt to subdue the whole island, although the Syracusans disowned them and tried without success to avert the war by negotiations. The decision to embark on this venture must have been the subject of much discussion at Carthage, as it was an even more radical departure from her policy during most of the fifth century than the intervention in 410; no doubt the decisive factors were the feeling of confidence produced by the victories of Hannibal, and a conviction that Syracuse was too much weakened by internal diversions to offer determined resistance. Both sides were active diplomatically; Syracuse sought help from all the Greek cities in Sicily and Italy and also from Sparta. Carthage also, as we learn from a recently discovered inscription, looked to Greece.[15]

An embassy was sent to Athens, where it was well received, and the Athenians sent envoys directly to the Carthaginian commanders in Sicily, asking for their friendship and alliance. Carthage had much to gain from a friendly Athens. She could hope that Naxos and Catane, old Sicilian allies of Athens, would refuse to send help to Syracuse—and they did in fact take no part in the war. Further, if the Athenians, who were now in a desperate position in their war with Sparta, could nevertheless be stirred to further vigorous resistance, the Spartans would be deterred from sending forces to the west. In this respect also the hopes of the Carthaginians were realized, though it may be doubted whether the Spartans would have allowed anything to deflect them at the moment when final victory was within their grasp.

From the Athenian point of view there were obvious advantages to be gained from an understanding with Carthage, though it is unlikely they can ever have been so optimistic as to expect material help. However, the campaigns of Hannibal had already brought about the withdrawal of the Syracusan contingent from the Aegean, and it was essential that it should not reappear. The principal objection to the alliance, that it might assist a non-Greek power of proven barbarity to subdue famous Greek cities, can hardly have had much weight at this time, even though the Athenians had justified their rule over the Greeks of Asia Minor with the argument that they were defending them from the Persians. Both Athens and Sparta, incapable of winning the war on their own, had sought the help of the Persians, in spite of the fact that they were far more dangerous to Greek freedom than any other power. In return for this help Persia required the recognition of her rule over the Greeks of Asia Minor, which Athens could not concede; she accordingly favoured Sparta, who was prepared to sacrifice the Greeks in spite of her claim, frequently repeated, to be fighting for the independence of all Greek cities.

The new evidence confirms that from the time of the Athenian invasion of Sicily Athens also was prepared to call in the non-Greek, no doubt the more willingly in the case of Carthage, since the two states had never been in conflict. The fact is that although consciousness among the Greeks in general of their difference from and, as they believed, superiority to non-Greek did not diminish as contacts between the two became more frequent, there was less and less reluctance on the part of individual Greek states to enter into close political relations with non-Greeks when it was opportune. This is why appeals to a common Greek feeling as it were to defend 'Greek civilization', made by states threatened by their non-Greek neighbours, often had so little effect.

We know nothing of the terms of the final agreement, if any, between Athens and Carthage; in any case it had no effect on the result of the Peloponnesian War, and Athens capitulated to the Spartan alliance in 404. Meanwhile the Carthaginians recruited an army even larger than their previous one. Our sources[16] give an impossible figure of 120,000 men; we can only say that in fact it probably outnumbered the 35,000 brought against it. The number of triremes given, 120, is much more likely to be correct. Hannibal was placed in command of the expedition, an obvious choice because of his earlier success, but in view of his age he insisted on taking with him a relative named Himilco as colleague. An advance force of forty triremes was sent ahead as a diversion, and though fifteen of these were lost in an engagement off Mt Eryx, the great fleet of transports under the protection of the rest of the triremes crossed safely to some point near the south-western tip of Sicily.

Hannibal's first action must have been the restoration of the position in the area which had been under attack by Hermocrates. This was quickly done—we hear nothing of any fighting at Selinus, and may assume that on hearing of the arrival of the Carthaginian expedition all Greeks who had ventured to return to the city at once withdrew. The next objective of the Carthaginians was Acragas, the nearest Greek city to Selinus, and a few miles inland from the southern coast of the island. For many years it had been exceedingly prosperous, largely owing to a careful neutrality in the various Sicilian wars. Among the many states with which it had traded was Carthage itself.[17] Acragas had a widespread reputation for wealth and luxury and had some of the most notable public buildings in Sicily. Hannibal first invited it to enter into an alliance with Carthage, or, if this was not acceptable, to remain neutral in the forthcoming conflict with Syracuse. Both proposals were rejected. The Acragantines were reinforced by a force of 1,500 mercenary hoplites under the command of Dexippus, a soldier of fortune from Laconia though not a full Spartan citizen; of more doubtful use were the 800 Campanians who had served with Hannibal on his earlier campaign but had gone over to the Greek side because they were dissatisfied with their share of the plunder.

Acragas was very strongly situated on a group of precipitous hills which had been fortified at weak points; below, to the west, the River Hypsas made a direct attack from that side particularly difficult. It was

natural, however, that Hannibal should try to take it by assault as he
had Selinus and Himera. He placed his main camp with his siege train
to the west of the city and a secondary one to the north in order to
prevent any help from Gela and Syracuse getting in. Two siege towers
were then brought up against the weakest section of the west wall, but
after some success they were both destroyed by a sally made during
the night. The next move was the destruction of the tombs and sepul-
chral monuments which lay to the south of the city, and the use of the
stone to fill up the bed of the Hypsas in order to facilitate further attacks.
While this work was going on, one of the tombs was struck by light-
ning, and the morale of the Carthaginians, which was affected by this
ill-omen, was further lowered by an epidemic of an unknown nature
in which Hannibal himself died. Himilco, who took over the command of the expedition, stopped the desecration and after sacrificing a
child to appease the gods, carried the work forward by other means.

Before a decisive attack could be launched, a substantial Syracusan
force approached from the east along the coast road. It numbered
30,000 foot-soldiers and 5,000 horse, and was commanded by one of
the newly-elected generals named Daphnaeus; the Syracusan fleet sailed
along the coast keeping in touch. Himilco ordered the troops in the
secondary camp to intercept the Greeks and prevent them entering
Acragas. A battle took place near a river to the east of the city and the
Carthaginians were defeated with losses amounting to 6,000. Daphnaeus checked the pursuit, remembering how three years before the
Himerans had suffered a disaster through losing their ranks after an
initial victory. The garrison of the city had an opportunity of attacking
the Carthaginians on the flank as they made their way to the south of
the city towards their main camp, but the Acragantine generals failed
to take it. Many of the citizens streamed out by the eastern gates and
joined with Daphnaeus and his troops; an impromptu assembly was
held, at which passions were so roused by accusations of bribery made
against the generals, as an explanation of their failure to attack, that
four out of the five were stoned to death on the spot and Dexippus only
narrowly escaped because of the prestige of the name of Sparta.

It was now the Carthaginians who were on the defensive. Supplies
from Gela were brought into Acragas, while the Syracusan cavalry prevented anything from entering Himilco's camp; he had been too confident of the speedy capture of the city to make adequate preparations
for his own supplies. Learning of the approach of a convoy of provision
ships from Syracuse to Acragas, he summoned forty triremes from
Panormus and Motya to intercept it. The Syracusans were not taking

the proper precautions, because of the previous inactivity of the Carthaginian fleet, which they felt made its appearance altogether unlikely now that winter was coming on. As a result, Himilco's ships sank eight of the Syracusan escort ships, drove the rest on to the shore, and captured all the provision ships.

This reversed the position a second time, since the Carthaginians now had ample supplies, while Acragas began to go short; in addition to the difficulties of getting the provisions into the city, the other Sicilian states must have found it very burdensome to supply their populous neighbour. The Campanian mercenaries of Acragas, judging their side's position to be hopeless, went over to Himilco on receipt of a bribe of fifteen talents. Worse still, Dexippus brought about the withdrawal of the Greek allies and mercenaries. He was suspected of being bribed, which may perhaps be no more than a reflection of the low estimate held of the honesty of the Lacedaimonians once they were freed from the austere regulations of their homeland; his own briefly-recorded reason for leaving was that owing to the lack of supplies it was better that the war be settled somewhere else. No doubt there was more to it than this, but it is clear that in the view of Dexippus, and presumably other generals on the spot, the only hope was to stand a long siege in a better position than Acragas, and hope the Carthaginians would give up first. It could have been argued that a largely mercenary force like Himilco's was not likely to be patient of a long period of siege operations, but this purely negative thinking shows a lack of confidence in the ability of the Greek hoplite army to match a more numerous but heterogeneous enemy.[18]

As a result of these misfortunes, and the memory of what had happened at Selinus and Himera, the morale of the Acragantines collapsed; it was decided to abandon the city. The operation was carried out with great speed, even though there was no imminent danger, and was entirely unhindered by Himilco. At first the refugees were sheltered by Gela, but they were later given a home at Leontini by the Syracusans. The Carthaginians entered an almost deserted city which contained a vast amount of booty. A considerable part of this consisted of works of art of every description, and the most valuable were sent to Carthage. It is a remarkable fact that it was about this date that the import of Greek products of many kinds into Carthage became common again after more than half a century; there were several reasons for this, as will be shown later, but the sudden influx of Greek works of art from Acragas played its part in changing the taste of the Carthaginians. A parallel occurred two centuries later after the sack of

Syracuse by the Romans in 212; it was from the loot brought into Rome from Syracuse that Roman taste became enthusiastically philhellene.[19]

The Carthaginians had been seven months before Acragas, which fell in December 406, but they now had comfortable quarters for the rest of the winter and an advance base for further operations. The future looked very black for the rest of Greek Sicily, and some people emigrated to the Greek cities in Italy, others to Syracuse. The internal political disorders, which had partly been the cause of the war, continued. The general opinion was that the Syracusan generals had been responsible for the loss of Acragas, which, in the sense that in spite of having by far the largest contingent in the field they had nevertheless accepted the advice of Dexippus and withdrawn, was justified. With the citizens in a state of mingled fear and anger, an assembly was held to discuss the situation. It was addressed by a former supporter of Hermocrates named Dionysius, who had served bravely before Acragas in a subordinate position.

There can be little doubt that from the first he sought to utilize the crisis in order to achieve supreme power for himself. He was a man of great cunning and ruthlessness, but one who was able to win the support of men of very different character. In his attack on the generals delivered in the assembly he was supported by one of the richest Syracusan citizens, even though his own popularity derived partly from his humble origin as opposed to the generals who were men of substance. The latter were deposed and new ones elected, among whom was Dionysius himself. He then got the assembly to recall political exiles, many of whom like himself had been friends of Hermocrates, thus increasing the number of his supporters. Next, he went to Gela, where the cautious Dexippus was in command, in spite of his poor showing at Acragas. Some kind of political struggle was in progress between the mass of the inhabitants and the rich; Dionysius intervened on the side of the former, and through his own prestige or the presence of his Syracusan soldiers procured the execution of many of the rich and used their property to pay arrears owing to Dexippus and his men. This action increased his popularity amongst the masses at Syracuse, and on his return there he continued to work on the fears of the people by accusing his colleagues of negligence or treason in the face of immense Carthaginian preparations. Such accusations were sure of a sympathetic hearing in the circumstances, and even those who doubted their substance agreed with the argument that in the crisis full power must be given to one individual. The generals were deposed and Dionysius was chosen commander-in-chief with supreme powers.[20]

Such was the rapid rise of one of the most remarkable figures of the fourth century. The picture of him in our ancient sources is a very hostile one; he is portrayed as a typical tyrant of the demagogic sort, who rose to power by the exploitation of class-feeling against the rich and who had few good qualities or achievements to his credit. This is hardly the whole truth. Dionysius certainly used class-war tactics with great effect, but he had supporters among the rich also. The Syracusans lacked complete confidence in their democratic institutions, and even in time of peace the city had never had the stability of democratic Athens.

They had already permitted some restrictions on their freedom at the time of the Athenian invasion, but the powers given to Dionysius were such that it was likely to be a difficult task to restore the normal constitutional practice. The supporters of Dionysius quoted as a precedent the authority given to Gelon and the great victory he had won half a century before; they omitted to mention, and the Syracusans preferred to forget, that he had gone on to establish a tyranny.

Himilco remained in winter quarters at Acragas during the months that all this was going on. He realized that any marked activity on his part might strengthen parties or personalities able to direct the Syracusan operations more effectively. In the spring, however, he marched out and devastated the territories of Gela and its neighbour Camarina, and then pitched camp near the former to prepare for an assault. He used the same tactics as he had at Acragas, not investing it completely but placing a camp both to the west and east. By this time it must have appeared positively advantageous to leave the besieged a line of retreat, for Acragas had shown how little confidence the Greeks had in their defences. The Gelans, in spite of the weakness of their position and fortifications—the city was long and narrow in shape, and not naturally strong—held out until the approach of Dionysius and his army. This consisted of about 30,000 foot-soldiers, Italiots as well as Siceliots, and was accompanied by a fleet of fifty ships. Fixing his camp to the east of the city, he tried to force the Carthaginians to give up the attack by intercepting their supplies.

After three weeks had passed with no significant result, Dionysius undertook a direct attack on Himilco's western camp, the eastern one having been evacuated at the first approach of Dionysius because of Himilco's unwillingness to risk a defeat like that he had suffered in similar circumstances at Acragas. The plan was that the Syracusan fleet should land troops in the rear of the camp, where its defences were weakest; the Italiots, marching between the Gela and the sea, were to attack the south-eastern corner, and the Siceliots (including the

Syracusans), having passed to the north of the city, were to make for that side of the camp. Dionysius himself planned to go with his mercenaries through the city and emerge by the western gate, where the Carthaginian camp came closest to the walls. The success of this plan depended on each division attacking simultaneously; but things went very differently.

The troops from the ships attacked first, and drawing off defenders from the part opposed to the Italiots, allowed the latter to break into the camp. As the other divisions had not yet attacked, Himilco was able to concentrate his men, in particular his Campanians, at this point, and the Italiots were driven out with the loss of 1,000 men. When the Siceliots made their attack, Himilco moved the Iberian and Campanian troops to the newly-threatened quarter, where they joined the Carthaginian contingent; the Siceliots were then repulsed without much difficulty. As for Dionysius, who had the shortest distance to cover, he had not even passed through the city when he heard of the defeat of the other divisions.

No adequate explanation has survived of what delayed Dionysius, and it is not surprising that he faced the familiar charges of treason, specifically in risking the lives of the Syracusans and their allies while preserving those of his mercenaries. A more probable explanation could be this: the successful carrying out of simultaneous attacks has always been one of the most difficult operations of war, and Dionysius' army was a heterogeneous one with no experience of joint operations on the scale that he planned. In the fight for the camp, the Carthaginians had the advantage of fighting from prepared positions where troops could easily be moved about. Yet the only alternative open to Dionysius, if a serious attempt was to be made to save Gela, was a pitched battle in which the Carthaginians with their superior numbers might annihilate the Greek army and have the whole of Sicily at their mercy. He therefore chose the alternative which offered a way of retreat if things should go wrong. Furthermore, we have already seen the lack of confidence shown by Dexippus and others at Acragas, and now Dionysius' advisers were unanimous in opposing a pitched battle after the failure of the attack on the camp. Oddly enough, it looks as though Himilco also was reluctant to engage in a pitched battle. He had offered no resistance to Dionysius on his first approach to the town, remembering the reverse he had suffered at Acragas, and at no other time showed himself ready to risk a decisive engagement. The fact is that a Greek hoplite army, properly led, could be a formidable fighting force, and Himilco was cautious about staking everything on one battle; his conduct of the

Statue from sanctuary at Monte Sirai, sixth or fifth centur

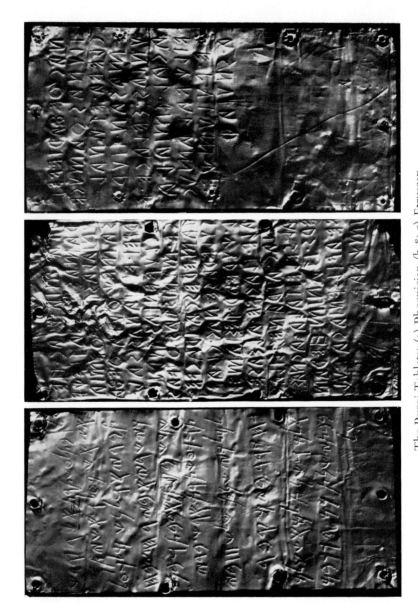

The Pyrgi Tablets: (a) Phoenician (b & c) Etruscan

Sicilian war both on land and sea marks him as an unadventurous commander.[21]

As soon as the failure of the attack was clear, Dionysius decided to evacuate Gela with all its inhabitants, and this was done the very next night; on the way to Syracuse, Camarina also was emptied of its inhabitants, as he was not prepared to defend it. Himilco's refusal to harry the retreating columns, which Dionysius' enemies took as a proof of collusion, was rather due to the Carthaginian's good sense. His mercenary troops would be inspired to still further loyalty by being given time to plunder, while the Syracusans (and Dionysius in particular) would be embarrassed by the crowd of refugees. Dionysius was faced with the same unpopularity into which he had done so much to bring Daphnaeus and others, whether people believed in the story of his treason or were simply humiliated by the lack of energetic resistance. The Italiots went home in disgust, and the refugees from Gela and Camarina settled at Leontini rather than put themselves directly in the power of Dionysius at Syracuse. The Syracusan cavalry, which was composed of the wealthier citizens, saw a chance of getting rid of the dictator, rode ahead of the main force, and took over the city. Then, through extraordinary negligence, thinking perhaps that Dionysius would be abandoned by the rest of the army, they dispersed. Dionysius came up, with a force of proven loyalty, and killed or drove out most of the dissidents.[22]

At this point there is a gap in our main source for this period of history; we have no knowledge of the movements of Himilco, or of whether he even began the siege of the last major city in Sicily outside his grasp. When the story resumes, we find that Himilco has offered terms to Dionysius which the latter has accepted. It appears that the epidemic which had attacked the Carthaginians at Acragas had broken out again, and Himilco is said to have lost half his men. A further reason for the conclusion of a peace treaty was the end of the Peloponnesian War, with the victory of the Spartans and their allies over the Athenians in April 404, which left Sparta free to help her friends in the west if called upon, even if only by the supply of volunteers, in view of her own exhaustion. It can hardly be believed that Himilco would have made peace without an attempt on the greatest prize in Sicily if it had not been for some very compelling reason, and in fact this argument also goes against the hypothesis of Dionysius' treason; he could never have obtained the security of Syracuse by such means.

The treaty confirmed Carthaginian rule over the original Phoenician foundations in western Sicily, over the Elymians, naturally including

7

Segesta, and over the Sicans (a section of the native Sicilians). The people of Acragas, Selinus, and Himera, or what was left of them, could return to their shattered cities as subjects of Carthage; and those of Gela and Camarina could return to theirs, after the walls had been destroyed, and live as tribute-paying dependencies of Carthage. All the other states in the island, Greek or Sicel, were to be independent, and this included Leontini, which had been a dependency of Syracuse since 423. Finally a special clause (apparently) recognized Dionysius as dictator of Syracuse. This treaty was so much to the disadvantage of Syracuse that it must have been dictated by Himilco. The territory of Carthage in Sicily was now many times greater than it had ever been before, while Syracuse was prevented from improving her position in the future by subjugating her neighbours. The clause recognizing Dionysius as ruler of Syracuse was almost certainly his reward for not holding out for better terms, as he might well have done seeing Himilco's desire for peace.

Himilco returned home in triumph and disbanded his army; quite apart from the acquisition of a large tract of fertile territory and an increasing number of tribute-paying subjects, as the Greeks began to go back to their old homes to see whether living under Carthaginian overlords was any worse than existence as refugees, the Carthaginian treasury must have been greatly enriched by the booty brought back from the Greek cities. The loss to be set against these gains was the epidemic which now spread throughout Carthaginian territory, causing great loss of life.[23]

On the other hand, the Greek world had suffered its greatest disaster at the hands of non-Greeks since the suppression of Greek freedom in Asia Minor by the Persians a century before. Yet these Greeks had been liberated by Athens within a generation, and the fifth century had seen a succession of Greek triumphs. Now the tide seemed to be setting the other way; the Greeks of Asia seemed to be in as desperate a position as those of the west. Sparta, after her victory over Athens, was unable and unwilling to replace her as the protector of the Asiatic Greeks, and by the Peace of Antalcidas of 387 surrendered all of them to Persia. A parallel between this treaty and that made between Himilco and Dionysius was that it stipulated that all other states should be autonomous. Superficially this accorded with deep-seated Greek political principles, but in practice it tended to prevent them from combining in alliances to oppose the politics of major powers. The common Greek feeling against any form of alliance or federation which might submerge the autonomy of the individual state had been strengthened by bitter experience of the fact—a perennial one—that it was practically impossible to construct an alliance which was not sooner or later dominated by one of its members.

The chances of Dionysius surviving this humiliating peace must have seemed negligible to many. However, with the essential backing of a force of mercenaries loyal to himself personally, and through his own force of character, he was able within a few years to challenge the Carthaginians to an even more serious conflict than the one he had with difficulty survived.

Dionysius is often portrayed as one of the earliest rulers to see the limitations of the city-state system of the Greeks, especially when it was faced with attacks from states differently organized or in other ways more powerful, and to have established a large territorial state under centralized government simply for this reason. This may be so, but it may be suspected that his prime motive in the conquest of all the Greek and Hellenized states of Sicily and southern Italy was his own lust for power, and that he had very few genuinely constructive ideas. In any case it took more than a Dionysius and a generation of Carthaginian wars to destroy the Siceliots' love of autonomy, and the city-state had its last flowering in the west, not in Greece.

Dionysius was exceedingly ruthless in the pursuit of his aims. He destroyed Naxos, venerated as the first foundation in Sicily, and peopled it with native Sicilians; he established Campanian mercenaries in Catane, the first step—though he could hardly be expected to see this—in the Italianization of the island; and though most of his mercenaries and colonists were Greeks, there was a great deal of inhuman forced movement of population. It was not generally held by the Greeks that he was a champion of Greek civilization against non-Greeks, and at times he seems to have regarded the existence of Carthaginian power in Sicily as essential for the safety of his own position. No major features of the Syracusan constitution were altered by him, since all were subservient to his will; he contented himself with the style of 'general with full powers' for life, and the popular assembly regularly met to give formal approval to his measures, for ancient dictators knew well enough how to pay lip-service to liberal institutions while depriving them of all real significance.[24]

As soon as the Carthaginians had left, he built an almost impregnable fortress on Ortygia, the most easily defensible part of Syracuse, to which only his bodyguard and men of proven loyalty were admitted.[25] In the succeeding years he entirely ignored the provisions of his treaty with Carthage guaranteeing the autonomy of the Greek cities, and conquered in turn Naxos, Catane, and Leontini, bringing some of the inhabitants to Syracuse, admittedly giving them the rights enjoyed by the existing citizens; most Sicel states also acknowledged his supremacy.[26] In spite of these flagrant breaches of the peace treaty, the Carthaginians showed reluctance to go to war. With the country still suffering from the effects of the epidemic, the mercantile oligarchy was reluctant to undertake the huge expenditure needed to raise another mercenary army, unless forced to do so by a direct threat to a major interest; they were prepared to ignore Dionysius' conquest of Greeks, so long as he did not openly attack the Carthaginian sphere of Sicily. If they had reacted sooner, as they were entitled to do, they might have avoided some serious setbacks, because from 402 Dionysius began to make preparations on a large scale which everyone knew were directed to a major war against Carthage.

On the heights of Epipolae, from which an enemy could dominate Syracuse, he built a fort joined to the city by two walls, which was one of the strongest pieces of fortification in antiquity. Two hundred warships were added to the fleet, some of which were quadriremes (galleys with four rowers to the oar) said to be a development of his own. Engineers and armourers were attracted from all over the Greek world to make equipment suitable both for Greeks and mercenaries of various races and methods of fighting. Dionysius is also credited with the invention of the catapult, but his machines were used for the discharge of small stones and bolts, and it was only in later generations that they were made large enough to damage fortifications. Dionysius was a worthy follower of Hannibal and the eastern tradition of siege warfare, and the first Greek to have any success in it.[27]

Early in 398 the preparations were complete, and the opposition to Dionysius had almost disappeared in the new feeling of confidence and power which his preparations had created. In his speech to the citizens, Dionysius described the Carthaginians as the common enemy of the Greeks in general and the Siceliots in particular, and recalled the sufferings of the five subjugated Greek states. He argued that the enemy were only prevented from subduing all of Sicily by the plague, while conversely this accident had now provided the Syracusans with an opportunity to liberate the five states before Carthage could recover. Carthage was presented with an ultimatum to give up the Greek subject states or go to war. To this Carthage could only give one answer, in spite of her lack of preparations, since surrender of the cities would certainly be followed by a demand for the evacuation of the rest of Sicily. Recruiting officers were sent to the usual sources of mercenaries but before the troops arrived the position in Sicily grew very serious.

Carthage now reaped the hatred which Hannibal had sown among the Greeks by his atrocities. As Dionysius approached with his army, each of the Greek cities rose and massacred the Carthaginian residents and garrisons, torturing any who were taken alive. We are told that from this time onwards the Carthaginians learnt to be more civilized towards their prisoners. This was probably not the case; what is more certain is that the customs of war among the Greeks declined from the already harsh (though compared with some of their neighbours, humane) standards, in accordance with the rule that atrocity begets atrocity.[28]

Dionysius made straight for Motya, the strongest point held by the Carthaginians in Sicily and resolutely defended. Realizing that with his superiority at sea he had little to fear from the Carthaginian fleet, he beached his ships and the crews joined the army in the task of building a mole across the stretch of water separating Motya from the mainland, the defenders having destroyed the causeway, Himilco, again put in command of operations in Sicily, sailed 100 triremes into the lagoon in which Motya was situated, hoping to destroy the Greek ships while they were beached.

Dionysius was equal to the emergency; he placed archers and slingers on the nearest ships and catapults on a neck of land past which Himilco had to sail. The missiles so disconcerted the Carthaginians that they retreated, and as Himilco was unwilling to face the superior numbers and weight of Dionysius' ships in a naval battle, he returned to Carthage, leaving Motya to fend for itself. When the mole was completed, a new hazard faced the Greeks. Motya must have looked like an Italian city of the Renaissance, for many of the buildings were towers some storeys high. In order that the attackers should not be dominated from these, Dionysius built siege towers six storeys high and while soldiers up above provided cover, teams below attacked the walls with battering rams. When a breach was made, the defenders resisted with all the fire for which Phoenicians and other Semitic peoples were famous, making every tall house a fortress as the Greeks sought to move up the narrow alleys.

Diodorus Siculus writes:

After the Siceliots had breached the walls and seemed to be masters of the city, they were raked by missiles from men in higher positions in the houses; they accordingly brought up their wooden towers to the houses and equipped them with foot bridges which they could push out on to the houses and thus force a passage, towers and buildings being the same height . . . Such a determination filled the defenders that the Siceliots were in a very difficult position. As they were fighting from the suspended foot bridges they suffered heavily, because of the lack of space and the desperation of the Phoenicians, who had given up hope of living. Some were killed in hand-to-hand fighting, others, pressed back by the defenders, fell to their death off the bridges.

In the end the superior numbers of the Greeks told in a night attack. The massacre, fear of which had animated the resistance, followed, women and children included; a group of Greeks who had fought for Motya (there were certainly numbers of Greek residents) were crucified.[29]

The capture of Motya was Dionysius' outstanding military achievement, and opened the way for a new era in the history of ancient warfare, as there were now very few places which were strong enough to withstand determined assaults by properly trained besiegers. The operation was a model for a more famous siege in which again men of Phoenician race were the victims—Alexander's siege and capture of Tyre.[30]

The season was now far advanced and the army tired after the long siege, so Dionysius returned to Syracuse, leaving a small garrison at Motya and a fleet under his brother Leptines to try to intercept any Carthaginian attempt to put an army into Sicily. Early in 397, in fact, the Carthaginians had their force ready, mostly Libyans and Iberians. The usual exaggerated figures for its size are given in our sources, but it was probably little larger than the army of Dionysius who mustered something over 30,000. In the campaign of 398 he is said to have had 80,000 foot-soldiers, which seems too many; but much of this army had been disbanded in the winter, and did not take part in the next year's campaigns.

The Carthaginian ships sailed under sealed orders which directed them to Panormus, the transports directly, the warships by the nearest point on the Sicilian coast in order to divert attention from the transports. Leptines fell in with the latter and sank fifty of them with 5,000 soldiers and half the 400 chariots the Carthaginians were bringing over —a curiously old-fashioned weapon which had not been used in conflicts between advanced states for generations. What use they can have been in the hills of Sicily it is difficult to see. The majority of transports landed safely, however, and we hear of no engagement involving the warships. Dionysius had returned to the west of the island to undertake the siege of Segesta, one of the very few places which had remained loyal to Carthage. On the arrival of Himilco, he withdrew to the east, no doubt because he did not have a large enough force to oppose his enemy at such a distance from his base. Within a very short time all the states in the west who had defected from Carthage returned to their allegiance, and Motya was recaptured. It was never rebuilt; instead a new city was founded nearby on the mainland at Lilybaeum, which soon became as important as its predecessor.[31]

Himilco then showed his imagination in marching along the north coast of the island, accompanied by his fleet, to Messana, the object being to cut Dionysius off from the Italiots and from Greece itself. Messana was razed, though most of the inhabitants escaped into the interior of the island, and almost all the Sicels, who were always ready to strike a blow against the Greeks, joined him. As the direct coastal route to Syracuse was closed owing to an eruption of Mt Etna, Himilco marched his army round the west of the mountain, aiming to rejoin his fleet under its admiral Mago at Catane. Dionysius had made preparations to stand at Taurus, half-way between Syracuse and Catane, with 30,000 foot-soldiers and 3,000 cavalry, accompanied by his fleet of 180 ships, of which almost all were quinqueremes or quadriremes. Sixty of these were manned by liberated slaves, a resource only used by ancient states in moments of extreme danger. It is in fact difficult to account for his apparent shortage of men, and it is possible that there was some political factor involved, such as a weakening of support among the Syracusans, which made him reluctant to use the citizen body to the full.

When Himilco was separated from his ships, Dionysius thought he saw his opportunity to attack and sent Leptines with the whole fleet to engage. Mago, who outnumbered Leptines and may have had as many as 200 ships, was reluctant to fight in a position where there would be complete catastrophe if he were defeated, but finally decided to join. The battle was the greatest fought in western waters up to that date; after an initial success the leading Greek squadron was defeated, and the rest of the Syracusan fleet, ill-manned and without proper order, were no match for the lighter but more numerous and better handled Carthaginian ships. One hundred Syracusan ships were sunk or captured, with the loss of 20,000 men.[32]

The reversal of fortune was now complete, and there was nothing Dionysius could do except retreat to Syracuse. He was followed by Himilco and Mago, and the latter sailed with his fleet and transports into the outer harbour while the Syracusans remained impotent in the docks on Ortygia. Himilco pitched his camp to the south of the city at the mouth of the Anapus river. There could be no question of investing it entirely, because of the great length (seventeen miles) of the walls, and the building of Dionysius had rendered them impregnable even to Carthaginian technique. Himilco must have hoped that morale at Syracuse would collapse, and there were apparently no atrocities to his discredit which would make a negotiated peace unthinkable. In point of fact there was serious opposition to Dionysius during the winter, but he overcame this with the assistance of a Spartan officer who had come to help in the defence.

Syracuse was in fact saved a second time by an epidemic, perhaps of typhoid fever, in the Carthaginian army, which broke out in the summer of 396. The camp was in a low-lying marshy place, and the summer was particularly hot; the dangers of infection when a vast number of men were crowded together in such conditions were increased by the fact that the Carthaginian mercenaries did not practice even the elementary hygiene which the Romans did in their camps. Diodorus describes the scene.

The disease first attacked the Libyans who were at first buried as they died; but soon because of the number of corpses and the infection of those who looked after the sick, no one dared to approach the sufferers . . . From the stench of the unburied and the miasma from the marshes, the disease began with catarrh followed by swellings about the throat; then fever came on with pains in the spinal nerves and heaviness in the legs, followed by dysentery and pustules over the whole body. These were the symptoms in most cases, but some went mad and lost their memory, and wandered in a delirium through the camp striking at everyone they met . . . Death came on the fifth day or sixth at the latest, amid such pain that those who had been killed in battle were accounted lucky.

Dionysius was not the man to let such an opportunity slip; he attacked two of the three strongpoints of the Carthaginian camp, and captured both. One of these was Himilco's headquarters, the other on the outer harbour protecting some of the beached ships. These were now set on fire by the Greeks, a strong wind spreading the flames to some of the transports lying at anchor; at the same time the Syracusan fleet at last ventured from dock to pick off such Carthaginian ships as were launched to prevent their destruction on shore. All this took place in full view of the citizens thronging the walls. The effect was to make Himilco's position untenable; the camp as a whole had held, and there had been no great loss of men in the fighting, but the destruction of a large part of the fleet made it impossible to supply the army. On the fourth night after the attack, he embarked the Carthaginian element of the army on forty surviving triremes and slipped out of the harbour, losing a few ships in the process. The rest of the army was left to fend for itself; most of the Sicels who had joined him escaped to their own homes, and the Iberians resisted until Dionysius offered to take them into his service; the rest surrendered, or were captured and apparently sold as slaves. It was later rumoured that Himilco had bribed Dionysius to let him escape, but this is probably a hostile fiction against the Greek; while the Carthaginian still held one fort on the outer harbour and had ships, he could hardly be prevented from escaping.[33]

The effect of the defeat on Carthage was considerable. That all Sicilian states except the Phoenician colonies and one or two others immediately fell away was unimportant compared with a revolt of her African subjects. Their resentment at the harshness of Carthaginian rule was exacerbated by the desertion of the non-Carthaginian troops in Sicily, necessary though this had doubtless been in Himilco's eyes. The rebels were joined by thousands of slaves and seized the town of Tunis, from which they pressed the Carthaginians within their walls. However, little difficulty was experienced in bringing in supplies from Sardinia, and the rebels, a heterogeneous mass without leaders, later split up and returned to their homes.

The Carthaginians were also oppressed by a sense of divine anger against them; the disease which had struck the army in Sicily was attributed to the destruction of the temples of the two deities who enjoyed the greatest popularity in the island, Demeter, goddess of the fertile cornfields, and her daughter Kore or Persephone. It was decided to build a temple in their honour at Carthage, and some of the most distinguished citizens were chosen as priests; the rites were to be observed in the Greek manner and Greek residents were appointed to assist.[34]

This solemn introduction of a Greek cult into Carthage symbolized the beginning of a new era in relations between the two civilizations. Whatever the reasons for the relative isolation of Carthage from the Greek world in the fifth century, she was now inextricably involved in Sicily, and the repeated conflicts in the next century exposed her to Greek influence in various fields. It is notable that the earliest coinage of Carthage, which appeared at the beginning of the fourth century, was based on that of Syracuse, and although the goddess who is portrayed is presumably Tanit, she is represented exactly like Demeter or Kore.[35] Himilco was not the object of any prosecution, but felt the disaster so keenly that he deliberately starved himself to death; he was succeeded as Carthaginian commander by Mago who had had command of the fleet, and who was probably his nephew.[36]

In the next two years there was little activity in Sicily, as Dionysius was concerned in bringing order to the large territory which was now once again within his grasp. In 393 Mago led a force from the Carthaginian dependencies in the direction of Messana, but was defeated. The next year he tried again with a larger force, which was met by Dionysius with 20,000 men at the River Chrysas near the Sicel town of Agyrium. But both generals had good reasons for avoiding a pitched battle; Mago was far from his base, and the main object of his operation was to put sufficient pressure on Dionysius to obtain a reasonable peace, while Dionysius needed more time to consolidate his rule over Greek Sicily.

The terms of the peace are unfortunately only briefly recorded in our sources, but it seems that Carthage renounced all claims to Greek cities on the island, and gave up her alliances with Sicel states; she retained, beside the Phoenician cities, the Elyminas and the Sicans. Thus the territorial position was more or less the same as it had been before Hannibal's campaign, except that both protagonists had strengthened their hold on their smaller neighbours.[37] The peace lasted for eight years, during which Dionysius directed his expansive aims elsewhere; he made himself master of the Greeks in Italy, though he did little to strengthen them against increasing pressure from the native Italians, and made the Adriatic almost a Syracusan lake.[38] His influence was even felt in Greece itself, but he was unpopular with most of the cities and there were hostile demonstrations against his representatives at the Olympic Games of 384. He was so far from being regarded as a saviour of Greek civilization that he was compared with the King of Persia as a ruler who had reduced numbers of Greek states to slavery.[39]

As his power increased, Dionysius became increasingly complacent about the prospect of another war with Carthage, though in this case it looks as though he was content gradually to damage their interests, leaving them the decision whether they would in the end react strongly. In 384 he took advantage of the difficulties of the Etruscans, who were under pressure from both the Romans and the Celts, to lead a fleet into their waters, ostensibly to suppress their piratical activities. He looted an enormous treasure from Pyrgi, the port of Caere, and founded a base on Corsica which had the double purpose of protecting his own shipping and threatening the Carthaginians in Sardinia.[40]

In Sicily one Sican state after another was won over to Dionysius' camp, until at last Carthage decided on war, probably in 382. Unexpected support was found amongst the Italiots, some of whom were prepared to make common cause with Carthage out of fear of Dionysius, which shows that by this time the picture of Carthage as a national enemy was no longer universally accepted, if it ever was. Details of this conflict are obscure, partly because there were no really large engagements. Mago sent an army into southern Italy of whose activity nothing is known except that in 379-378 it restored to Hipponion the survivors of the destruction wrought there by Dionysius some years before. Inconclusive skirmishing with small losses on both sides marked the campaigns in Sicily till 375, when the Carthaginian army was defeated at Cabala, in the west of the island, losing 10,000 killed, including Mago himself, and 5,000 taken prisoner.

The surviving Carthaginian officers opened negotiations with Dionysius, who demanded the surrender of all Carthaginian positions in Sicily and the payment of reparations. The officers accepted these terms but said that they had to be ratified by the Carthaginian government, and a truce was arranged for this to be concluded. It seems clear that the Carthaginians in the field were hoping to gain time, since they must have been aware of the crucial importance attached to the possessions in Sicily and the unlikelihood of the government agreeing to their surrender without a further effort to retain them.

Mago's son Himilco, an ambitious and warlike young man, succeeded his father as commander in Sicily and revitalized the army in a period of intensive training. When he was ready, negotiations were broken off, and at a battle near Himera the result of Cabala was reversed. Dionysius was defeated with the loss of 14,000 Siceliots, including his brother Leptines; this was one of the few occasions in which a Carthaginian army defeated a Greek army of classic hoplite formation in the open field. Himilco's losses were also heavy, and he returned to Panormus, from which new negotiations were begun. This time Dionysius was willing to concede Carthage the advantage; three Greek cities—Selinus, Heraclea Minoa, and Thermae (the successor of Himera)—and a portion of Acragantine territory west of the River Halycus went to Carthage, with an indemnity of 1,000 talents to be paid in instalments. Carthage now controlled a third of the island, and in fact the division of Sicily more or less along the Halycus remained in force with only shortlived changes for a century.[41]

The last occasion on which Carthage contended with Dionysius was in 367, a year before the tyrant's death. A serious epidemic of some sort was raging in Africa, and there was unrest among her subjects there and in Sardinia, and Dionysius sought again to take advantage of the situation. A frontier incident was made the cause of the war, but our authority says that it was provoked by Dionysius, and the fact that it was fought in the Carthaginian sphere proves the point. Selinus and

Eryx went over to his side, and he undertook the siege of Lilybaeum, with little success. While it was in progress he was deceived by a false report of the destruction of a Carthaginian fleet coming to relieve the fortress, and divided his fleet, sending part of it back to Syracuse and beaching the remainder, 130 triremes, at Drepana, the harbour of Eryx. There they were taken by surprise by a fleet of 200 ships under a new Carthaginian commander, not of the Magonid family, called Hanno, who was later called 'the Great'. Most of the Syracusan ships were taken, and as it was now no longer practicable to besiege Lilybaeum, Dionysius returned to Syracuse. A truce was arranged, and though Dionysius died before a fresh peace treaty was concluded, this was done as one of his first actions by his successor, the territorial arrangements being the same as those in the peace of 375.[42]

For nearly forty years Dionysius had fought intermittently with Carthage, and he has sometimes been portrayed as the preserver of Greek civilization in Sicily. Yet it is clear that he started or provoked three of these conflicts; our sources make no effort to gloss over the fact, not so much because a charge of aggression was an additional count in their indictment of the tyrant as because fixing the responsibility for a war was of little interest to them, particularly when it was a case of a war between Greek and non-Greek, when an attack by the former was generally regarded as quite legitimate. No doubt his first war was popular because of the resentment of the Greeks at the atrocities of Hannibal, and in so far as the capture of Motya probably contributed to the Carthaginians' decision to have no more expansive adventures like that of Hannibal, it was beneficial to the Greeks. His second campaign also opened with the highest hopes of Greek Sicily, but like the last two was curiously ineffective in spite of the massive preparations and the advantage of getting in the first blow. The fact is that the substantial look of Dionysius' empire was deceptive; he was entirely unable to make use of what should have been the greatest advantage to him and to the western Greeks, namely the manpower it provided. Manpower, or at any rate manpower in the sense of military potential, was the greatest single power factor in antiquity, as the Romans realized; but Dionysius had aroused far too many resentments for him to be able to demand of his subjects the sacrifices which would have been necessary to create a dominating military force.

For their part the Carthaginians cannot have been dissatisfied with their military methods; their heterogeneous and hastily-organized mercenary armies had not proved markedly inferior to the classical Greek hoplite formations; the warlike traditions and constant practice of the mercenaries probably balanced the better cohesion of the Greek armies. Neither side made great use of their fleets—seapower in antiquity was not an easy thing to use to the full, because of the relatively unseaworthy character of the ships—and the Carthaginians were generally superior.

The effect of the wars on the way of life of Carthage, and her standing in the Mediterranean world, were profound; even though aggressive wars such as that of 409 remained unusual for Carthage, the attacks of Dionysius made it impossible for her ever again to isolate herself from the Greek world. Many members of the governing class through military or diplomatic service in Sicily experienced to the full the attractions of Greek civilization. During the century[43] there was a general resumption of imports from the Greek world, and much booty must also have been brought back from Sicily; there were Greek residents at Carthage, Greek cults were observed, and Greek mercenaries used. The way was open for Carthage in the following generations to intervene in the internal affairs of Siceliot cities at the request of Greek politicians; already a general such as Mago, the victor in the sea battle off Catane, had made a deliberate effort to attract the Siceliots by a friendly policy and had welcomed victims of Dionysius, and the same seems to have been true of Himilco.

5

The War against Timoleon and the Invasion of Africa by Agathocles[1]

THE peace treaty[2] which Carthage signed with Dionysius' successor, his son, also called Dionysius, enabled her rapidly to overcome the revolt of the Africans, but there was disunion in the city itself. An enemy of Hanno called Suniaton was condemned to death for having had treasonable correspondence with the Syracusans in the time of Dionysius the elder. We are told that as a result the Carthaginian government forbade any of its citizens to learn to read or write Greek.[3] This law has been doubted, on the ground that in fact Greek influence on Carthaginian life continued to grow, and clearly its more suitable position in the history of Carthage would have been in the early fifth century. However, the existence of a hasty and violent reaction against Greek culture, because of its apparent connexion with treason, is not disproved by the fact that the law clearly was a dead letter almost from the start.

The position of Carthage vis-à-vis the Siceliots improved, because of the growing hatred felt everywhere for the younger Dionysius. In particular, he had banished Dion,[4] brother-in-law of the elder Dionysius and one of his chief advisers. This man had been responsible for a remarkable experiment: he invited Plato to Syracuse to try to induce the younger Dionysius, who had a smattering of philosophy, to work towards the ideas expressed in the *Republic*; but the young man tired of the advice of the elderly philosopher. Dion took up residence at Athens and continually intrigued against Dionysius. He was supported by the Academy, the influential philosophical school of which Plato was the head, though not by many Syracusans, who saw only a change of masters in view.

In 357 he set sail with only 1,500 men for Sicily. He was blown by the north wind down to the African coast, and made his way with some difficulty to Heraclea Minoa, in the Carthaginian province of Sicily. He knew what he was about, for he had many contacts among the leading men of Carthage, dating from the days when he had been an adviser of Dionysius. Carthage foresaw nothing but advantage in a struggle for power at Syracuse, and the commander at Heraclea (who was a Greek) gave his support to the venture. In the event, the situation at Syracuse underwent a series of bewildering fluctuations, as there were at least three competing interests, those who remained loyal to Dionysius, those who welcomed Dion, and those who wanted a democratic régime.

In 355 Dion obtained full control, though not before the city had been plundered and half destroyed by Dionysius' Campanian mercenaries.

Within a few months Dion was assassinated, as it appeared to many that he in his turn was seeking to establish himself as tyrant. There followed ten years of anarchy, which had its effect on the rest of Sicily. Syracuse came successively under the control of other sons of the elder Dionysius, and in 347 again under that of Dionysius the younger. Almost all her dependent cities became independent, most of them falling into the hands of miltary adventurers, Greek, Sicel, and Campanian, whose policies were entirely selfish and almost wholly pernicious.

It was in such a period of Siceliot weakness that Plato wrote[5] of the probability of the Greek langugage in Sicily being supplanted by Phoenician or Oscan (the language of the Campanians), a prediction which came half true in the sense that Greek civilization in Sicily was bound up with what happened in Italy, and finally gave way to Italians, though Latin not Oscan speakers. The interests of Carthage were well served by the collapse of the Syracusan Empire, and several important

Siceliot states, including Acragas, Gela, and Camarina, became in some
degree dependent on her. There was no open hostility, and the Carthaginians avoided taking any action which might frighten the Greeks into
some sort of unity.[6]

It must have seemed that if such a state of affairs continued it might
be possible to dominate all Sicily through the medium of well-
disposed tyrants dependent on Carthaginian support. Such a policy was
common prudence, and testifies to the caution of the mercantile aristocracy in control, for whom open warfare was always unwelcome; it
shows also that the acquisition and exploitation of a tribute-paying
empire (except among their own race and primitive peoples) was not
part of the Carthaginian scheme.

Carthage was not without her own political troubles about this
time, which perhaps strengthened her determination not to force the
pace in Sicily. The leading figure at Carthage since the last years of the
elder Dionysius had been Hanno 'the Great'[7]; what this epithet implies
is not clear, as there were two later figures also called Hanno who were
given the same nickname. They may have been the same family, or
perhaps it represents some Phoenician term only half understood by
Greeks and Romans. Some time in the 340s, Hanno, who was said to be
the richest man in Carthage, plotted to make himself tyrant. A romantic
but improbable account of the plot is given in our sources, but from it
we can see his methods. There was an attempt to gain popularity
amongst the masses by distributions of food, and when forced to take
armed action—perhaps prematurely—Hanno called on the slave population, African subjects, and a chieftain of Mauretania. The attempt
does not appear to have posed a great military threat to Carthage;
Hanno was captured and tortured to death with the savagery the
Carthaginians generally used against political offenders, and most of
his family were executed as well.[8] However, we find the survivors
exercising power again in later generations; the influence and prestige
of leading Carthaginian families was difficult to destroy entirely, as the
earlier example of the Magonids had shown.

A new situation arose out of an extraordinary incident in 345. On
the return of the younger Dionysius to Syracuse, a number of the surviving aristocrats fled to Leontini, where they co-operated with Hicetas,
a former friend of Dion and the most powerful figure in Leontini. This
group, in despair at the situation in Sicily in general and Syracuse in
particular, sent an embassy to Corinth, as the mother city of Syracuse
and other Siceliot cities, asking for her help in putting down the tyrants
who were responsible for the existing weakness and anarchy. They

Vessel of East Greek provenance, part of
'Foundation Deposit' at Carthage

Phoenician pottery from the Tophet at Motya

alleged that a Carthaginian attack was imminent, but although a force was present in the west of the island putting down a revolt at the Sican town of Entella, there is no real evidence that Carthage was meditating a change in her policy towards the Siceliots.[9]

Corinth was no longer a power of any consequence, and though the invitation was gratifying to her pride, only 700 soldiers were sent, under the command of an aristocrat named Timoleon, whose reputation as a hater of tyrants was founded on an incident in which he had organized the assassination of his own brother, who had made himself master of Corinth. The Carthaginians sought to prevent his landing, not so much on the principle of opposition to outside intervention in Sicily as from a fear that he might have some success in putting an end to the anarchy among the Greek states. Their plan was to co-operate with Hicetas, who had successfully concealed from his Syracusan supporters his ambition to supplant Dionysius as tyrant. In the early part of 344, Hicetas, with a small amount of assistance, made himself master of all Syracuse except Ortygia, to which Dionysius retreated. When Timoleon reached Rhegium a few days later, he found twenty Carthaginian ships there to bar his passage into Sicily and a message from Hicetas saying that as Syracuse was now almost entirely liberated, Timoleon's presence was no longer required, except perhaps as an adviser; in any case, the Carthaginians would not let him cross. Timoleon, however, slipped through the blockade and landed at Tauromenium.[10]

Greek Sicily now had two competing liberators, neither of whom at first aroused much enthusiasm. Timoleon's slender force was increased by the support of Mamercus, the tyrant of Catane, who as a Campanian had the reputation of that people for treachery and brutality; he then came to an understanding with Dionysius to help him defend Ortygia against Hicetas, from which it must have appeared that he had no real interest in the suppression of tyrants. Hicetas, who up to now had tried to keep his obligations to Carthage to a minimum, at length asked for substantial assistance, as he saw no chance of reducing Ortygia without it. His request was granted; it appeared to the Carthaginians that their policy of dominating Greek Sicily through dependent tyrants was about to achieve its greatest success.

In the spring of 343 a fleet of perhaps 150 ships and some thousands of soldiers was sent to Syracuse under the command of Mago, presumably the successor of Hanno the Great, and entered the Great Harbour without opposition. But a good understanding between the Carthaginian and Hicetas was never reached, as each was trying to use the other for his own purpose—it was no part of Hicetas' plan to be a

8

dependant of Carthage. The commander of a section of the Carthaginian fleet through incompetence allowed some Corinthian reinforcements for Timoleon to cross from Italy to Sicily, while Mago seems to have lacked the courage to attempt an assault on Ortygia, in spite of his numerical superiority. At the same time, the defenders of Ortygia established contact with Hicetas' Greek troops, and affected their morale by arguing that it was disgraceful to collaborate with the Carthaginians to subdue the chief city in Sicily. Mago used this as an excuse, and when Timoleon's relieving force was only a day's march from the city he sailed away, having accomplished nothing. He later committed suicide rather than face an inquiry into his conduct of the operation. It is true that by this time, regardless of the circumstances, failure could bring about the crucifixion of a Carthaginian general, but in Mago's case, in spite of the confused account of these episodes that we have, we can deduce that he was entirely lacking in the initiative necessary to make use of the opportunity presented to Carthage. Hicetas escaped with a substantial force to Leontini.

On his entry into Syracuse, Timoleon showed that his previous collaboration with tyrants had been mere opportunism, forced upon him by the weakness of his position when he arrived in Sicily. Dionysius was sent into exile at Corinth and the liberation of Syracuse was symbolized by the destruction of the fortifications of Ortygia where the tyrants had had their residence, and the construction of courts of justice in their place. In 342, however, Timoleon made little progress in expelling other tyrants, and was even driven to the expedient of raiding the Carthaginian territory in the island to obtain plunder to pay his troops.

At the same time the Carthaginians were engaged in their usual activity when faced with a major campaign, raising an army from the African subjects and from sources of mercenaries. This time the important decision was taken of sending to Sicily the élite corps of Carthaginian citizens called by the Greeks the Sacred Band; it numbered several thousand heavily armed soldiers trained more or less to fight like a Greek hoplite force. This army landed at Lilybaeum in the summer of 341 under the command of two officers, Hasdrubal and Hamilcar, the former apparently the senior. Timoleon reacted quickly against this threat and patched up his quarrel with Hicetas, still his chief opponent in Greek Sicily. With not more than 12,000 men he entered Carthaginian territory and met the opposing army at the River Crimisos, not far from Segesta. He reaped the reward of his courage, for there is no doubt that his army was far outnumbered by that of the

Carthaginians, and if it had lost, the conquest of Sicily would this time have been inevitable.

The Carthaginian commanders were surprised at the speed of Timoleon's approach, and were attacked as the army was in some disorder while making the crossing of the river. The chariots, in which the Carthaginians still placed some faith, had been sent across first, but were useless against the well-drilled infantry. The Sacred Band, which had also crossed, put up a fierce resistance, but cut off as it was by the river from the rest of the army, it was gradually overwhelmed and finally put to flight. Then, as the rest of the army was crossing, torrential rain drove directly into their faces; the river rose with great rapidity, swollen by torrents coming down from the hills, and swept away many, thus completing the Greek victory.

If Plutarch is correct in saying that the loss of 3,000 citizens of Carthage was the heaviest they had ever suffered in a battle, we can see clearly on how few occasions the citizens were committed. The remnant of the army made its way back to Lilybaeum, but its position was by no means desperate; many of the tyrants, who had probably expected a Carthaginian victory but had done nothing to help, now turned to active operations against Timoleon, correctly expecting that fortified by his remarkable success he would redouble his efforts to rid Sicily of tyrants and that he would be widely supported.

Hasdrubal was replaced for his failure, and in the difficult situation in which they found themselves the Carthaginians turned to Gisgo, a son of Hanno the Great. He had escaped the fate of the rest of his family, and is said to have been exiled, but it is perhaps more likely that this exile was self-imposed. He had a good reputation as a soldier and was now recalled, to be sent with seventy ships and a force of Greek mercenaries to Lilybaeum. The aim was to help the friendly tyrants, in particular Hippo of Messana and Mamercus of Catane, whose alliance with Timoleon had been pure opportunism, but Timoleon was assisted by the general dissatisfaction of their subjects and dealt with them before assistance could be brought. Gisgo was doubtless also authorized to see if a reasonable peace could be secured, and the opportunity for this was easy to find. The Carthaginian government was obviously reluctant to pay for more reinforcements to meet the now formidable army of Timoleon, while the latter was eager to proceed with the destruction of the remaining tyrants. The terms of the peace seem to have resembled those of 375 and 367, the River Halycus to mark the boundary of Carthaginian territory.

Timoleon went on to rid Sicily entirely of its tyrants, with the exception of Andromachus of Tauromenium, to whom he owed a debt of gratitude for a friendly reception when he first arrived in Sicily. More than this, he made great efforts to attract settlers from all over the Greek world to Sicily, to restore the cities which had been half ruined in the preceding decades, and some tens of thousands answered the call. His own political views were unsympathetic towards a completely democratic system, and this outlook was strengthened by the fact that Sicilian democracies had been particularly prone to fall under the sway of tyrants. The constitution adopted by Syracuse and no doubt other Siceliot states, under his guidance, was consequently aristocratic, or more exactly timocratic. The annually chosen chief executive had to come from one of the most distinguished families, and the main business of government was carried on by a council of 600 members, to which only the wealthiest citizens could belong. To prevent successful military leaders from seizing power, it was laid down that in a campaign of any consequence, a general should be invited from Corinth to take command.

Having carried through these measures, Timoleon, who had gone blind, resigned his extraordinary powers in 338 and lived the rest of his life as a private citizen at Syracuse. He appears as one of the most disinterested men of the fourth century, an age noticeably lacking in such people; the material forces at his disposal when he arrived in Sicily were negligible, but he possessed qualities of a high order essential for success in his environment. In particular he showed an astute opportunism, almost cunning, in manipulating the competing interests and jealousies of his enemies, such as is usually found in persons willing only to use such a talent in a bad way. Further he had the personal courage and inspiring self-confidence so necessary in an age when generals took the field at the head of their men.

It is often said that his work was largely ruined at the end of twenty years by the rise of Agathocles to the tyranny of Syracuse; but these twenty years were almost certainly a period of political and social tranquillity of an order which Sicily had not enjoyed for over a century, and more than this was hardly to be expected in a period of relatively rapid historical change. It was ironic that it was in Sicily, where the system of fully autonomous city-states had so often showed its worst side in political violence and instability, that it had its last period of success, for the year of Timoleon's resignation was the year of the battle of Chaeronea, at which Philip of Macedon effectively ruined for ever the autonomy of the cities of Greece.

Of the effect on Carthage of this period we know very little. Her attempt to dominate Sicily through an opportunist use of the tyrants had failed, but apart from the heavy losses suffered in the destruction of the Sacred Band, she was no worse off than before. The political complexion of the 'liberated' states was also not threatening to her. It was true that the governments which replaced the tyrannies could not but have feelings of hostility towards a power who had supported the discredited régimes, but an important historical fact played in favour of a peaceful coexistence of Greek and Carthaginian in Sicily. Greek aristocratic or oligarchic governments were in general less prone to indulge in adventurous foreign policies than those of other complexions, since power rested in the hands of those who had least to gain and most to lose by war; it was clearly recognized that war and its attendant instability was one of the causes of tyranny. Again, the type of government now in power in the Siceliot states was not unlike that at Carthage itself, and to the extent that class feeling played a part in relations between states, this fact also made for easier relations; indeed in 330 Carthage intervened in support of the Syracusan aristocracy.[11]

On the military side, the Carthaginians had little to be satisfied about, and in particular they had entirely failed to utilize their superiority at sea, for it is clear that the Syracusan fleet was no longer the power it had been in the days of the elder Dionysius. The idea of using their ships not simply to transport armies to western Sicily but to land troops and achieve surprise in the midst of enemy territory had apparently not occurred to the generals, and the adherence to archaic weapons such as chariots gives the impression that to them the old tried ways were the best. Finally, it might be said that it was at this period that Carthage reached as near the status of a civilized power in Greek eyes as any other non-Greek state in the period of Greek independence. It was now that Aristotle had much to say in praise of the Carthaginian system of government, the only non-Greek one which could properly be compared with a Greek city's constitution. To those that could see, it was no longer Carthage, but the warlike and backward Italian tribes that were the greatest threat to the western Greeks.[12]

The featureless history of Sicily in the years following Timoleon is accentuated by the stupendous events which took place in the East. There, a few years after the assassination of his father, Alexander had resumed the plans already drawn up for what was characterized as a war of revenge against the Persian Empire for its various injuries to the Greeks, and of liberation for its Greek subjects. Whether the original plan went beyond the conquest of the Aegean coast of Asia Minor may be doubted, in spite of the Greeks' confidence in their ability, given proper leadership, to defeat a Persian army of any size, but as Alexander pressed on with uninterrupted success, ever wider vistas opened before the king and his small army of Macedonians and Greeks. Within a space of ten years, the Persian Empire was extinguished, and Alexander marched his men from the Hellespont to the Indus. This military and political cataclysm was the most rapid and far-reaching in antiquity, where changes were normally slow. Greek civilization, though altered in the process, was given a field of operation infinitely wider than it would ever have had otherwise; without the conquests of Alexander there would have been no Alexandria, no Antioch, no Constantinople.

The scale of the changes in the east was so vast that it was not appreciated by men of the west for some time. Carthage, however, was directly affected sooner than most, through the destruction of her mother city. Sidon and Byblos welcomed the arrival of Alexander, but Tyre, confident in her insular defences, remained loyal to Persia. Its capture was essential to Alexander before he advanced into Asia, as he would otherwise leave a fleet in his rear. The siege lasted seven months, a more desperate version of Dionysius' siege of Motya. Among the few survivors in the city were some Carthaginian envoys, who had come to bring the traditional offering to their founder. From this circumstance there arose a tradition that Carthage had been preparing to help Tyre, which was certainly not the case. Other stories that Carthage was among the western states which Alexander was planning to conquer, when he died in the prime of life, belong to the mass of legends which soon grew up around this brilliant and romantic figure.[13]

After the destruction of Tyre, Sidon became the most important city of Phoenicia, now part of the empire of Alexander and later of the Seleucid dynasty, descended from one of Alexander's generals who made himself master of Syria after the conqueror's death. Greek civilization, even in the fifth century more influential in Phoenicia than at Carthage, made still more rapid progress, while at the same time the Phoenician language rapidly declined in the face of Aramaic. Thus Carthage was now not only cut off from any material or moral help from Phoenicia—this had been the case for a long time—but was in effect the last surviving part of the Phoenician race.[14]

The end of the period of relative quiet in Sicily came with the overthrow of Timoleon's political arrangements at Syracuse. Opposition to the aristocratic régime grew in spite of its merits, and a leader was found in the person of Agathocles. He had been born at Thermae of parents exiled by Dionysius from Rhegium; his family emigrated to

Syracuse at the time of Timoleon. Agathocles had a reputation for military ability, but was twice exiled for his opposition to the aristocratic government. About 320 he found a welcome in some small places near Syracuse, made himself master of Leontini, and posed a threat to Syracuse itself. Carthaginian policy had been to support the status quo in the island; in 330 the aristocracy at Syracuse had been overthrown by a democratic revolution, and the exiled nobles were helped in a small way, though it was through Corinthian intervention that the aristocracy was restored.[15]

In 319–318, however, Hamilcar, the commander in Sicily, judged that the aristocractic régime was unlikely to survive and expediency demanded that an attempt be made to get on friendly terms with Agathocles. Through his mediation, an understanding was reached between political parties at Syracuse, involving the recall of Agathocles, who was then given military command over the areas he was in fact occupying. Such a compromise was unlikely to last; some of the aristocrats resorted to arms, and were massacred out of hand by the supporters of Agathocles, who far outnumbered them. Agathocles then observed the forms which had become conventional when military dictators seized power. He told the assembled people that having restored their democratic liberties, he would now retire. On the inevitable opposition to this taking place, he allowed himself, with a decent show of reluctance, to be elected sole general with full powers for an unlimited period.[16]

Thus Syracuse fell once more into the hands of a popular dictator, the hatred of the Syracusans for the aristocrats being far more potent than their liking for genuine democratic liberties. The reputation of Agathocles is as black as that of Dionysius in our sources, because of their standard dislike of tyranny, but there is no doubt that throughout his life he enjoyed the enthusiastic support of the mass of the Syracusans; they were not the victims of his cruelties, which were generally directed against aristocratic opponents in Syracuse and elsewhere.[17]

To Hamilcar, the rapid rise of Agathocles was mortifying. As he soon got control of several Sicilian cities, he seemed to be well on the way to establishing once more a powerful Siceliot state. Carthage therefore directed her attention to preventing Agathocles from absorbing any of the major states. Thus in 316 he was obliged to give up an attack on Messana, through diplomatic intervention.[18] In the following year, Messana joined with Acragas and Gela in an alliance, but when the Spartan prince they chose to lead them proved a failure, they too were in a dangerous position. Again peace was made with Agathocles through Carthaginian intervention, though Messana refused to accept the terms and fell to the dictator.[19]

Hamilcar had preserved the independence of Acragas, the most powerful Siceliot state after Syracuse, but his government began to use him as a scapegoat for the revival of Syracusan power. One source,[20] almost certainly false, said that he had a secret agreement with Agathocles, whom he had helped to power in Syracuse and to whom he had handed over most of Sicily, his object being to get Agathocles' help in his own design to become tyrant of Carthage. The more likely version is that he was heavily fined for negotiating a treaty which, while it saved Acragas, recognized Agathocles' control over much of Greek Sicily.[21] It seems also that he was superseded by another Hamilcar,[22] this one the son of Gisgo, who had taken over after the disaster of the Crimisus. During this period of the rise of Agathocles, the Carthaginians confined themselves to diplomatic measures, having no army in Sicily beyond the limited forces normally kept in the west of the island.

Though the Carthaginian authorities were unjust to Hamilcar, whose bargaining position was weak, they were doubtless correct in their estimate of the aggressive intentions of Agathocles. In 311 he led a large army in an attack on Acragas, which was only saved by the arrival of a fleet of sixty Carthaginian ships. He then attacked the region beyond the River Halycus. Thus another war between the two powers broke out, the sole responsibility for which rested on Agathocles, with the less excuse considering the general direction of Carthaginian policy for a long time past. This time, there could be no possible claim that the existence of Greek civilization was at stake. If Carthage had been able to get control of all Sicily, the effect upon her of Greek civilization would have been even more considerable than it was on Rome when she conquered the Greek states.[23]

In 310 Hamilcar son of Gisgo brought over from Africa a force of 14,000 men, including 2,000 Carthaginian citizens. Though he lost a number of ships in a storm, the size of his army probably trebled when his Sicilian and Siceliot allies joined him. His camp at Ecnomus at the mouth of the River Himeras was attacked by Agathocles from his position across the river. The Greek was probably over-confident because of the often-proved superiority of Greek infantry over the Carthaginian armies, but on this occasion it failed. The assault was driven back, and large numbers of Greeks were killed as they tried to make their way back across the river. After this defeat, city after city, both Sicilian and Greek, went over to Hamilcar, who made every effort to show that the Carthaginians were generous and civilized rulers. Soon Agathocles was left with nothing but Syracuse itself, and his position became desperate; his fleet was no match for the Carthaginian and was unable to prevent a blockade of the city.[24] No help could be expected from the rest of the Greek world, where the successors of Alexander were too busily engaged in their own struggles for supremacy. As a last hope, he staked everything on a stroke of great hazard—a counter-invasion of Africa, which, if the initial stages were successful, might at least force the Carthaginians to give up the blockade of Syracuse. He put 14,000 men, of whom 3,000 were Greek mercenaries and 3,000 mercenaries of Samnite, Etruscan, and Celtic provenance, on sixty warships, and with some difficulty eluding the Carthaginian fleet set out on 14th August, 310. After six days' sailing he arrived at a placed called 'The Quarries', probably near Sidi Daoud on the west coast of Cap Bon. Having too few men to leave a guard on the ships, he burnt them and set out for Carthage.[25]

The Carthaginians had never had to face an attack on this part of Africa after they had conquered it in the early fifth century, and consequently there were very few strongpoints or garrisons. Diodorus Siculus[26] gives a description of its great wealth and prosperity:

> It was divided into market gardens and orchards of all sorts of fruit trees, with many streams of water flowing in channels irrigating every part. There were country houses everywhere, lavishly built and covered with stucco, which testified to the wealth of their owners. The barns were filled with all that was needed to maintain a luxurious standard of living, as the inhabitants had been able to store up an abundance of everything in a long period of peace. Part of the land was planted with vines, part with olives and other productive trees. Beyond these, cattle and sheep were pastured on the plains, and there were meadows filled with grazing horses. Such were the signs of the prosperity of these regions where leading Carthaginians had their estates.

The prospects of the vast amount of booty they could obtain buoyed up the soldiers in spite of their lonely isolation, and after storming the towns of Megalopolis (an unidentified place) and Tunis, Agathocles pitched his camp a few miles from Carthage.

In the city there was at first great confusion and alarm as conflicting reports of what was happening in the country arrived. Two generals were appointed by the government, Hanno and Bomilcar, the latter son of the Hamilcar who had been fined in 314. It seems that the city was divided into factions—the two men were bitter enemies—and that agreement could not be reached on a single appointment.

Without waiting for reinforcements to come in from overseas or

from African territory not yet touched by Agathocles, the generals put
into the field their available force, 40,000 foot, 1,000 horse, and 2,000
chariots; most of these troops must have been Carthaginians, and it
was presumably hoped that superiority in numbers would compensate
for lack of experience and training. The battle took place somewhere
between Tunis and Carthage; the crucial point was the struggle on the
Carthaginian right wing between the Sacred Band under Hanno's
personal command and a picked force of hoplites led by Agathocles.
After a hard struggle, the Greeks proved superior, and Hanno was
killed, fighting to the last. Bomilcar ordered a general retreat, for which
he was later accused of treachery, but this seems to have been unjust;
Carthaginian losses are nowhere put at over 6,000, and were probably
not more than 3,000; the greater part of the force was therefore preserved in good order, and in fact Agathocles did not carry out a
resolute pursuit.[27]

Thus the extraordinary position was reached in which each army,
on the two sides, was directly threatening the other's city, though the
Carthaginian position was much safer, since they could bring in by sea
whatever they wanted, and the small force of Agathocles could never
attempt to storm the formidable defences across the isthmus of Carthage.
However, the reaction of the Carthaginians to the invasion of a territory which they must have regarded as inviolable was extremely
sombre; they saw in it divine punishment for neglect of the gods. In
the first place, a large amount of treasure and precious offerings was
sent to the god Melkart at Tyre, now reoccupied after its destruction by
Alexander. It is to be presumed that the despatch of even nominal
offerings to the god had been stopped after this occurrence, but now
it appeared necessary to make amends. The anger of the Carthaginian
deity, Baal Hammon, was found to have been caused by the fact that
children of slaves had often been substituted for those of the nobility
at the human sacrifices offered to him. Accordingly, 200 children from
the most noble families were chosen by the authorities and sacrificed;
these were presumably from those about whom the fact of substitution
was well known. In addition, 300 children were voluntarily surrendered
by parents who were only suspected. This incident was probably
instrumental in delaying the relaxation of the Carthaginian sacrificial
system under the impulse of Greek civilization, the substitution of
slave children having marked only the first stage in the process.[28]

Hamilcar was ordered to send help to Africa as soon as possible;
before he did so he made a final attempt to take Syracuse. He sent into
the city envoys with the metal rams which had been saved from the

destruction of Agathocles' ships, to spread the story that the expedition had met with disaster. The authorities were not convinced, and soon a despatch boat, built by Agathocles after his victory, arrived with the truth. After an attempt to surprise the defenders while the citizens were celebrating the good news had failed, Hamilcar sent 5,000 men to Africa. This small number shows that it was still intended to keep the pressure on Syracuse, and that the Carthaginians had not given up hope of a double success in Sicily and Africa. In the latter, Agathocles fortified a camp near Tunis and set out with part of his force to overrun further territory, in order to deprive Carthage of revenue and supplies. He stormed Neapolis and won over a native chief of the region, but while he was proceeding against Hadrumetum, he heard that the Carthaginians had made a sally, had taken his camp, and were besieging Tunis. Dividing his forces again, he tricked the Carthaginians into believing that he was returning with all his troops, and they abandoned the siege, being unwilling to risk another pitched battle. When the reinforcements from Sicily arrived, another attempt was made on Tunis; this time Agathocles, who had meanwhile taken Hadrumetum and Thapsus, came upon them by surprise and inflicted heavy losses.[29]

Thus after a few months' campaigning, Agathocles was master of much of the east of Tunisia; he was credited with the possession of 200 'cities', though all but a few of these were no more than native villages.

These setbacks to Carthage were followed after the winter by a disaster in Sicily. Hamilcar, whose winter quarters were to the south of the city, decided to move round to the north side, perhaps to try an assault at a place which had not been attempted before. While making his way up the Anapus valley, he was taken on his right flank by Syracusans coming down from their positions on the Epipolae and from Euryalus. With his troops unable to manoeuvre in the narrow valley, and encumbered by the presence of numerous camp-followers, Hamilcar could not organize an effective resistance. His army broke and he himself was taken. The Syracusan authorities handed him over to those who wanted to take vengeance on him; he was tortured to death and his head was sent to Agathocles.[30]

This defeat was catastrophic to the Carthaginian position in the island. Acragas and her other Siceliot allies broke away and campaigned against both Carthage and Syracuse at the same time. The traditional strongpoints held firm, but during the next few years Carthage was unable to do anything to damage Syracuse except blockade it with the fleet.[31] What was worse was that she had now lost her principal bargaining point in the struggle with Agathocles; he would obviously not now leave Africa after a negotiated peace, but only if defeated in a decisive battle. The threat to Carthage increased with the determination of Agathocles to amass a force large enough to attempt the storming of the city. He formed a project which connected Carthage and Sicily with the new Hellenistic states of the east and showed the wide vistas open to ambitious leaders in the generation after Alexander.

One of Alexander's officers, Ptolemy son of Lagus, had acquired Egypt in the division of empire which followed the king's death. In 322 he appointed as his governor of the Greek cities of Cyrenaica (which went with Egypt) Ophellas, who had been a member of Alexander's bodyguard. Agathocles now proposed that Ophellas join him in annihilating Carthage; when this had been done, Ophellas could have the whole of Carthaginian North Africa, while Agathocles ruled Sicily. This prospective division gave Ophellas the best of the bargain, but was presumably the minimum required to get his support; in any case, Agathocles probably appreciated the difficulty of controlling any part of Africa from Sicily, and the rest of the Carthaginian Empire in Sardinia and Spain was presumably included in his share.

Ophellas set out with an army of 10,000 and a large number of civilians, for it was confidently expected that another large territory was about to be added to the Greek world and opened up for colonization. The march from Cyrene to Agathocles' camp near Tunis through the hostile and forbidding country famous in recent history took only three months, and was a remarkable achievement. But the two leaders soon differed; a former companion of Alexander was not the man to take orders from a mere Siceliot tyrant, especially when they concerned dispositions in a territory already promised to him by treaty. Agathocles rid himself of this opposition by treacherously killing Ophellas in his camp; for the army which Ophellas had brought with him, separated from home by more than 1,000 miles, there was nothing left but to join Agathocles, whose strength was now doubled.[32]

We are told that at exactly the same time there was serious unrest in Carthage and that each side was unable to take advantage of the other's divisions because of its own. The cause of the unrest in the city was an attempt by Bomilcar to seize sole power; he had presumably remained as sole general after the death of Hanno.

The report of Diodorus, which comes from a good source, is given in full since it describes one of the very few incidents to have taken place within the city of which we have such a detailed account.

When Bomilcar had reviewed the soldiers in the place called the New City, a short distance from Old Carthage, he dismissed most of them, but kept back those that were in the plot, five hundred citizens and a thousand mercenaries; he then proclaimed himself 'tyrant'. His men were divided into five groups, who attacked and killed anyone in the streets who resisted. In the tumult which spread throughout the city, the Carthaginians at first believed that the city had been betrayed [to Agathocles] but when the true situation became known, the young men joined together in groups and proceeded against Bomilcar. But he swept them aside and rapidly advanced to the main public square in Old Carthage, where he slaughtered many unarmed citizens. However, many of the Carthaginians occupied the tall buildings which surrounded the square, and showered missiles on the rebels below, who were all within range. After suffering many losses, the rebels closed their ranks and forced their way through the narrow streets back to the New City, though under continued fire from the houses they passed. They then occupied a position on a hill, but the Carthaginians had by now taken up their arms and were drawn up against them. Finally some of the oldest citizens, who were best suited to the task, were sent to the rebels offering an amnesty, and an agreement was reached. Because of the external dangers to the city, no action was taken against the participants, with the exception of Bomilcar, who was tortured and put to death regardless of the agreement.[33]

Although Agathocles was unable to take advantage of this episode directly, it was apparently as a result of Carthaginian preoccupations that he was able to extend his activities to the west of the city, capturing Utica and Hippo Acra. The latter was particularly important because of its magnificent harbour (Bizerta). Here Agathocles began to build a fleet, as he had realized that Carthage could never be taken unless he had enough ships to defeat her at sea. This occupied the winter of 308–307, but early in the new year he had to divert some of his force; he embarked 2,000 men on the first ships that were completed, and sailed to Sicily to try to improve the position of Syracuse, which was under pressure from the independent Siceliots led by Acragas. In Africa, where he left his son Archagethus in charge, there were successful plundering expeditions into the interior as far as Thugga.[34]

But in the absence of Agathocles, the Carthaginians took heart. The senate decided to send out three armies of 10,000 men each, one to the east coast, one to the south of the city, and one to the south-west. The main purpose was to restore the Carthaginian position among the native tribes won over by Agathocles; it could be hoped that the Greeks would divide their forces in order to retain their hold on the territory they had conquered, in which case pitched battles could be risked, since the defeat of at any rate one Carthaginian division would not be fatal.

The plan had great success: the division moving to the south of the capital under another Hanno ambushed an opposing Greek force and killed 4,000, including the commander. That going to the south-west had to encounter a plundering expedition led by Archagethus. Himilco, the Carthaginian commander, concealed half his force in a native town and met the Greeks with the rest. At a certain stage in the fighting he withdrew in pretended disorder, so that the concealed troops could break out and attack the Greeks as they broke ranks in pursuit; almost the whole force was destroyed. As a result of these successes, most of the allies and dependent states returned to their allegiance, and Archagethus was shut up in Tunis with his surviving troops.[35]

When Agathocles heard of the events in Africa, he decided to return at once. With seventeen Syracusan ships and eighteen from his Etruscan allies, he defeated the Carthaginian blockading fleet, which had been reduced to a mere thirty ships by other demands made upon it, and so freed Syracuse from anxiety about its supplies. He then sailed to Africa and took over the army which at this stage consisted of 6,000 Greeks, a force of 6,000 Celtic, Samnite, and Etruscan mercenaries, and 10,000 Libyans. The latter were of little use, however, and when Agathocles met one of the Carthaginian divisions they deserted, and 3,000 of the rest of his force were killed.

With this defeat, all hope of conquering Carthage was lost. Agathocles was in grave danger of being lynched by his now mutinous soldiers, who saw their hopes of getting home with enormous booty rapidly diminishing, and he deserted his army with two of his sons as he fled secretly back to Sicily. The soldiers then elected new commanders and entered into negotiations with Carthage. Since there was now no question of compromising with an enemy but simply a desire to get a body of alien troops as quickly as possible, Carthage offered reasonable terms. All the places still in the possession of the invaders were to be given up, and in return 300 talents would be paid. Any who chose could enter Carthaginian service at the regular pay for mercenaries, and the rest were allowed to settle at Solus in Sicily. The few who rejected the terms were soon overpowered and used as slaves to bring back into cultivation the devastated land. A peace was signed soon after with Agathocles; Carthage was eager to devote her energy to restoring the prosperity of Africa, while Agathocles was hard pressed by his Siceliot opponents. The Carthaginian possessions were confirmed once more along the usual boundary, the River Halycus, and Agathocles even received a nominal payment for giving up parts of it which he had occupied.[36]

Carthage thus survived the greatest danger she had yet faced, though its extent is sometimes exaggerated. Agathocles was no Alexander, in either genius or resources; it is easy to forget that what looks like a stroke of real strategic merit, the counter-invasion of Africa, was in fact a desperate gamble, his only hope of avoiding destruction. His initial successes resulted chiefly from the unpreparedness of the Carthaginians. The latter were not in real danger of extinction so long as they had superiority at sea, and this was not challenged by Agathocles until it was too late.

It may be noted that in spite of their defeats, the defection of their allies and subjects, and the devastation of their lands, the Carthaginians never considered negotiating with Agathocles so long as he was in Africa. The ruling aristocracy, often accused, sometimes justly, of excessive devotion to its material interests, was prepared to put up with the devastation of its landed wealth in order to procure the annihilation of the invader. In this they were following a correct long-term policy. Quite apart from the surrender of Carthaginian Sicily, which would certainly have been the least demanded by Agathocles as the price of a withdrawal from Africa, such an agreement would have encouraged future imitators of the tyrant; by their standing firm and finally destroying his army, a salutary example of determined resistance was presented. It might be said that Carthage could have gone on to defeat Agathocles in Sicily and take Syracuse, but this was not the Carthaginian way. The difficulties of such an enterprise even in times of Syracusan weakness were now well known through earlier reversals of fortune in Sicily.

The peace made with Agathocles demonstrated once again that the Carthaginian conception of their interests in the western Mediterranean did not include the acquisition of an extensive empire beyond what had been held for a century or more. It is true that Carthage was ultimately destroyed by a power which did have expansive aims and whose strength derived from large conquests, but at this stage Rome was but a small cloud on the horizon; in any case, foreign policies are not determined by threats which may appear generations ahead.

6

The City of Carthage and its
Economic, Political, and Religious Life

THE thorough destruction of Carthage by the Romans in 146 was followed, after a century, by the growth of a new city on the same site which in the end no doubt equalled its Phoenician predecessor in size. As a result, our knowledge of the topography and still more the buildings of the earlier city is extremely sketchy.[1] There are a number of references in ancient authors to the appearance of Carthage and some of its buildings, and we can make some inferences from discoveries in other Phoenician settlements in the west, particularly about domestic architecture; but whether the temples found at Motya and on Sardinia closely resembled those of Carthage is unknown.

The economic heart of Carthage was its harbour. There are a number of difficulties in the descriptions of it in ancient sources,[2] and its identification on the ground has been often discussed. In spite of these difficulties, it remains probable that it is represented today by the two lagoons lying to the north of the bay of Le Kram and less than a mile below the hill of St Louis. The lagoon nearest the bay is roughly

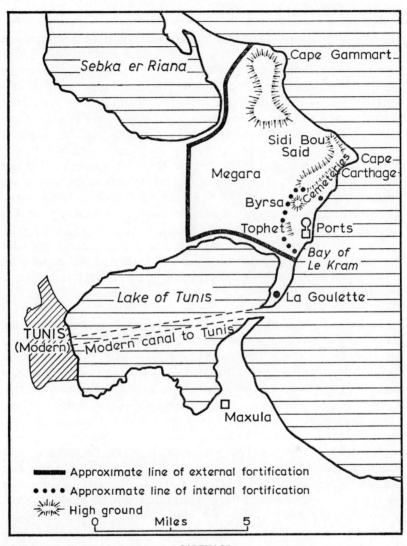

Sebka er Riana

Cape Gammart

Sidi Bou
Said

Cape
Carthage

Megara

Cemeteries

Byrsa

Tophet

Ports

Bay of
Le Kram

Lake of Tunis

La Goulette

TUNIS
(Modern)

Modern canal to Tunis

Maxula

━━━ Approximate line of external fortification
•••• Approximate line of internal fortification
⚡ High ground

0   Miles   5

CARTHAGE

rectangular, and the one behind it is crescent-shaped; its outlet to the sea to the east is recent and was made for reasons of public health.

According to our sources, the harbour in antiquity was a double one, the two parts being connected with each other, and there was a single entrance to the open sea seventy feet wide, which could be barred with iron chains. The outer part of the harbour was for merchant ships; it was rectangular, about 1,600 by 1,00 feet in dimension. From it a narrow channel led to the inner division, which was circular, about 1,000 feet in diameter, and reserved for warships. In the middle of this was an island, on which was the naval headquarters building. This was of a sufficient height to give a clear view over intervening buildings in the direction of the sea, but activity in the naval harbour could not be seen from outside, even from the mercantile harbour, because it was surrounded by a double wall. All round the island and the circumference of the harbour were quays and sheds to hold 220 warships, as well as arsenals and ship-building and repair yards.

It is obvious that both harbours were very small when we consider the size of the Carthaginian fleet and her trading interests, but they followed a traditional Phoenician pattern of small man-made ports at important places; there was one at Hadrumetum and another at Motya. The word 'cothon' was used by our sources to transcribe a Phoenician word for such ports. At Carthage it was apparently used strictly of the naval harbour but loosely of the whole establishment. The construction of these harbours was a work of great magnitude, though it is not beyond the bounds of possibility that there was already in existence a lagoon with which to make a start. The security of such a 'cothon' must have more than made up for the expense of its construction and the difficulties of entering and leaving, particularly during the winter, when navigation practically ceased.

The entrance to the harbour was from the south. To the east of the entrance, and stretching north along the shore, was a large structure known to archaeologists as 'Falbe's quadrilateral' after its discoverer in the early nineteenth century. It covered several acres, and was massively built, using in places existing outcrops of rock. It appears partly to have protected the entrance to the harbour, but may also have served as a quay when it was not necessary for merchant ships to enter the cothon itself. The quadrilateral, which was outside the city proper, had a substantial parapet on its seaward sides. Its traces now under water still remain, stretching over 300 yards south of the Lazaret.

Carthage was defended, as might be expected, by walls of great strength, which were proof against all assaults till the last Roman attack; in fact it was so strong that Agathocles could not seriously consider making an attempt on it. The total length of the wall was twenty-two or twenty-three miles, which would have been impossible to defend with the manpower available to Carthage had not the greater part of it been along the shore.[3] All this part could not be attacked except by an enemy with complete command of the sea, and Carthage had little to fear till the last decades of her existence.

The crucial sector of the wall was therefore that across the isthmus leading to the mainland. This was about two and a half miles at its narrowest point, which was some three miles to the west of the cothon and the densest area of settlement. In this sector—the only one of which we have any knowledge—the wall was over forty feet high, not counting the battlements and towers, and nearly thirty feet thick; the towers were placed at intervals of sixty or seventy yards and were four storeys high. Inside the walls there were stables on two levels; the lower were for 300 elephants, the upper for 4,000 horses; there were presumably ramps for these to go up and down. In addition there were storehouses and barracks for 20,000 infantry and 4,000 cavalrymen. In front of this formidable structure was a smaller rampart of unknown character and beyond this again a ditch sixty feet wide backed by an earth rampart strengthened with timbers and stone. It is not surprising that this sector was proof against all Roman assaults and that they finally breached the walls in places where they bordered the sea and were less strong.[4]

The course of the wall to the north of the city is uncertain, because of changes in the formation of the Sebka Er Riana, which, as previously mentioned, was a gulf of the sea in ancient times. The high ground about Cape Gammarth was probably included in the defended area, and the wall then followed the coast as far as the cothon. Somewhere in this region it turned west, cutting across the tongue of land separating the sea from the lake of Tunis, then followed the shore of the lake most of the way to the narrowest point of the isthmus. The wall was longer than another famous defensive work of the same period, that of Dionysius of Syracuse, which was about seventeen miles long, but the Carthaginian one had a much shorter sector liable to attack from the land. There is no evidence of the date of this work; its great size does not exclude its being early, even sixth century.

There was also a wall round the hill of Byrsa, which thus formed an inner citadel.[5] The enceinte here is said to have been two miles in circumference, which means that it included more than the hill of St Louis. The name Byrsa was applied also to the oldest section of the city, that between the citadel itself and the cothon. As already mentioned, only a short distance to the west of the cothon the sanctuary of Tanit was established, probably by the earliest colonists, but the development of the city beyond this is almost unknown; in the last century of its existence a small temple to some other deity existed in the area.

Between the cothon and the citadel was the principal public place or square, equivalent to the Greek *agora* or Roman *forum*. It is however unlikely that it presented the regular appearance of such places in the Greco-Roman world. Near it was the building in which the senate usually met, and outside this the sufets dispensed justice in the open, as was common in much of the Mediterranean world.[6] We hear of three streets leading from the public square up to the citadel. This would appear to be the limit of the older section of the city, because a vast area of cemeteries stretched along the slopes of the hill of St Louis itself and its neighbour, called the hill of Juno by archaeologists of the last century, and extended to the sea with the hill Bordj Djedid. Graves of the seventh and sixth centuries have been found in all these regions, and it is clear that for some time they marked the limit of the inhabited area.[7] At the end of the fourth century, however, there was in existence a substantial new quarter apparently beyond the cemeteries and including the area of Sidi bou Said. It was from here that Bomilcar made his attempt to make himself tyrant. The word '*megara*' was used by our authors to distinguish an area which extended up to the walls of the city and which was almost rural in appearance, the houses being interspersed with fields and market gardens. This area was very large, but whether it included all the west and north of the space enclosed by the walls is unknown.[8]

The aspect of the old city was probably by no means unlike that of many eastern Mediterranean towns of today which are little touched by modern civilization. The streets were narrow and winding, the houses in some parts were up to six storeys high. This type of building is known from other Phoenician cities[9] like Motya and Tyre, where they were necessary because of the lack of space, and its appearance at Carthage where there was plenty of room was doubtless the result of tradition; this Phoenician model was probably the origin of similar buildings erected in large Hellenistic cities and also at Rome when space became limited. There were other buildings of smaller dimensions which had roofs surrounded by balconies, or sometimes vaulted roofs.[10]

From the remains of the houses at Dar Essafi on Cap Bon,[11] and some scanty foundations found on the hill of St Louis, it seems that the houses were of simple whitewashed appearance from outside, with the walls almost blank except for a door on to the street; the centre of the house was an interior courtyard. The masonry was of large dressed stones of poor quality from the quarries on Cap Bon, but in the majority of cases these did not rise above the foundation level, the rest of the house being built of unbaked brick. In Hellenistic times there was some increase in the amount of decoration and probably also in comfort. The floors came to be made of a pink cement with fragments of white marble mixed in, and the interior walls were covered with stucco. There were probably other features of Hellenistic building used, such as columns; we know that in the naval harbour each of the sheds housing the warships was flanked by Ionic columns, so that they presented the appearance of a continuous portico.[12]

As for the temples, which are said to have been numerous and which were such a feature in the aspect of Greek and Roman cities, the Carthaginians in general remained faithful to the traditional concept of a sacred enclosure in which were deposited the offerings or the stelae which in some sense represented the deity. This type of sacred enclosure is best typified in the sanctuary of Tanit—remembering that it was also sacred to Baal Hammon. It is significant that there appears to have been no substantial building associated with this enclosure; traditional attitudes presumably dominated the Carthaginians' attitude to these favourite deities.[13]

The finest and richest temple at Carthage at the time of its destruction was that of Eshmoun, identified with Aesculapius, which was on the Byrsa. Its surrounding precinct was approached by a flight of sixty steps.[14] It is difficult to believe that the temple to the Sicilian Demeter and Kore erected after the disaster of 397 was not built on a Greek model, and the wealth of the statues and gold and silver offerings which the Romans captured testify to the elaborate nature of at any rate some of the temples in the latter days of the city.[15]

The population of ancient city-states is very difficult to determine, because of a lack of figures and the different ways of making an estimate. We are told by Strabo[16] that the total population of the city alone (apparently excluding Megara) was 700,000, which is an impossible density. A safer figure to work back from is the 50,000 who were the survivors of the three years' siege of 149–146. During this war the walls were defended by 30,000 men and there was another force in the country for a while. This would indicate a total population of some 200,000, including slaves who were freed in the crisis. But it must have been much larger than this at the height of Carthaginian power in the early third century, and it would be surprising if it did not approach 400,000, including slaves and resident aliens, which was the population

of Athens in the late fifth century.[17] Stabo's figure may be correct for
the population including the Cap Bon peninsula and the area in the
immediate vicinity of the city, all of which had a status different from
that of the interior whose inhabitants were subject to Carthage. It is
unlikely that there were more than 100,000 people of more or less
pure Phoenician descent in Africa outside the capital; with such a
limited manpower did Carthage face the might of Rome.

Carthage was the city in the Mediterranean in which commerce
played the largest part: when a Greek or Roman of Hellenistic times
thought of a typical Carthaginian he thought of him as a merchant.
It was agreed that it was through her commerce that Carthage had
become rich, even the richest city in the world, as some believed. Yet
this commerce has left very few traces to be discovered by the archaeologist; indeed, if we relied on archaeological evidence alone, we would
deduce that commercial activity at Carthage played a smaller part than
in a number of other Mediterranean cities. This is an illustration of the
fact that deductions about trade and commerce from archaeological
discoveries must be made with caution. It is obvious that it is primarily
artifacts which survive, and that the perishable materials which comprised such a large proportion of ancient trade have left no trace; foodstuffs of all sorts, metal in unworked state, textiles, skins—and slaves.
The problem of Carthaginian trade is that much of it was obviously
in such goods; her imports and exports of manufactured articles
accounted for only a small part of the whole.

There can be no doubt that the trade from which Carthage drew the
most profit was that which she inherited from the early Phoenician
traders in the western Mediterranean—trade with backward tribes from
whom the precious metals, gold, silver, tin, and presumably iron (since
Carthage is known to have manufactured her own weapons) were
obtained. The conditions for this trade even improved in Carthage's
favour as she was able to maintain a monopoly in the western Mediterranean till the loss of her fleet in the first war with Rome. During the
Carthaginian period the native populations with whom most of this
trade was carried on did not move into a higher economic state which
would have diminished Carthaginian profits. The effectiveness of
Carthaginian control of this trade is shown by the vast armies she was
able to raise throughout the fourth and third centuries, quite apart
from the general testimony of ancient authors. More concretely, a
study of the Carthaginian gold coinage of the second half of the fourth
century attests vast stocks of gold and an enormous mintage far in
excess of that known for other advanced states.[18]

The report of Hanno shows the participation of the Carthaginian state in a venture which was designed to obtain or to reinforce control over the West African gold trade. It is not impossible that such trade was in fact a monopoly of the state, just as there were many state trading monopolies in Egypt. A classic definition of Carthaginian trading policy is that it aimed 'to open markets by force or by treaties or by the foundation of colonies; to exercise a monopoly in countries where it was possible to avoid all competition; to regulate through agreement stipulating reciprocal advantages in countries where this monopoly could not be exercised; and to protect navigation, the colonies and the trading posts against piracy'.[19] We know that Carthage had commercial as well as defensive treaties with Etruscan cities, and there can be no doubt that they were like those she made with Rome, of which we have details concerning the conditions on which the Carthaginians were able to insist before allowing citizens of other powers to trade within their sphere.

Carthaginian monopoly in the western Mediterranean was profitable in another way. The products of Egypt, Greece, and Campania which are found on North African sites and in Sardinia and Spain must have been brought there in Carthaginian ships. It was for this reason that foreign traders were allowed to visit Carthage but not proceed further west; the goods they brought would be re-exported by Carthaginians. Carthage took stern measures to check piracy; her own practice of sinking any foreign ships found in her sphere may look like piracy under another name, but Carthage seems to have exacted recognition of her claims from other states.

Little has so far been found in western sites to show what the native peoples wanted in exchange for their metals. Presumably the pottery at Mogador once contained wine or olive oil and another well-known article of Carthaginian trade was cloth.[20] We find numbers of Etruscan bucchero vases in Africa and Sardinia, which reflect the commerce with Etruria known from literary sources.[21] These long-lasting remains are only a small trace of a much larger commerce; Selinus grew wealthy from trade with Carthage, but in what this consisted is not known.[22] Perhaps foodstuffs played a part, as Carthage must have imported a great deal before her conquest of territory in Africa. No doubt cereals and meat could be obtained from the native peoples, but wine and olive oil must have come from outside. In the fifth century itself these products were imported from Acragas.[23] Carthaginian merchants did not cease to frequent the Greek ports, and we hear of a number of them established at Syracuse in 398.[24] Continued traffic with Tyre is attested in literary sources, and with Egypt in discoveries in Africa[25]; the objects imported from the latter were mostly of small value, as indeed were the majority of Carthaginian imports; there are none of the finest products of Greece such as were sought after by the Etruscans and which even found their way into central France.

The Carthaginians naturally had industries of their own, some of whose products were exported. There must have been a considerable force of metal workers, in view of the extraordinary production of hundreds of sets of arms per day in the last struggle of Carthage against Rome,[26] but it is difficult to trace their activity in other ways. Few objects of metal which are certainly Carthaginian have been found in Europe and it is probable that many of the exports went to the Libyan and Numidian tribes. The export of these and other products of Carthaginian industry became much commoner in the fourth century, and particularly after the conquests of Alexander. This conquest, and the establishment of the Hellenistic kingdoms, brought about an economic revolution in the eastern Mediterranean, and there was a new market for all sorts of cheap manufactured goods which the Carthaginians were well equipped to exploit. They shared with the Phoenicians themselves a lack of artistic talent, at least when compared with the Greeks, and their products lacked individuality, but their mixture of various styles was very suitable for trade in the cosmopolitan cities of the Hellenistic world. After the resumption of close contacts with the Greek world, it is not surprising that the Carthaginian merchant became a familiar figure in the east; inscriptions recall their presence at Athens and Delos, two of the greatest markets in the Aegean; but better evidence of their widespread activity is to be found in the fact that there were Greek comedies in which the central character was a Carthaginian trader. These are lost, but the Latin author Plautus wrote a play *Poenulus* based on one of these Greek originals. The scene is in Aetolia and the 'hero' is Hanno, a pious trader of small goods searching for his daughter who has been kidnapped from Carthage. In spite of the fact that the play was produced shortly after the Hannibalic War, the Carthaginian is a figure of fun and is not presented as an object of hatred. The articles in his cargo include shoe-straps, pipes, nuts, and panthers, a list designed to raise a laugh from the fact that a Carthaginian could be expected to trade in anything. Apart from this, we hear of articles made of ivory and textiles for which the Carthaginians had a wide reputation. There can be little doubt that Carthage exported substantial quantities of corn and other foodstuffs, the import of which into the eastern Mediterranean became increasingly

Phoenician pottery from Monte Sirai, sixth century

Silver coins of Carthage

Punic coins of Spain

Gold coins of Carthage

necessary as urbanization increased. A surplus for export is attested for Carthage in the last fifty years of her existence[27] and was undoubtedly available before. Another significant event was the creation of the Hellenistic Empire of Egypt under the Ptolemaic dynasty; this included Cyrenaica, Cyprus, and for a while Phoenicia; it adopted the Phoenician standard for its coinage, instead of the Attic which had been general before. This made Carthaginian trade with the area easier, since the coinage of Carthage, which began early in the fourth century, was naturally on the Phoenician standard. Imports from the Greek world became common again during these centuries,[28] and to them were added the products of Campania—pottery vessels of all sorts, lamps, terracottas, and bronzes.

The vigour of Carthaginian commerce is finally attested in the last fifty years of her existence, when, deprived of her sources of metals and her monopoly in the west, she was nevertheless able to preserve a measure of prosperity while paying a heavy yearly indemnity to Rome. There can be no doubt that the export of foodstuffs was more important than ever in this concluding period.

If the wealth of the city was founded on its trade, as all ancient sources asserted, the same must be said of the wealth of the aristocracy, but what form their participation in trade took can only be conjecture, for lack of evidence. It is to be presumed that the nobles financed, or more probably owned, numbers of ships engaged in trade, and took their profits from the voyages, the most profitable no doubt being those to the west. It is not to be supposed that the Hanno of Plautus was numbered among the senators of Carthage, even though he is described as rich and noble. It is also possible that some wealthy Carthaginians had interests in Carthaginian industry. But after the conquest of the northern part of Tunisia there was another source of wealth, land.

It is sometimes assumed[29] that a landed interest grew up in Carthage which was at times hostile to the merchants, but there are some considerations that make this uncertain. Those who participated in the original conquest had made what wealth they had in trade and commerce, and the acquisition of land was simply an added source. The Magonids themselves, who are taken as examples of early 'merchant princes', participated. Further, the estates of the Carthaginians, though worked largely by slave labour, do not seem to have been of great size. They were apparently concentrated in the Cap Bon peninsula and the immediate vicinity of Carthage, and confined to the production of olives, fruit, and livestock; this at any rate is what appears from the

description of the area in our sources. Further, we have the evidence
of the treatise of a certain Mago on agriculture. He was a Carthaginian
writer probably of the third century, with a knowledge of Greek
agricultural practice; his work was so highly regarded that when Carthage was destroyed a copy was translated into Latin for the use of
colonists going to Africa. Only a few quotations survive, but these
give the impression that the type of estate Mago was considering was
one of modest size specializing in fruit growing and stock rearing. The
cereals that were exported came from the plains in the valley of the
Medjerda and other rivers, which were apparently left in the hands of
Libyans. Mago advised that a man who bought a farm should live
on it and give up his town house, but it remains a fact that there is
no evidence to support the view that there was a substantial section
of Carthaginian society who derived its wealth solely from the land.
We ought rather to envisage the merchants as owning properties in
the country, from which they no doubt drew some profit and to which
they retired in the heat of summer, but which were not their main
concern.

A very rough analogy is the practice in England in the sixteenth
and later centuries when merchants bought landed estates while con-
tinuing in business—though their descendants for social reasons not
present in Carthage tended to become identified with the original
gentry.

There was a great interest among the Greeks, and to a lesser extent
the Romans when they came under Greek influence, about the constitutions in force in the numerous communities of the Greek world.
So intense was the preoccupation with constitutional forms that some
came to believe that the construction of a theoretically logical and
balanced constitution would produce good results in a city which
adopted it, regardless of its particular circumstances. This was not such
an unreal hope as it sounds, because the similarities in material status
and in social and religious ideas among the Greek states were such that
it could easily appear that some form or other would be valid for all.
Another motive which drove political thinkers to look for some universally valid constitution was the desire to overcome the instability which
had become a feature of Greek political life in the fourth century; it
was widely believed that constitutional reforms on the correct lines
would put a stop to this.

Among non-Greek states, Carthage was almost unique in possessing
a constitution[30] which was widely admired by Greek political writers.
It was the only non-Greek constitution to be included in a collection

of studies of constitutions made on the orders of Aristotle.[31] In the third century the geographer Eratosthenes,[32] protesting against the Greeks' assumption of their superiority over all non-Greeks, said that the Romans and Carthaginians could not be considered to be 'barbarians', because they had such excellent constitutions; and these writers were followed by many others, including Roman authors, who praised the Carthaginian constitution at least in the form it had up to the time of Hannibal.[33]

Unfortunately, the lack of sources makes it difficult to describe it in any detail; Aristotle's study is lost, as is that of another Greek writer of unknown date, Hippagoras.[34] We are left with a few brief remarks in Aristotle's *Politics*, and in Polybius, together with what can be drawn from incidental references in other writers, chiefly the historians.[35]

The Carthaginian constitution was generally put in the category of mixed constitutions, which were said to combine the best elements of monarchic, aristocratic and democratic régimes. There was no question of separation of powers, a notion in general alien to ancient politics, or even checks and balances except in a loose way. A strong executive was held to form the monarchical element, a permanent deliberative council the aristocratic, and popular assemblies with elective and some legislative rights, the democratic. This was obviously a very simplified way of looking at political institutions, but then politics in ancient city-states were relatively simple, and there is a certain amount of sense in the observation that different types of government have their own virtues and defects. The trouble with a mixed constitution was, as the realist Tacitus observed, that it was very difficult to bring into being, and if it were, it would not last long. In point of fact, the constitutions praised in antiquity as 'mixed' were aristocratic or oligarchic. This was universally admitted to be the case with Carthage, and was why such constitutions were praised; most of the people who wrote about politics were from the upper classes of society and so in favour of them.[36]

Hereditary kingship was the general rule in Phoenicia down to Hellenistic times, and it may be considered probable that at any rate in early times Carthage had the same institution: there were kings in Cypriot cities of Phoenician origin.[37] Our Greek sources all use the Greek word for king—*basileus*—of a number of Carthaginian leaders from the sixth century onwards; for example, apart from shadowy figures in the sixth century, Hamilcar, defeated at Himera, Hanno, leader of the voyage down the African coast, Hannibal son of Gisgo, leader of the intervention in Sicily in 410, Himilco his successor in Sicily, followed by Mago. All these belonged to the Magonid family;

from the fourth century we know of Hanno the Great and two of his grandsons both named Hamilcar. Although these two families predominate, the early monarchy appears to have been elective, or at any rate not in principle hereditary. Herodotus says[38] that Hamilcar (480) was chosen king 'because of his courage' and the elective nature of the Carthaginian monarchy is attested for the fourth century by Aristotle. Greek usage recognized such a form of monarchy which was lifelong but not strictly hereditary. All the kings known to us from this early period are shown acting as generals, but this is due to the nature of the evidence; there can be no doubt that their functions were primarily sacral and judicial.

Roman historians Latinized one Carthaginian political term—'sufet'.[39] In the third century and after, the sufets were elected annually, and were at least two in number.[40] Sufet is the same word as the Hebrew 'shophet', generally translated 'judge' as in the Book of Judges, but it is clear that in both Carthaginian and Hebrew usage the word meant more than judge and designated the chief man, or men, in the state. Carthaginian sufets were indeed judges, but are known also to have had the right to summon the Senate and the popular assembly.[41] On the other hand, unlike the Roman consuls, but like the archons of Athens, they had no military powers. It is by no means clear whether the annual sufets of the third century had replaced entirely, or were no more than a later development of, the life-kings of the early period. Although sufets do not seem to have existed at Tyre, it might be supposed that the term was used in early days to designate a governor of a colony when it was still subordinate to Tyre, and that the term continued in use to designate the leader of the city, now chosen by its own people. We can envisage the development, common to early Greek and Roman politics, whereby royal power was gradually reduced by an aristocracy. But the only text which equates sufets with kings is highly suspect.[42] It may be that sufets always existed alongside the kings, and gradually extended their power, reducing that of the kings to merely formal and religious functions. Apart from the sufets, there was a state treasurer, and apparently a censor of morals and there must have been officials to take care of practical matters like the upkeep of the harbours, markets, and public buildings.[43]

One of the stages in the weakening of the royal power is described by Justinus, a late and often unsatisfactory source, but probably in this case having a part of the truth. Referring to the Magonid family in the middle of the fifth century, he says[44]:

as this powerful family weighed so heavily on the public freedom and controlled both policy and justice, a court of 100 judges, chosen from among the senators, was instituted; after each war, generals had to give an account of their actions to this court, so that fear of sentence and respect for the laws which they had to obey at Carthage would inspire them to recognize the state's authority when they commanded overseas.

Hanno, king at the time, was apparently exiled together with his brother Gisgo, but the family clearly remained powerful and rich enough to appear in a leading role again at the end of the century. Aristotle[45] compared the court of one hundred with the ephorate of Sparta, no doubt precisely because the Spartan ephors' most important function was to prevent the kings becoming too powerful; and indeed we hear of Spartan kings being convicted and exiled, as happened at Carthage. Further diminution of the royal power perhaps occurred after the attempt by Bomilcar to make himself tyrant, that is, a true despot, in 308, the second member of his dynasty to take this action.

Birth and wealth were equally important in the choice of the kings, and no doubt of the later sufets as well. In the later period at any rate, the full citizen body almost certainly had a say in the election, but if there is one thing we know for certain about Carthaginian politics, it is that they were always dominated by the rich; Aristotle, although no great friend of democracy, considered the part played by money at Carthage to be deplorable.[46] It was from the wealthiest class that the Carthaginian Senate, as it is convenient to call it, was drawn. No doubt from early days there had been a body of senior and respected citizens to advise the kings and—later—other officials, and we have definite evidence from the fourth century. It discussed all matters of importance —foreign policy, war and peace, recruitment of the armies and the administration of subject territory are all referred to. If the senate was in agreement with the kings or sufets, matters did not have to be submitted to the assembly of citizens.[47] In the third century there was a body of (at least) thirty senators who formed a permanent committee of the senate.[48] Whether its powers were different from those of the senate is not known, but it may be assumed that it looked after day-to-day and urgent matters and probably, as is the habit of small committees, obtained a leading part in the business of the senate as a whole. In the third century, a few of its members apparently accompanied the generals overseas, to exercise some control over political matters which might come up.

Members of the senate held office for life; it is not known how vacancies were filled, but simple co-option is probable. The senate also provided the panel of one hundred judges already referred to (the exact number was apparently 104, but the round figure is generally used). After Aristotle's time, the court's judicial power extended over all state officials, and when Hannibal reformed it in 196, it members held office for life, though this may have been a late development. At some stage the election of members to fill vacancies was put in the hands of a number of *pentarchies*, boards of five members. These boards are only mentioned by Aristotle; they were self-perpetuating bodies, whose members did not hold other offices and who had as their chief business the supervision of some part of the administration, but not military or imperial affairs.[49]

The amount of power which was exercised by the assembly of citizens was limited in practice if not in theory. If the senate and kings (or sufets) disagreed on a proposal, it was remitted to the assembly. On occasion a popular vote was asked for by sufets and senate in order to obtain general support for hazardous measures. Even if the requirements of wealth and distinguished ancestry were practical rather than legal requirements, they were, as far as we know, always adhered to. In this respect there was a similarity to the practice in Rome, where, in spite of the electoral freedom of the citizen assemblies, claims of birth almost always secured election. The citizen body was divided into groups which met at times for common feasts, a practice for which there are analogies in the Greek world, and which probably had political as well as social significance.[50]

In the sixth to the fourth centuries, most of those who held command in the field were kings, but in the third and second centuries the generalship was entirely divorced from civil office at Carthage. The earlier arrangement was typical of monarchies in the Mediterranean world, the kings of Sparta and Macedon, for example, being the leaders of their armies. However, the language of the sources indicates that in each case the attribution to the king of military authority was a special arrangement for a specific campaign or emergency, and that the basic separation of military from home authority existed in principle at an early date. This was not due to any theory about the wisdom of separating military from civil power but to the fact that the Carthaginian way of life was essentially one of commerce and that since she had no enemies of consequence in Africa, the wars which took place were generally abroad and could be regarded as temporary crises to be dealt with by temporary appointments. There was no limit to the length of time the appointment could be held. Several families, the

Magonids in the early period and the Barcids later, developed a military tradition.

The Carthaginians are said to have regarded their generals as potential overthrowers of the state, and there was certainly an obvious danger since the mercenary armies can have had no loyalty to Carthage other than as a paymaster. On analysis, however, we find that no such attempts were made, and in the plot of Bomilcar in 308, of which we have a relatively full account, the attempt was made with only a small body of picked troops.[51] There were other plots to overthrow the constitution in which generals or former generals were concerned, but precisely when they appear not to have been in command of an army. All the commanders of really large forces of which we hear were entirely loyal—a record which compares very favourably with, for example, the Siceliot generals. It may be supposed that the supervision by the court of one hundred was effective. On the other hand, Carthage became notorious for the severity with which unsuccessful generals were punished, there being a number of instances of exile and even of crucifixion.[52] This probably encouraged the emergence of men of cautious and unenterprising temperament, but the fact that Carthaginian generals remained in command for many years provided them with greater experience than many of their Roman enemies.

This is all we can be in any sense clear about in the Carthaginian constitution, and it is obviously very little compared with what we know of Rome or Athens; we have also taken on trust our Greek and Latin authors who may well have misinterpreted some of its features because of superficial resemblances to those of the Greek world. However, it is obvious that internally Carthage had evolved in a way by no means dissimilar to that of Greek colonial foundations and for that matter Etruscan and Italian city-states, a fact which demonstrates again the essential unity of the Mediterranean area. This impulse towards a type of constitution similar to those of the Greco-Roman world was remarkable at Carthage, because in Phoenicia the institutions apparently remained archaic to the time of Alexander, in spite of Greek influence in other spheres. We are not to see a Greek model behind any Carthaginian institution, however, in spite of the fact that it was compared in a general way with that of Sparta as well as Rome. Aristotle's chief criticism was that pursuit of wealth, the principal occupation of the Carthaginians, made the constitution tend towards oligarchy, his technical term for states governed by a class whose only qualification was wealth.[53] This criticism was undoubtedly justified. The popular rights which were held to mitigate the tendency towards oligarchy were of little practical value, and there is not a trace of the influence of the mass of the citizens on Carthaginian policy until the late third century.

The fact is that compared with Greeks and Romans the Carthaginians were essentially non-political. It was noted that the Carthaginian masses were generally submissive to the ruling class, and they were late in developing a sense of solidarity. Aristotle said that the oligarchy was careful to treat the masses liberally and to allow them a share in the profitable exploitation of the subject territories.[54] No doubt these measures played a part in preventing the growth of dissatisfaction. Furthermore, Carthaginian citizens were immune except on rare occasions from military service; as a result, they did not have the opportunity of acquiring that consciousness of the importance of solidarity and mutual support which was essential in ancient infantry warfare, and which was a most potent if unexpressed factor in the growth of Greek and Roman democracy—and popular dictatorship. This links up with what was one of the most highly-praised features of Carthaginian internal history, the lack of serious movements of unrest leading to the creation of tyrants;[55] it is indeed a fact that none of the recorded attempts by powerful politicians to obtain supreme power at Carthage was based on a widespread popular movement. Ultimately, in the last quarter of the third century, the Carthaginian people began to play a larger part than before, but their interest seems to have been not in economic or political reform but in the imperialist policy in Spain of the Barcid family. Only when the aristocracy's corrupt handling of affairs became intolerable in the economic distress which followed the Hannibalic War, was there a movement of reform headed by the great general himself.[56]

The Carthaginians were notorious in antiquity for the intensity of their religious beliefs, and in this respect they did not differ from the Semitic peoples from which they had sprung. In fact, our knowledge of their deities has been advanced by archaeological discoveries in their homeland.[57] At Ugarit (Ras Shamra) have been found a number of inscribed clay tablets, dating from the fourteenth century B.C., which contain mythological poems concerning Phoenician deities. Before this discovery it was held that each Phoenician city, including Carthage, had its own particular protecting deities, but that there was no Phoenician pantheon resembling in any sense the familiar Olympian pantheon of the Greeks. It now appears that this was incorrect, and that some gods appear under different names and with some different attributes in various places. The Ras Shamra tablets do not mention deities later popular in Phoenicia such as Melkart or Eshmoun, but many centuries

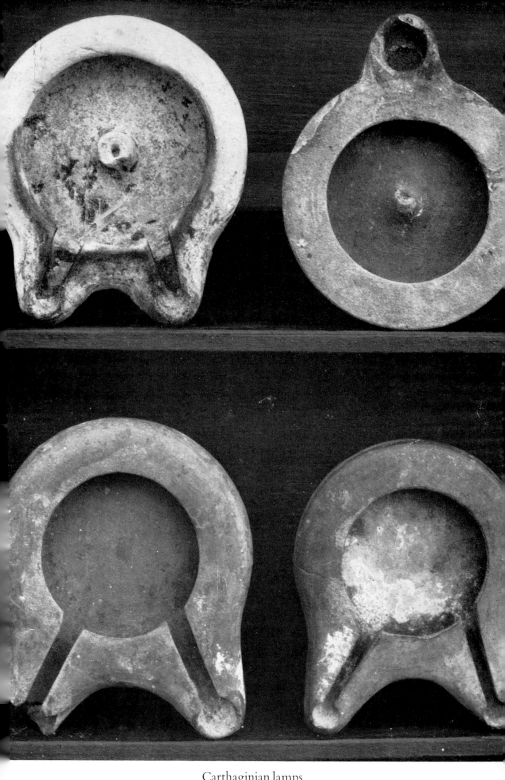

Carthaginian lamps

Terracotta protome

between their date and the later information we have about Phoenicia.

During this time there were the great folk movements in the east which had their effect in widespread changes in cult, to which all ancient religions were particularly susceptible. Furthermore, in spite of their religious conservatism, it was inevitable that in the course of time the deities worshipped at Carthage should appear in a somewhat different form from that which they had had in Phoenicia. In common with most ancient Semitic peoples, the Phoenicians had a supreme male deity, a 'Baal', meaning 'Lord' or 'Master'. At Carthage he was known as Baal Hammon. The meaning of the epithet is not entirely clear, but it appears to mean something like 'burning' or 'fiery', and to derive from one of his characteristics as a solar deity. The epithet was used to avoid pronouncing the true name of the god. Baal Hammon was no doubt regarded, as was the Phoenician supreme deity El and the Hebrew Yahweh, as the creator of the universe. It was a sign of the sombre character of Carthaginian religion that when the Greeks came to equate Carthaginian deities with their own, they identified Baal not with Zeus, 'father of gods and men' as Homer called him, but with Kronos. The latter was a survival from an early stage of Greek religion and was represented as a cruel tyrant who devoured his own children, a trait which recalled the human sacrifices at Carthage which the Greeks found so distasteful.[58]

Baal Hammon remained the supreme god as long as Carthage existed, and later had a long history in North Africa under his Roman identification as Saturn. But in the early fifth century he was outstripped in popular worship in Carthage and most of her dependencies by a goddess known as Tanit. It is not clear whether Tanit is even a Phoenician name—it may be Libyan. Tanit represented in some degree the goddess Asherat (Astarte) of the Ras Shamra tablets. She generally had an added epithet 'Pene Baal', meaning 'Face of Baal'. The most likely explanation is that she was regarded, in spite of the difference in sex, as a more approachable manifestation of Baal, the invisible and utterly distant creator. It seems likely that her popularity was due to the acquisition of the rich African land and the feeling of the need to worship a deity who brought life and fertility.[59] She probably owed much to the cult of Hera among the Greeks of the west, and also to that of Demeter. Symbols of fertility such as the palm tree, pomegranates and doves appear on numerous stelae in her honour, but she was more than a fertility goddess. Whereas representations of Baal Hammon are extremely rare, there are a number of surviving terracotta statuettes of female figures which apparently represent Tanit; more common

10

was the 'sign of Tanit', a rough engraving on hundreds of stelae from Carthage and many other sites of a woman with arms raised in blessing.

When the Romans conquered Africa, Carthaginian religion was deeply entrenched even in Libyan areas, and it retained a great deal of its character under different forms. Even human sacrifice continued, though clandestinely and infrequently.[60] The deities received the names and epithets suited to them in Latin, and temples on a classical model replaced the open sanctuaries of the Carthaginians, but they were often on the same sites, even at Carthage itself, in spite of its destruction. Baal-Kronos became Saturn, Tanit became Juno, often with the epithet 'Caelestis' to show her position as a sky goddess. The cult of both was common throughout Roman Africa, and Caelestis was supreme at Carthage itself until the triumph of Christianity, just as Tanit had been in pre-Roman times. The Emperors had to use soldiers to destroy her vast temple agglomeration in A.D. 421.[61] Baal-Saturn acquired a new attribute as 'lord of the harvest', suited to the increasing prosperity of Roman Africa; among the Libyans he rapidly outstripped Caelestis in popularity, and his cult tended to reduce all others to insignificance.

One of the most widely worshipped deities in the east was a fertility goddess with the name of Astarte in Phoenician; at an early date she was identified with the Greek Aphrodite, whose home significantly was on Cyprus, where Greek and Phoenician met. In the story of Elissa, the priest and sacred prostitutes from her temple on Cyprus join the expedition to Africa. However, her cult was not widespread in the Carthaginian world, since her most important function, the assurance of fertility, was taken over by Tanit. The most famous place for her worship in the west was admittedly in the Carthaginian sphere at Elymian Eryx, where a pre-Carthaginian goddess of fertility became identified with her Phoenician and later Greek and Roman equivalents. She had a temple at Carthage, and there may be truth in the tradition which said that the town of Sicca on the border of Numidia was founded by people from Eryx (naturally under Carthaginian direction). The temple of Venus, her Latin equivalent, had a special position there in Roman times, and at an earlier date free women, as opposed to slaves, had taken part in temple prostitution. This is the only attested mention of this practice in Africa, and it is to be doubted whether it was a feature of Carthaginian religion, even though it was well known among various Semitic peoples in the east.[62]

Other deities were likewise overshadowed by Tanit and Baal Hammon, but mention may be made of a few of some importance. Eshmoun, identified by the Greeks with Aesculapius the divine Healer, and popular at Sidon, had a temple at Carthage which was said to be the largest and richest in the city, and occurs elsewhere in the west. Melkart, the lord of Tyre, was widely worshipped, and it is presumed that every Tyrian foundation had a cult of Melkart as one of its earliest institutions. He was identified by the Greeks with Hercules, which is perhaps why so many of the latter's exploits were located in the far west.[63] On Carthaginian coins issued in Sicily are symbols which appear to belong to a warrior god, identified with Ares in the list of deities in Hannibal's treaty with Philip of Macedon. Under what name he went in Carthage is not known, and it is to be doubted whether his cult was widespread in view of the unwarlike nature of the city.[64]

A striking discovery of Carthaginian archaeology has been that of a sacred enclosure or 'holy place' a few yards west of the cothon. This enclosure is generally called the Sanctuary of Tanit, and in it were found thousands of urns containing the burnt bones of children with stelae of various forms, most of them inscribed, to mark the place of deposition. This discovery put beyond doubt the reality of the human sacrifices, particularly the sacrifices of young children, which our sources attribute to the Carthaginians. The enclosure is also sometimes called the 'tophet', this being the Hebrew for a place near Jerusalem also used for human sacrifice.[65]

Two Old Testament texts are of particular interest to the whole subject:

And [King Josiah] defiled Topheth which is in the valley of the children of Hinnom, that no man might make his son or his daughter to pass through the fire to Molech (2 Kings 23:10).

And:

[The children of Judah] have built the high places of Tophet which is in the valley of the son of Hinnom, to burn their sons and daughters in the fire, which I [the Lord] commanded them not (Jer. 7:31).

In these texts our version makes 'Tophet' a place-name, when it really means no more than a sacred enclosure; more important is the misunderstanding in the translation 'to Molech' (or Moloch); there was no such god.

The Hebrew word, the same as the Phoenician word on many of the commemorative stelae from the sanctuary at Carthage, was MLK and meant something like 'sacrificed offering', and so 'to Moloch' should really be rendered 'as a sacrifice'. The sacrifice in Judah as in Carthage was made to the local Baal, or supreme god, as another text makes clear:

They have also built high places of Baal to burn their sons with fire for
burnt offerings to Baal, which I commanded not . . . therefore behold the
days shall come, saith the Lord, that this place shall be no more called
Tophet, nor the valley of the son of Hinnom, but the valley of slaughter
(Jer. 19:5 and 6).

In Roman times in North Africa, the Phoenician word survived in a
compounded MLKMR which was transcribed in Latin *molchomor*, and
meant 'sacrificial offering of a lamb'.[66]

It must be stressed that in spite of the Old Testament references, no
'tophet' has been found in the east, nor is there other evidence of human
sacrifice in Phoenicia itself. It was the case that the early Hebrews were
influenced by Canaanite religion, which was presumably akin to that
of the Phoenician cities at the time, and therefore the practice must
have been brought from their homeland by the Phoenicians. Nevertheless the possibility remains that it died out at a relatively early date
in Phoenicia while lasting for centuries in Carthage and other western
settlements.

The Cathaginian 'tophet' was in use from the earliest days of the
colony down to its destruction, as the changes in the styles of the urns
and ceremonial stelae prove. Furthermore, human sacrifices also were
made in Carthaginian dependencies of Phoenician origin elsewhere in
the west; tophets have been found in Hadrumetum, Motya, Calaris,
Nora, and Sulcis, with dedicatory stelae and urns in every way comparable with those found at Carthage. The sacrifices were originally
made to Baal Hammon alone, and in the famous description in Diodorus
of the sacrifice of hundreds of children of the aristocracy, the god concerned is said to be Kronos, with whom the Greeks identified Baal
Hammon, but from the fifth century we often find Tanit associated
with Baal, and usually named first.[67]

Human sacrifice was the element of Carthaginian life most criticized
by the Greeks and Romans. While it is true that a number of Mediterranean peoples practised it at times, most of the more advanced left
it behind in their very early days; this was the case with the Greeks.
At Rome it lingered somewhat longer, and in times of great disaster,
when religious feeling was intense, it was occasionally resorted to, as
happened after the battle of Cannae in 216, when two Gauls and two
Greeks were buried alive on the forum.[68] It was the regular and official
nature of the sacrifice, and the number and age of the victims at
Carthage, which impressed the rest of the Mediterranean. It was alleged
that Darius, the king of the Persians (and thus himself a 'barbarian' to
the Greeks), and Gelon, the victor of Himera, both attempted to stop

the practice, but this is probably legend.[69] At Carthage itself no king or prophet arose to denounce it, as they did in Judah, and the decline in the strict performance of the sacrifices seems to have been gradual and probably due to contact with the Greek world. It is remarkable that Roman 'war propaganda' in the third century, in which any aspect of Carthaginian life was open to criticism, made little of such a target. Diodorus' account of the sacrifice of 500 children of the aristocracy in 310 reveals not only the fanaticism of the Carthaginians but the neglect of the practice in the preceding years. In the tophet at Hadrumetum the urns of the earliest levels (sixth and fifth centuries) contain human bones only, but in the fourth century animal bones occur mixed with human or alone, and in the latest levels there are only animal bones.[70]

According to our sources, some rather doubtful, the sacrifices took place annually, were always of male children, and were an obligation laid on the leading families of the city. It is, however, not clear to what extent there was a legal compulsion on any particular families to surrender a child for sacrifice. It is likely that in theory all full citizens should have participated; amongst the Canaanites, of whom the Phoenicians were originally a part, and also their neighbours the Israelites, there was an obligation on all to offer 'first-fruits' to the gods, and this included first born children.

The impulse behind the practice was an exceedingly primitive one; the 'virtue' of gods had to be maintained by a continued supply of blood, in order that their protective and fertilizing activity should continue. The disasters suffered at the hands of Agathocles were attributed to evasion of sacrifice by those on whom at least a strong moral obligation lay. Almost all the stelae appear to record that the sacrifice was performed in fulfilment of a vow on the receipt of divine aid, but this does not mean that the basis of the sacrificial system was merely contractual. The whole character of Carthaginian religion was one of the weakness and submission of human beings in the face of the overwhelming and capricious power of the gods, and the necessity of appeasing them.

This is made clear by the personal names of Carthaginians.[71] Unlike those of Greece and Rome, the great majority of Carthaginian names were of religious significance; they reflected a submissive attitude to the gods, the child when named being committed in a fatalistic way to them in the hope of some protection. It is interesting to note that such an attitude was manifested to all the main deities irrespective of their attributes, as far as these are known. Baal appears as a compound in some sixty personal names, Melkart, the next most popular, in over twenty. Tanit is very rare, presumably because nomenclature tends to be conservative and her rise in popularity was late. Some examples are Hamilcar, 'favoured by Melkart', Hasdrubal, 'helped by Baal', Hannibal, 'favoured by Baal', Bomilcar 'in the hand of Melkart', Bostar, 'in the hand of Astarte'.

The priesthood at Carthage was probably divided into two main groups. There were those whose whole life was dedicated to the service of the deity, and who were surrounded by numerous taboos. If we may believe a Roman poet, Silius Italicus,[72] the priests of Melkart at Gades were celibate, had their heads and faces shaved, and wore distinctive robes; entry to the temple was forbidden to women and pigs. Various taboos of a similar nature probably had to be observed by those going to other temples. In Roman times those who wished to enter the temple of Aesculapius (Eshmoun) had to abstain from sexual intercourse for three days and from eating beans and pork. Other sacred posts were held by members of the aristocracy who otherwise lived a normal life.

Inscriptions tell us that some of the priesthoods were in effect hereditary in certain families, as was the case of Phoenicia itself. There were certainly grades of priesthood, as in the inscriptions we find not only 'cohen', a simple priest but also 'rab cohenim', chief of the priests. It is probable that each temple had its chief priest with a number of subordinates. and the same is true of priestesses for whom the distinction is known. There was a college of ten senatorial members with the duty of general supervision of religious affairs, and it must be the case that it was an extremely important body in such a society.[73]

The importance of human sacrifice in the traditional picture of Carthage tends to obscure the fact that the sacrifice of other objects, in particular animals, was an essential part of the religion, as it was of the Hebrews and for that matter of the Greeks and Romans. The sacrifices not only secured the continuation of divine favour; they paid for the organization of priests, who maintained this contact between the people and their gods. Several important though fragmentary inscriptions refer to the division of the sacrificed animals among the priests according to a regular tariff. Bulls, calves, sheep, lambs, kids, and poultry are enumerated.

There were various categories of sacrifice: a holocaust in which the entire animal was consumed by fire, a sort of sacrifice of communion in which part of the sacrificed animal returned to the giver, part going to the priest, and a third in which the priests retained all of it. In addition the priests were paid, probably in silver by weight, according to the importance of the victim, the most expensive being the bull. These payments apparently applied only to those who brought their own victims, since the priests could not claim payment from those who had no livestock or poultry; such persons presumably could purchase sacrificial animals at the temple. In addition to animal sacrifices, other sorts of foodstuffs were offered, and incense, which figured largely in the cult of Baal Hammon.[74]

Unlike the Egyptians, the Carthaginians seem to have attached little importance, at least for the greater part of their history, to the idea of life after death, in spite of centuries of contact with Egypt and the introduction of some Egyptian deities into Carthage, or at least into their personal names which generally reflected religious feelings. Their eschatology was probably little more developed than that of the early Hebrews; the dead had a brief existence in the tomb itself and were accordingly provided with a few essentials, and luxuries, such as they had been used to when alive. Apart from isolated instances, inhumation was the rule, and the wealthy at any rate were often buried at the bottom of deep shafts in tombs of well-dressed stone; in the later period of Carthaginian history there was much use of marble sarcophagi from the Greek world.[75]

Tombs at Carthage, and also at settlements in Sardinia, Sicily, and Spain, have provided numerous examples of characteristic Carthaginian products whose precise significance is mysterious. These are terracotta masks of various types.[76] Strictly there are two main classes, masks with holes for eyes and mouths, and masks having no such holes, generally referred to as *protomai*. They are found in fairly rich tombs, never on the face of the dead, and some tombs have several. The earliest, dating from the seventh century are fearsome grotesques; subsequently *protomai* of both male and female features became common till the fourth century after which the usage declined rapidly. The antecedents of these products are various, both Egypt and Mycenae being included; the closest parallels to the grotesques are in the east Mediterranean and particularly Cyprus, recalling the place of the island in the legendary accounts of the foundation of Carthage, but there are also parallels to the later *protomai* in the Greek world. It has been suggested that they had some ritual significance, but it seems unlikely that the masks were ever actually used as masks. It is possible that the grotesques were believed to frighten off evil influences, while the *protomai*, particularly the female, often thought to represent Tanit, were likewise believed to protect the dead in some way.

The influence of Greek civilization on the thought of the Carthaginians is obviously difficult to assess, since we have no Carthaginian literature, but it was probably less than its influence on the externals of Carthaginian civilization; an exception may be made of a part of the upper class who were influenced by Greece in the same way that their fellows in Rome were.

The cult of Demeter and Kore was officially installed in the city, but it does not seem that the same privilege was given to other Greek deities, though these must have had their votaries among the residents from the Greek world who became numerous in the city in the fourth century. But the conservatism and the intensity of Carthaginian religion prevented a mass desertion of the native gods such as tended to happen in the larger cities of the Mediterranean.

Nor is there evidence that Greek literature and philosophy made much impact. No doubt as Carthage became increasingly at home in the Hellenistic world the number of those who knew Greek grew, and some must have read and brought back to Carthage Greek books. We hear of libraries in Carthage at the time of the destruction of the city, and these may have contained Greek as well as Carthaginian works. The only one we know of is the work on agriculture in twenty-eight books by Mago, who knew Hellenistic studies in this field.[77] Works of this practical nature, which were common in the Hellenistic period, will have appealed to the money-conscious Carthaginians. But their education never became dominated by Greek as did that of the Romans, and it has in fact been suggested that the priesthoods took care to retain a dominating influence on what there was of Carthaginian education, apart from the practical accomplishments handed down from father to son. It is surprising to find that there was a school of later Pythagoreans at Carthage in the last decades of the city. Their system, by now a form of mysticism rather than a philosophy, had always been popular among the Italiots and it was from there that it may have been imported.[78]

Lastly we know of one Carthaginian who achieved intellectual fame outside his own country; this was Hasdrubal, who took the Greek name Cleitomachus. He was a pupil of the head of the Academy at Athens, Carneades, and in 129 himself became head of this establishment; fortunately he had been established at Athens before the sack of Carthage.[79]

From what has been said above, it can be seen that the Carthaginians retained to the end of their days a way of life very different, in spite of superficial similarities, from that of most of the rest of the Mediterranean world. There can be no doubt that their adherence to traditional modes of thought gave them a sense of solidarity and was a source of strength to them, placed as they were in the midst of more numerous and often hostile peoples, but it also affected their capacity to develop in new ways and to do away with practices belonging to a primitive age. They were always strange to their neighbours, who were the more ready to judge them harshly, as in the hostile summing up of Plutarch, writing in the second century A.D., but using some earlier writer:

> The Carthaginians are a hard and gloomy people, submissive to their rules and harsh to their subjects, running to extremes of cowardice in times of fear and of cruelty in time of anger; they keep obstinately to their decisions, are austere, and care little for amusement or the graces of life.

This could be criticized in detail, but has perhaps as much truth in it as such characterizations of a people by its enemies can be expected to have.[80]

7

The First War with Rome[1]

AT this point something must be said about the
rise to power and the institutions of the state
which was now about to encounter Carthage
and eventually destroy her. The establishment of Roman supremacy
in Italy, besides being the essential foundation of the Roman Empire
in its extended form with all that that meant to European history, was
a remarkable phenomenon in its own right. It was the only successful
example of a city-state acquiring a large and stable territorial empire
which was used rather than exploited by the dominant power. There
were territorial states of greater size such as the Persian Empire or the
kingdoms of Alexander's successors, but these had resulted from the
rapid conquests by absolute rulers of heterogeneous and usually 'non-
political' states of a type not found in the western Mediterranean.

In Italy the Romans had won dominion over a large number of
communities more similar to city-states than anything else, though not
so highly developed as those in Greece, and this was the more remarkable in that there was not much sense in Italy of belonging to a common

civilization. There were Ligurians and Etruscans who were non-Indo-European, Umbrians, and Oscans, hill dwellers of the Apennines who spoke an Italic dialect but whose marauding way of life was very different from that of the Romans, peoples akin to the Illyrians on the shores of the Adriatic, and finally a ring of Greek colonies on the coast from the Bay of Naples to Taranto. Each of these groups, and others as well, was divided into a number of more or less autonomous units.

Rome herself was originally only one of some fifty villages of the Latins in their small land south of the Tiber, and as late as about 500 there were still a dozen of these left. The preponderance of Rome among them had been established by her Etruscan kings of the late sixth century, and though it was shaken when Etruscan domination was thrown off, Rome was again the leading Latin state by the middle of the fifth century. For the whole of this, the Latins were almost exclusively concerned with defending their fertile land against marauding tribes coming down from the hills which surround the Latin plain. Rome's leadership was again temporarily destroyed in 390, when the city was sacked and burnt in an invasion of Gauls and the people had to ransom themselves. It was at this point that the rugged determination of the Romans in face of disaster first became apparent. In the next generation she slowly re-established her position, making full use of the territory north of the Tiber which she had conquered in a war with the Etruscan city of Veii. By 358 she was strong enough to force the Latins to agree to a new treaty by which the control of the League of Latin states was firmly and permanently vested in Rome.

The crucial date in the history of Roman expansion in Italy was 338. This year marked the end of a revolt of the other Latins against Roman domination. In the settlement which was then made, Rome abolished the Latin League; some of the surviving Latin towns had to accept separate treaties with Rome, in which their obligations to provide military help for the ruling city were an important item. Local autonomy was allowed them, but there could be no question of independent foreign policies. The Latins were forbidden to have relations with each other but the old Latin Rights *vis-à-vis* Rome continued in force; basically this meant that a Latin could obtain full Roman citizenship if he took up residence in Rome. Other Latin towns were incorporated in the Roman state, not as slaves or a subject people but as full Roman citizens; a certain limited amount of self-government was allowed them also, though their full identification with Rome was rapid.

The massive breach in the usually exclusive attitude of the city-state towards the extension of citizenship was not all, however. The

Campanians, who had supported the Latins, were (apparently) given Roman citizenship without voting rights. Under this arrangement, the Campanians suffered no more diminution of their autonomy than would have been insisted upon in an ordinary treaty—deprivation of the right to independent foreign policies was the chief—and in addition they enjoyed the rights and privileges of Roman citizens, except the right to vote, which, however, they could obtain if they became resident at Rome. Their chief obligation, undoubtedly a heavy one, was the requirement to undertake the same military service as full Roman citizens and also to pay the same taxes.

The Romans were now fully embarked upon a policy of prudent generosity, the aim of which was to bind defeated states to them by liberal treatment.[2] On the one hand the manpower at their disposal would increase with every settlement of this kind, while on the other there would be no need to disperse their strength in maintaining garrisons amongst embittered and vengeful subjects. It is true that in earlier days Rome had sometimes annihilated a defeated state completely, in order to satisfy the land-hunger of an increasing population of active peasants, and in future times policy or greed led on occasion to similar acts of ruthlessness, but in general the more sensible policy prevailed in Italy. In the fourth and third centuries, only small amounts of land were taken from defeated states, generally for the use of colonists who were sent out to act as garrisons at strategic points; indiscriminate massacre and looting was not general.

Most states were bound to Rome by treaties which differed in detail but followed a similar pattern. They were allowed to retain their independence except in foreign policy, and paid no tribute; they were, however, required to furnish troops, or in a few cases ships, to the Roman army when called upon to do so. Rome in return went to their aid if they were attacked by a state outside the increasing circle of those bound to Rome. It is obvious that the advantage of Rome's protection to these dependent allies decreased as Rome absorbed potential enemies, but it was important for many till the late third century, because of repeated attacks by the Gauls of the Po valley, who were regarded as aggressive and dangerous enemies by all Italians.

By the middle of the third century, a number of states had been given the Roman citizenship with or without the vote, and Rome controlled what was in effect an Italian confederation including all states south of a line roughly from Pisa to Rimini.

The Roman achievement has been minimized by some scholars on various grounds, the thought behind the arguments being, however, little more than that Rome's treatment of the defeated was dictated by prudent self-interest rather than by genuine liberal sentiment. This is doubtless a fact, but it could be said that prudence in the calculation of self-interest is not so common among major powers that it ought not to be recognized when it occurs. The Romans later compared their liberal attitude towards their subjects with that of the Athenians, who, it was said, alienated and soon lost their empire as a result of their exclusiveness—an over-simplified view, but with truth in it. An Athenian might have replied that it was easier for the Romans to extend their citizenship to others than it was for the Athenians, because in the fully-developed democracy in the Greek city the almost day-to-day participation of every citizen in the task of running the city made his rights too valuable to extend indiscriminately; in Rome, even in her most democratic days, the emphasis in the conception of citizenship was on legal and constitutional safeguards of civic rights against abuse by those wielding power, not in participation in the government, though this was also present.

There was in addition the simple fact, rooted in the past of both peoples, that the attachment of the various groups of the Italians to autonomy was subtly different from that of the Greeks; it was strong but not so intense, so die-hard; the Italians recognized the limitations of the system, and were more prepared to accept the leadership, in effect the domination, of a power which respected their dignity and allowed a sufficient amount of local responsibility. In a very large number of cases realism made for the acceptance of one defeat as final, an attitude which, given the concessions which were customary and the need for united action against the Gauls, was not necessarily inglorious. Far more Italians were bound to Rome by alliances than were incorporated as citizens, and (at least in the period under discussion) this was as much due to the wishes of the Italians as of the Romans; an alliance, even if it meant a *de facto* diminution of sovereignty, was less drastic than incorporation in the Roman state. The attractiveness of the Roman citizenship and the demands of all Italians for it are later history.

The Romans of imperial times looked back to the third century as a golden age in internal politics, and ascribed their successes in the great wars against Carthage at least partly to the system of government. Only a few words can be said here about this remarkable institution, formless and replete with archaic survivals, yet effective. What struck many of the observers was the amount of power, judicial, executive, and military, vested in the two annually elected consuls, though several safeguards such as a right of mutual veto and the prohibition of im-mediate re-election were designed to prevent the establishment of an autocracy.

But in spite of their great powers, the effectively dominant body in Rome was the Senate of about three hundred members, to which all Romans elected to any public office belonged for life. The Senate could only advise, not legislate, but such was its prestige through the experience of its members, its permanence, and its often proved ability to provide Rome with coherent policies, that it was rare for its recom-mendations to be rejected. Its dominance became greater as Rome grew and political problems more complex, so that many decisions had in effect to be made by the Senate, which alone could satisfactorily discuss them.

Finally there were the popular asemblies; in fact, as a result of his-torical survivals, Roman citizens could be called upon in four different forms of assembly, three of which had similar powers. In the third century, the assemblies between them decided on war and peace, were fully sovereign in the field of legislation, and elected the consuls and other officials. Originally the consulship and membership of the Senate had been restricted to a hereditary aristocracy, the patricians, but in the course of political struggles lasting over two centuries this mono-poly had been broken, and the plebeians, the non-patrician citizens, could hold any office. However, this mostly benefited the wealthier plebeians, and it was always the practice of the Roman voters to elect men of substance and standing.

The Roman constitution was thus superficially like that of Carthage, but in practice there was the great difference that the Romans were politically-minded people. Strong social pressures impelled all of any consequence through birth or wealth to take an active part in politics, and amongst the mass of the citizens, most of whom would be liable for military service until the age of forty-five, questions affecting the issues of war and peace at least were hotly discussed. It was further recognized that whatever the form of the constitution, it was the good intentions and will of the people that made it work; at a later date these were lacking, and politicians were able to use defects in the constitutional structure for their own ends. In the earlier period, how-ever, the Romans had a common-sense approach to politics. They ob-served that their social conflicts never degenerated into vicious outbreaks of massacre and counter-massacre, which had marked the class struggles of many Greek states. The very anomalies in the constitution produced at this time a frame of mind among political leaders which prevented them from pressing controversial views to the limit out of egoistic adherence to principle, and the powers of the popular assemblies were sufficient to prevent the emergence of a new exclusive and arrogant governing class. This is not to say that the Romans never failed in their choice of leaders or policies. On the contrary, almost every major war had in it some story of disaster caused by the negligence, inefficiency, or plain stupidity of the elected leaders, or by hasty decisions in Senate or assembly. It was in such times that the qualities of the Romans were most evident; there were no recriminations or resorts to panic measures, but a sinking of differences, a disciplined determination to stand fast and persevere until the tide turned, as it invariably did.

Such was the power with which Carthage came into conflict in the third century. The two states had, however, entered into relations a long while before. The historian Polybius had access to two early treaties, copies of which had circulated among his friends in the Roman Senate in the years immediately before the final Punic War. Unfortunately he does not give an exact Greek translation of the texts, but does provide what amounts to a paraphrase.[3]

The first treaty was dated by Polybius to the first year of the Roman republic, which he put in 508–507, and he adds the remark that the original Latin text was in such old-fashioned language that only the cleverest could understand it, and that with some difficulty. The terms of the treaty and the form in which they are put testify to its antiquity. The Romans agreed not to sail beyond, i.e. west of, the Promunturium Pulchrum (Cape Farina), and if they were forced there by storm, not to trade, and to leave within five days. They could trade with the rest of Africa and Sardinia, provided that the business was carried out before an official, and with the Carthaginian province of Sicily (and Carthage itself) on the same terms as anyone else. The Carthaginians agreed not to attack certain Latin towns subject to Rome, and if they took any other Latin town they were to hand it over to Rome; they would not build any fort in Latium.

The terms of the treaty which in this early stage of international relations, when nothing could be taken for granted, was in effect little more than mutual recognition, indicate clearly the interests of the two sides. The Carthaginians were insistent on the proper regulation of trade and the exclusion of all foreign shipping from the coast of North Africa and by implication from the far west of the Mediterranean. Rome, on the other hand, was interested in the recognition of her rights in Latium, which had been won for her by her late Etruscan rulers.[4] The treaty was probably similar to others known to have existed between Carthage and Etruscan cities, among which Rome had been and perhaps still was numbered. Contacts between the two must have been negligible for a long time, as Roman overseas trade declined, if anything, in the fifth century, while the only thing which would have brought Carthaginians to Latium would have been piratical attacks on her ships passing between Etruria and Sardinia.

A second treaty was signed in 348 and was apparently designed to bring relations closer and take account of changed situations.[5] In this treaty the Romans agreed not to plunder, trade, or colonize not only west of Cape Farina but also south of 'Mastia of the Tartessians', which was apparently Cartagena. Further, the Romans were now excluded from Sardinia and the whole of Africa as well, and had to leave within five days if driven there by accident. Only at Carthage itself and in the province of Sicily was a Roman permitted to trade. Carthage agreed that if the Carthaginians raided any city of Latium not subject to Rome they could keep the plunder but would give up the city to Rome. Both sides agreed not to use provisions obtained from a dependency of the other side to damage any of the other's allies. The strength of the Carthaginian position is obvious from the extension of the area in which Rome recognized her monopoly of trade. The recognition of the possibility of Carthaginian raids on Latium is probably to be connected with the inhabitants of Antium, who were notorious pirates at this date. Rome's prime interest in the territory is, however, recognized and also the system of allies which both Rome and Carthage led.

It was only a decade after the signing of this treaty that Rome disbanded the Latin League and incorporated most of Campania. There followed almost a generation of warfare with the most important people of southern Italy, the Samnites, an Oscan-speaking tribe from whom the Campanians themselves had sprung. This war was crucial for Roman dominance in southern Italy, but her contacts with the outside world of Hellenistic states and Carthage itself would not be great until her power impinged upon the Greek colonies of southern Italy. By the end of the fourth century these had greatly declined in strength, as a result of pressure from Italian peoples such as the Lucanians and Bruttians and the expansive policies of more than one Syracusan tyrant. The most powerful which still survived was Tarentum, which was head of a League comprising most of the rest.

This League was increasingly unable to provide for effective resistance to the Lucanians, and had adopted the expedient of inviting warlike princes from Greece to help them. The first of these was Archidamus, king of Sparta, the more welcome since Sparta was the founder of

Terracotta 'Mask'

Terracotta 'Mask'

Tarentum. He came in 342–341, and brought some relief before he was killed in a battle with the Lucanians in 338.

A few years later more help was needed, and this time Tarentum urned to Alexander of Epirus, an uncle of Alexander the Great. From 334–331 he achieved startling successes throughout southern Italy, reducing several Italian tribes and exercising control as far as Arpi and Posidonia. He even became an ally of Rome, which was looking for friends in view of the growing hostility of the Samnites. But the Epirotes were hardly regarded as a Greek people at all, and it was not surprising that their king had ideas of his own about the future of the Italiots; they were to become part of an empire in the west, such as his nephew controlled in Greece and was winning in Asia. The Tarentines dissolved their alliance with him, and his venture ended ingloriously when he was assassinated by a Lucanian serving in his army.

The Tarentine assertion of the traditional Greek feeling for autonomy appeared to be justified for a time, since her enemies had been shaken by Alexander's success and were concerned in the war between the Romans and the Samnites. During this war Rome extended her power through alliances right up to the Tarentine territory, and in circumstances which are not clear we find that in 303 the Tarentines were engaged in a war with the Lucanians, who were this time assisted by Rome. Recourse was again had to Greece, and the Spartan Cleonymus came over with a force of 5,000 mercenaries. The quarrel can hardly have been considered a serious one by Rome, for a peace was signed between the two sides and Cleonymus left Italy of his own accord.

Thus the gap between the areas in which Rome and Carthage were interested was gradually closing, and this was shown again in the opening years of the third century, when the old enemy of Carthage, Agathocles, also had his way in southern Italy; he was invited by the Tarentines to assist them against the Bruttians, and campaigned with some success till 293. His heart was not fully in this war, because he was planning yet another attack on Carthage with the particular aim of conquering western Sicily. He realized that his previous failure had been due to his weakness at sea, and he brought the Syracusan fleet to a strength of 200 ships, the highest it had been since the time of Dionysius. He also concluded alliances with major Greek states in the eastern Mediterranean, but died in 289 just when his preparations were complete.

Within a few years the Tarentines brought Rome and Carthage into a temporary alliance through their fourth—and last—invitation to a ruler in Greece though the Romans were partly responsible for this

11

peculiar circumstance. In 282 the Italiots of Thurii, Tarentum's chief rival in the west, appealed to Rome for help against the Lucanians. This placed the Romans in a difficult position, because of their former alliance with the Lucanians, while at the same time there had grown up a tradition of slightly patronizing friendship for Greek states, which had resulted in alliances with Massilia and Neapolis. The fact is that in the period of Samnite wars the Romans had become allies of some states which in times of relative peace were an embarrassment to a power which increasingly prided itself on being the protector of the weak against more powerful neighbours, particularly if the latter could be portrayed as aggressive disturbers of international order, as the Lucanians certainly could. The appeal of Thurii was accepted, and a fleet was sent to help them. This aroused the furious resentment of the Tarentines, first because their own traditional position as protectors of the Greeks had been overlooked, and second because there was in existence a treaty with Rome in which the latter agreed not to send warships into the Gulf of Tarentum. They launched their ships, sank four of the Roman ships, and captured one.

There is no doubt that the Romans, now beginning to show an arrogant complacency resulting from great power, had never expected the Tarentines to react on the basis of a treaty probably dating from the time of the expedition of Alexander of Epirus when circumstances had been very different. A substantial body of opinion in Rome was apparently prepared to overlook the incident except for compensation, until the Tarentines rashly insulted the Roman envoys and invited King Pyrrhus of Epirus to their aid; he arrived just in time to prevent the Tarentine aristocracy, which was pro-Roman, from acceding to Roman terms.[6]

The new 'liberator of the Greeks' was one of the most remarkable figures of the age, in the prime of life, a relative by marriage of Alexander the Great—and Agathocles—and well known as a leader of men. It was confidently expected that he would build an empire in the west like that of Alexander. His army of 25,000 men was made the more formidable by the presence of twenty elephants, the use of which had been learnt by Alexander in India, and without which no Hellenistic army was complete; the Romans, however, knew nothing of them. In 280 and 279 he won victories over the Romans, but these were so costly to him that they provide the proverbial phrase 'pyrrhic victories'. He therefore welcomed Roman approaches for peace, the more so since there were now two other spheres of activity where he might hope for easier conquests.

One of these was Sicily, where several cities clamoured for his help against renewed Carthaginian pressure. The situation in the island had moved entirely in favour of Carthage since the death of Agathocles. There was no one to carry on his scheme for another war against Carthage, and there was civil strife in Syracuse between those who wished to restore a republican régime and the leaders of Agathocles' mercenaries. Carthage supported the latter, to the extent of helping to bring about an agreement whereby all Syracusan exiles returned and the mercenaries were given land and civic rights.[7] Most of the states which had been subjects to Agathocles became independent, falling into the hands of adventurers of all sorts, just as had happened in the years following the death of Dionysius. Disorders continued in Syracuse, and the city fell into the hands of another tyrant named Hicetas.

The leading position of Syracuse was increasingly challenged by its old rival Acragas under its ruler Phintias, who extended his power over much of the west of the island. He did not come into open conflict with Carthage, though the latter undertook the support of at least one state, Enna, which felt its independence threatened. Finally Phintias took the title of 'king', which in effect was a claim to be master of all Greek Sicily; but he was defeated in battle by Hicetas, who could not accept the domination of the Acragantine tyrant. This battle took place about 280, and subsequently Hicetas felt himself strong enough to make an attack on Carthaginian territory in the west of the island; we know nothing of the course of the war which followed, but the reaction of Carthage must have been swift and effective, as Hicetas was decisively beaten in 279 as far to the east of Sicily as the River Terias in the territory of Leontini.[8] As a result of this defeat he was deposed by a rival named Thoenon. This man, however, did not receive the confidence of the Syracusans and was shut up on Ortygia, while the people appealed to Sosistratus of Acragas for help. It seems that Acragas had given no assistance to Syracuse in the war against Carthage, which indicates yet again the particularist policies of the Siceliots, especially when they were ruled by tyrants.

For Carthage, the junction of Syracuse and Acragas under one ruler would have meant that once again there was a powerful Siceliot state to threaten her position in the island, and it was decided to follow up the victory over Hicetas with a full-scale assault; in 278 a hundred ships and a powerful army began the siege of Syracuse, divided as it was into competing factions.[9] So Carthage seemed to be in a position finally to complete the conquest of Greek Sicily, but once again it was an opportune moment presented by Greek divisions, rather than the adoption of a policy of open conquest, which determined her action. With such a prospect now open to them, the Carthaginians naturally sought to take every precaution against intervention by other powers, which in effect meant Pyrrhus, who—as must soon have become known —had entered into negotiations for peace with Rome during the winter of 279–278. Mago, the Carthaginian admiral in charge of the impending operations, was sent to Rome with a fleet of 120 ships to try to persuade the Romans to continue the war against Pyrrhus. The great fleet, the largest any Roman can have seen, strengthened the hand of the party at Rome which had prevented peace with Pyrrhus on an earlier occasion, after his first victory, with the argument that Rome should never negotiate with an undefeated enemy on Italian soil; perhaps as important was a substantial gift of silver bullion, with which the Romans could pay for the help she was receiving from her allies over and above what was required by treaty.

The agreement finally reached between Mago and the Romans was, however, limited.[10] It simply stated that if either side made peace with Pyrrhus, its terms were to include a clause allowing Rome (or Carthage, as the case might be) to go to the aid of the other if attacked. In either case the Carthaginians would provide the ships, but each side would pay its own men. Carthage also undertook to help Rome by sea if needed.

Apart from the gift of silver, the Romans were thus assured of naval assistance against Tarentum if it was needed, which was important, as they had no fleet of any substance, but were not bound to send help to the Carthaginians. The latter had at least prevented a peace with Pyrrhus, and even if the clause about Roman help was not binding on the Romans, it might at least intimidate Pyrrhus from taking action in Sicily. In point of fact the limit of collaboration between the two sides was the transport by Mago of a small body of troops to Rhegium. Further, in the face of their common danger, the two sides at Syracuse sank their differences and appealed to Pyrrhus to come to their help; he agreed without bothering to come to terms with the Romans, rightly calculating that they would still have more than enough on their hands in southern Italy to think of sending help to Sicily.

So the Carthaginian plan had failed, and the consequences were disastrous.[11] Late in 278 Pyrrhus brought 10,000 men to Sicily unopposed, and the number was trebled by contributions from the Siceliots. The enthusiasm with which he was greeted seems to have outstripped that which Timoleon had aroused in his days of success. He was hailed as king and commander-in-chief of the Siceliots, and in 277 won an extraordinary series of successes. In addition to Greek cities, Heraclea Minoa and Segesta joined him freely, and first Eryx then Panormus were taken by storm, until the only foothold still left to Carthage in the island was Lilybaeum.

One state remained friendly, or at least hostile to Pyrrhus; this was Messana, which later played such an important part at the beginning of the Punic War. It had been seized by Campanian mercenaries of Agathocles shortly after their employer's death;[12] the citizens had been expelled or killed, and the women, children, and property divided. Calling themselves Mamertini (from Mamers, the Oscan form of the Latin Mars), the Campanians settled down to a life of uninhibited brigandage throughout the north and east of Sicily. It was natural that they should oppose Pyrrhus, as a man who might bring some sort of order to Sicily. However, the Carthaginians considered their position so desperate that they sought peace on the basis of a surrender of all their possessions in Sicily except Lilybaeum; Phyrrus was dissuaded from agreeing to this by his Siceliot advisers, who argued that to leave Lilybaeum in Carthaginian hands was to allow the continued existence of a threat to Greek Sicily. Yet the Siceliots were not willing to take their fair share in the difficult and costly task of reducing the fortress, whose strength was so formidable that it held out against the Romans for years in the first Punic War. Pyrrhus also demanded men, ships, and money for an attack on Africa. As opinion turned from him and he resorted to repressive measures against defaulting friends, several states returned to the Carthaginian alliance, and others even joined the Mamertines.

In spite of a victory in the field over a Carthaginian force, Pyrrhus finally decided that he had little to hope for in Sicily, and in 276 he returned to Italy, where his allies were being hard pressed by the Romans. On the way the Carthaginians made a successful attack on his fleet and he lost 70 out of 110 ships.[13] This blow was decisive; the next year, after another minor action against the Romans, he sailed back to Epirus to another field of adventure. Such was the end of the last hope of a consolidation of the Greek position in the west in the face of various enemies.

The defeat of Pyrrhus by the Romans—for such it was held to be—caused a great deal of comment among the Greeks of the eastern Mediterranean, and in 273 Ptolemy Philadelphus of Egypt established friendly diplomatic relations with the Roman state, which at the time ranked among the barbarians. The failure of the Greeks in the west, in spite of efforts by various rulers from Greece itself, is remarkable, and by the time of Pyrrhus one thing was clear: their greatest enemies were not Carthaginians but Italians. The former could now be regarded as essentially a power of the same order as the major Hellenistic kingdoms of the east, which had attained a relatively stable balance of power. The Italians were only just emerging from what to the Greeks was barbarism, and presented to the Italiots, as they were later to do to the major Greek powers, a novel military threat; they could not equal the Greeks in some of the advanced military techniques, but they more than made up for this in reserves of disciplined manpower and a long tradition of warlike activity. It is notable that when the Italiots became subordinate allies of Rome they provided ships, not soldiers; this was not simply because the Romans had no naval tradition of their own and so got their ships elsewhere, but because they considered the military qualities of the Italiots, and later of all Greeks, to be distinctly inferior to their own.

Within a few years of the departure of Pyrrhus, Rome and Carthage were engaged in a war which lasted almost a whole generation and produced the heaviest casualties of any war known up to that date. The question of responsibility for this is a difficult one, because to all intents and purposes we only have the Roman point of view.[14] The problem of 'war-guilt' was one which exercised the Romans both because of their own traditional attitude to war and because of a deep-felt need at certain periods of justifying their supremacy to the Greek world, which they knew resented and criticized it, and the good opinion of which they badly wanted. It is to be noted that the Romans sought to show that all their wars had been undertaken with proper justification in defence of themselves or their allies against aggression. Gibbon ironically remarked of the writer who consistently put forward this view of Rome's wars: 'according to Livy, the Romans conquered the world in self-defence'. But this attitude, which it is easy to regard as hypocritical, was by no means common in antiquity, and, more important, it had its effect at times on Rome's policy. There were substantial periods of Greek history when there was felt to be no need to justify wars; what mattered was that they should be successful.

The so-called 'fetial law' in early Rome, which governed inter-state relations, did not permit aggressive wars, and it was on the basis of this early law that views of what constituted a 'just war' were erected, with substantial influence down to modern times. It is too easy to reject out of hand the self-justification of imperial powers, and to assume that their conquests have always been the result of determined and

ruthlessly executed plans of aggression. In early days the fetial law—
which was common to the Latin states and presupposed a rudimentary
but sensible way of looking at war, at a time when by Greek standards
Latium was still quite barbarous—was generally observed. The difficulties arose when Rome became a major power, when her security
was affected in other ways than by attacks on her own territory or that
of her allies, ways which were not covered by the fetial law. Several of
Rome's wars from the fourth century onwards could be regarded
strictly speaking as unnecessary, when the right of defending an injured
ally was used as an instrument of policy, in fact so successfully that it
became traditional; the defence of a weaker friend was satisfying to
the Roman moral sense and often had the fortunate result of increasing
Roman power. It was not, however, the case that Roman policy was
directed towards the mere acquisition of territory in the early third
century.

It was an incident at Messana which was the occasion of the war.[15]
The Campanians there had continued their depredations after the
departure of Pyrrhus, particularly at the expense of Syracuse. At length
a new ruler of Syracuse, Hiero, inflicted a severe defeat on them, probably in 265, and forced them to retire to their city walls. Fearing that
they might be unable to resist, the Mamertines asked for and received
a Carthaginian garrison. It appears, however, that there was a section
of the Mamertines who preferred a Roman alliance, or else that the
community as a whole thought it would be desirable to have Roman
protection as well as Carthaginian, not realizing that although all three
had been opponents of Pyrrhus, the situation was now different; Carthage or Rome, but not both, could protect them. An embassy was
sent to Rome to ask for protection, an act which in Roman eyes constituted a technical submission to Rome. It was the decision of the
Romans to accept this request that led to war.[16]

The historian Philinus, who wrote a history of the first Punic War
favourable to Carthage which was used by Polybius as a major source,
argued that acceptance of the Mamertines' request constituted aggression by Rome, as there was in existence a treaty in which Rome and
Carthage undertook not to engage in Sicily and Italy respectively.[17]
This was presumably the argument which he got from Carthaginian
informants. Polybius flatly denied[18] that the treaty existed, and to a
great extent judgement on the existence of the treaty must be sub-
jective. Either of the two could have been misinformed, but it was not,
perhaps, so easy to conceal a document of this type from Polybius as
has been supposed; it seems as though all the documents concerning

the early period of Roman–Carthaginian relations were being circulated amongst members of the Roman aristocracy about 153–150, when Polybius was writing.

In spite of Polybius' explicit statement, belief in the treaty survived, and several Roman authors felt it necessary to exculpate Rome by another method, namely that Carthage had previously violated the treaty by intervention at Tarentum, certainly a grotesque fiction.[19] Livy records a treaty, of which he says nothing, which he placed in the year 306, and those who accept the version of Philinus usually identify it with that of Livy.[20] However, it seems unlikely that at this date a treaty of such a sort could have been signed between the two; it was true that Roman alliances now reached to the borders of Tarentum, and consequently that she had some interest in all the south of Italy; Carthage, however, controlled only a third of Sicily at this date, and there could hardly have been envisaged a situation in which the Romans would be a threat to their position there.

On the whole, therefore, the statement of Polybius is to be accepted, in which case the Carthaginian informants of Philinus were either deliberately deceiving him, or perhaps more likely reducing to an over-simplified form their own interpretation of the treaty of 279. In this, it will be recalled, either side was permitted to send help to the others' territory on Carthaginian ships if requested. Carthaginians could argue that this implied a recognition of spheres of interest into which neither party could enter without the other's permission, and that Messana, by virtue of its acceptance of a Carthaginian garrison, could be regarded as her dependency. Obviously this would be very special pleading, particularly since the treaty was only concerned with the problem of Pyrrhus, but at least it can be said that interests are a fact even if they are not recognized in a treaty, and can only be ignored with some risk.

Some of the arguments of the Roman senators are reproduced by Polybius. Those against accepting the plea for protection argued that the circumstances of the Mamertines' conquest of Messana and their subsequent behaviour made it unjustifiable to support them. As recently as 270 the Romans had suppressed some Campanians whom they had sent to garrison Rhegium in the Pyrrhic war, who had seized the city and behaved as brigands, in imitation of and in association with the Mamertines. It was true that the Campanians of Rhegium were Rome's direct responsibility—they were Roman citizens—but Rome would certainly be inconsistent if she helped a community who had acted in the same way. Those in favour of the Mamertine request argued that self-interest required intervention; if Carthaginian control of Messana was consolidated, she would soon defeat Syracuse, and thus Sicily would be entirely under Carthaginian control. The Carthaginian Empire including Sardinia as it did, would encircle Italy and have an easy 'bridge' (the Straits of Messina) into Italy.[21]

It was perhaps plausible to argue that Carthage would soon be able to defeat Syracuse, though as has been seen there had been times in the past when the situation had been even more favourable yet Syracuse had not fallen. But that the Carthaginians were a threat to Italy was specious. Quite apart from the past history of Carthaginian policy, there was the fact that in the preceding generation Rome's strength had increased enormously, while Carthage had no more than she had had for a century. The only reality behind the fear of Carthage was perhaps that now a major power controlled one side of the Straits of Messina, and that Pyrrhus had shown how easy it was for a state with a powerful navy to land an army in Italy. The Romans, however, were by no means unique in magnifying potential threats. Another argument which was certainly used was that it was the general policy of Rome to accept into her alliance and protection any state which offered or asked to join the system, and when the Syracusans joined the Carthaginians immediately after the start of the war, Hiero accused the Romans of expansive policies disguised under the cloak of this respectable sentiment.[22] There were, however, others who whatever the morality of the case were opposed to a policy of activity overseas while there was still a great deal to do in Italy.

The upshot of the debates in the senate was that it was unable to reach a decision, and the matter was turned over to the popular assembly for consideration without a senatorial recommendation. This was a very rare occurrence in a matter of such importance, and must mean an almost equal division of opinion among the leading senators. In point of fact, however, this was likely to sway the vote in favour of accepting the Mamertines, because the consul who happened to be in Rome, Appius Claudius Caudex, was in favour of it, and a consul's opinion expressed before the assembly always had great weight. He argued that the safety of Roman Italy required the alliance, and also held out the prospect of great plunder (i.e. if war should result).[23]

At first sight these arguments look contradictory; if Carthage was such a threat to Italian security, how could she be easily defeated and provide much booty? Yet Polybius says that at the time the Romans were war-weary, and so they must either have been persuaded that war was unlikely or that it would be soon over. It is tempting to suggest that Appius stressed the fact that it was Syracuse, a city of enormous wealth and unwarlike inhabitants, which was attacking the Mamertines and thus the immediate object of Roman arms if they were needed. Yet when Appius left for Messana he carried the authority to declare war on the Carthaginians if they refused to give up their position. At best, therefore, Roman acceptance of the Mamertines' request was based on an exaggerated notion of what was essential to the security of Italy, and can be described as adventurist or even reckless. There was a substantial element among the senators who regarded the prospect of war with equanimity, believing that it would bring them political and military distinction, while many voters saw the prospect of material gain.

On the Carthaginian side the question was simply whether to accept the Mamertines' change of alliance or to resist. Acceptance would entail recognizing a complete alteration of the balance of power in Sicily which had lasted so long, since the state which now controlled all central and southern Italy would have a foot in the island and control both sides of the straits. It required very little knowledge of the methods of Roman expansion in Italy to foresee that Messana would be only the first step in the incorporation of other Sicilian states in the Italian confederation. It would be open to any state within the Carthaginian sphere to put itself under Roman protection and then ask for help if Carthage tried to assert her supremacy.

It is probable that if we had better information about the first year of the war it would appear that Carthage tried for a while, through diplomatic means, at least to keep a Roman force from Messana, but much of the information we have (apart from Polybius' narrative) is from late Roman sources and untrustworthy. The Mamertines seem to have got rid of the Carthaginian garrison before the arrival of the Roman army, and the unfortunate commander was later crucified for his lack of firmness. They then decided to invite Appius formally to send in a Roman force.

At about this time, Hiero and the Carthaginians sank their differences and formed an alliance, beginning a joint siege of Messana. Whether he, like the Carthaginians, feared the advent of a new major power in Sicily cannot be known, since negotiations for the alliance may have begun before the decision of Rome to intervene became public. Both Syracuse and Carthage had an interest in suppressing a community of brigands like the Mamertines, and Hiero could have thought little of the morality of the Romans, whom he had helped against the Campanians of Rhegium. When Appius arrived at Rhegium he sent an embassy with an ultimatum to the Carthaginians and Syracusans; it was presumably in answer to this that Hiero made his remark about Roman bad faith. Appius got his force into Messana in spite of the Carthaginian naval blockade, but it was late in the year, and he achieved nothing decisive during his term of office, the victories attributed to him belonging in fact to the consul of 263–262, Manius Valerius. He was of a family hostile to the Claudii, but was no less a supporter of the war, and is said to have been the first Roman to see that Carthage would never be defeated unless the Romans built a fleet. The unusual step was taken of sending both consuls to Sicily with a full year's levy of two legions each and allied contingents in proportion, making a total of some 40,000 men. Valerius defeated the Carthaginians and Hiero at Messana; and when his colleague Otacilius joined him, the two proceeded against Syracuse, while many dependants of both Syracuse and Carthage went over to the Roman side.

Hiero had nothing like the force needed to meet such a formidable army again, neither had the Carthaginians yet enrolled one of their large mercenary armies. He might have sustained a siege, since there was nothing to prevent the Carthaginians from sending in supplies by sea. But he calculated that the prospects of the Romans were superior to those of his allies, and determined to change sides. Opinion in Syracuse, never enthusiastic about the alliance with Carthage, waned rapidly at the Roman successes. The prudent Valerius offered very generous terms; Hiero was allowed to retain some of his dependencies, and became an ally of Rome. The indemnity of one hundred talents was small, and the principal obligation was the provision of supplies to the Romans in Sicily; Hiero reigned as a faithful ally of Rome for some fifty years with hardly any interference. Before the winter set in further Carthaginian dependencies deserted, including Segesta.

By now, Carthage had begun to collect a mercenary army of some size, hiring Ligurians, Celts, and Iberians. It was essential to put up more resistance in the face of the blow suffered by the defection of Hiero, which relieved the Romans of any anxiety about supplies; but it was felt to be impossible to meet the Romans in the field. Selected strong points were therefore chosen as centres of resistance, in particular Acragas. This strategy was based on previous experience; pressure from the east of Sicily had always been beaten off in the end, even though on occasion all but a very few places had been taken. In June 262, a new pair of consuls came again with four legions and began the siege of Acragas, which was vulnerable because it was not on the coast. The city was so strong that no attempt was made to take it by storm, and the garrison commander held out for five months till famine brought about great distress.

At this point, the newly enrolled army arrived from Africa under a commander called Hanno, who had taken part in the siege of Messana in 264. Figures for the size of this force are uncertain.

Philinus gave 50,000 infantry, 6,000 horse, and 60 elephants, all of which figures are perhaps exaggerated. Making his base at Heraclea Minoa, Hanno cut the Romans' supply route to the east, though sufficient got through to prevent the Romans giving up the siege. After two months of inactivity, the position in Acragas became such that an attempt had to be made to relieve it. In the battle which followed, Hanno's force was driven from the field but did not suffer particularly heavy losses, while it had so engaged the Romans that the garrison commander was able to withdraw from the city without loss. The Romans then sacked the defenceless city and enslaved the survivors. This, although the common practice after severe sieges, was resented by the rest of the Siceliots, since only the garrison had been Carthaginian, and the friendliness with which Rome had been greeted by a number of places gave way to hostility.

Carthage gained substantially from this change of feeling, and the Romans made little progress in Sicily in the next year. Some further towns in the interior went over to the Romans, but more of those on the coast (who could be helped by the Carthaginian fleet) returned to their former alliance, and the Roman effort was dispersed in keeping control of the areas which they had so far won. Further, in 262 naval reinforcements were sent to Sardinia from Carthage and in 261 they made frequent raids on the Italian coast. The increased vigour of the Carthaginians was due in part to the arrival of a new general, Hamilcar, sent to replace Hanno who was fined for his failure to retain Acragas.

Yet in the long run, the year 261 marked a turning-point in the war, for the Romans decided to build a fleet. Polybius states that the capture of Acragas led the Romans to aspire to the conquest of the whole of Sicily, and that their failure to take the coastal towns made them realize they could hardly do this without a fleet. It is, however, possible that some Romans had previously hoped for the conquest of the whole of Sicily without a fleet, and that the decision to build one was more a result of the humiliating raids on Italy than Polybius admits; these raids ceased when a fleet was in being.

The Roman achievement was one of great magnitude, for Rome had no naval tradition whatever and always felt uneasy at sea. The setting up of a small organization to look after naval matters came as late as 311, and the ships and their rowers came from allied states, chiefly Greeks. The total naval strength did not amount to more than twenty ships (triremes), and the ships were laid up when not required. After the Pyrrhic war, another twenty-five ships became available from the Italiots who were known as 'naval allies'. Now, however, a force of quinqueremes was built, ships with between twenty-five and thirty oars on each side, with five rowers to each oar. Ships of this size had first been used in Phoenicia or Cyprus shortly before the time of Alexander the Great, and had been in use at Carthage for some time. No Italiot states possessed any, and it seems unlikely that Syracuse did either.

We are told that the Romans built one hundred quinqueremes (besides twenty new triremes) on the basis of a Carthaginian ship which had been captured in 264, though this may be an example of a traditional article of Roman pride, willingness to learn from enemies. The ships were by no means identical with those of Carthage. In particular, they were more heavily built (and consequently slower) because they had to carry a device which it was hoped would neutralize the superiority of Carthaginian seamanship. This was a boarding-bridge thirty-six feet long and four feet wide, with a slot twelve feet from one end; through this slot was fixed a pole twenty-four feet high and ten inches in diameter. The whole device was mounted in the prow of the ship. At the far end of the boarding-bridge, on the under side, was an iron spike, and on the upper side a ring, from which a rope passed through a pulley at the top of the pole. By this means it was possible to raise the bridge to an angle of about forty-five degrees from horizontal, and the aim was to lower it sharply so that the spike became embedded in the deck of the enemy ship and the Roman marines could cross. It is clear that the bridge could be man-handled round a certain distance and could be lowered over the sides of the ship, but not the stern. The whole device was popularly known as a '*corvus*', or 'crow', and its adoption shows clearly that the Romans felt their only chance of winning at sea was to turn naval battles into land battles, in which their superior training and weapon handling would be manifest.

It is true that boarding tactics were used by other powers in naval warfare at this time, but it was possible to win battles at sea by seamanship as well, by ramming the enemy ships or rendering them helpless by breaking their oars. Each Roman quinquereme had a permanent guard of forty 'proletarii'—men from the poorest section of the population, who were excluded from service in the legions—and when at sea had eighty legionaries. Thus a fully manned quinquereme carried not far short of 400 men in all, and losses to a defeated fleet were liable to be tremendously heavy.

Tradition said that the ships were built in sixty days, which must be an exaggeration even when their rough heavy construction is taken into account. But they were certainly built in a season, with skilled labour from various naval allies, who also provided many of the rowers, and the Romans considered they were ready to venture into the new element. The Carthaginians must have been aware of what was going on, but felt confident in their ability to overcome the novices. Their confidence was increased at the first encounter.

One of the consuls for 260, Cnaeus Cornelius Scipio, was sent with seventeen ships to Lipara, a Carthaginian naval base, where there was a movement in favour of Rome. The commander at Panormus, the Hannibal who had garrisoned Acragas, sent a squadron of twenty ships, which blockaded Scipio in the harbour at Lipara; there followed a most un-Roman panic, and the entire force was taken without a blow. A few days later, however, Hannibal lost many ships out of a force of fifty, through over-confidence when reconnoitring the main Roman fleet as it was sailing south. He did not regard this as a cause for alarm, and was eager for a battle in which the main forces would be engaged. This took place off Mylae, near Messana. The surviving consul, Duilius, had 143 ships against Hannibal's 130, but the latter engaged without even arranging his ships in proper battle order. The Romans sailed in two lines, the rear line being designed to prevent the Carthaginians who evaded the 'crows' of the front line from wheeling round and attacking from astern. Hannibal and his fleet had no answer to this; some were caught by the front line, others by the second. When they finally broke away, they had lost thirty-one ships captured and fourteen sunk, with 10,000 men taken or killed. It is not surprising that this first naval victory had a great moral effect in Rome, and a famous inscription set up by Duilius has survived.[24]

However, Carthage could if pressed put a fleet of 200 ships into the water, so there was no question of the war being over. In any case, the Romans suffered a serious reverse from the hands of Hamilcar near Thermae in 259, and fared little better at sea. The fleet was sailing under Lucius Scipio, brother of the consul captured at Lipara, in the Tyrrhenian sea. He took Aleria in Corsica but did not venture on a major battle when he approached the colony of Sulcis in Sardinia. This had been reinforced by Carthage through the despatch of a number of ships under Hannibal. Next year this officer met his end after his train of failures; he lost a number of ships in an engagement with Sulpicius, the consul of 258, and was crucified by his own men for incompetence. Sulcis remained in the hands of Carthage, however, as did the rest of the Sardinian colonies, in spite of Roman strength in these waters, while in Sicily, although Hamilcar was confined increasingly to the west of the island, Rome had to keep a force of 40,000 men permanently.

The year 257 was a period of relative calm before the storm. It was the eighth year of the war, but Carthage had suffered little except financially, and her Sicilian territory was still not as limited as it had been in the worst year of Pyrrhus' attack. It can hardly be doubted that at this point Carthage would have been prepared to recognize the Roman position in Sicily. The easy victory which had been hoped for by the Romans had not come about, there had been heavy losses, and there was the prospect of more. But Rome was reluctant to offer peace terms to an enemy unless she had won a really commanding position.

It must have appeared obvious to the senate for some time that a more rapid way of bringing Carthage to give up Sicily than the dogged sieges of Sicilian towns was needed, because the naval victories in themselves were indecisive. The plan of invading Africa was therefore formed, but it had to be carefully handled because of the great reluctance of the land-bound Italian peasantry to engage in such an apparently hazardous adventure. The year 257 was accordingly passed in building a fleet which would outnumber that which Carthage could put into the water, and in 256 the great armada was ready. It seems to have consisted of 230 warships, outnumbering the Carthaginians by thirty. In addition there were about a hundred transports for the horses and supplies. The fleet, under the consuls Manlius Vulso and Atilius Regulus, left the Tiber early in the year, passed through the Straits and along the east coast of Sicily, round Cape Pachynus (Cape Passero), and put in near Cape Ecnomus (Monte Rufino) to pick up the legionaries who were to take part in the expedition. By this time the Carthaginians knew very well what was afoot; they calculated correctly that the Romans would sail along the south coast of the island to the point at which the crossing of the open sea to Africa was shortest, and accordingly based their fleet at Heracles Minoa in order to intercept them. The engagement took place somewhere between this town and Cape Ecnomus.

The Roman fleet sailed along the coast in three lines, of which the first consisted of two squadrons each commanded by a consul, with the two flagships in the centre of the line; the second towed the transports, and a third brought up the rear. The tactics of Hamilcar, the

Carthaginian commander, are not altogether clear. His ships were drawn up in a single extended line overlapping both the Roman flanks, so presumably some sort of enveloping movement was envisaged, probably with an attack on the rear of the Roman front line if it could be drawn away from the second. This was a distinct possibility, as the second line was encumbered by the transports. In fact the Roman front pressed back the Carthaginian centre, assuming a wedge-shaped formation, but the Carthaginian wings failed to take it in the rear. The reason for this is not known; it may be that the Roman second line, which slipped the transports, was able to close the gap. The battle instead resolved itself into three separate engagements, in which the two centres were interlocked, the Carthaginian left engaged the Roman second line and the right the Roman third line, which was now standing by the transports. The Roman centre was victorious in its engagement; the fact that it was led by the two consuls probably indicates that it comprised the major part of the Roman strength. Regulus then took his squadron to the assistance of the third line and the transports, and drove the enemy out to sea. Lastly, the third Roman line was pinned with its back to the shore, but the Carthaginians were unable to drive it aground, because they were prevented by fear of the 'crows' and the superior quality of the Roman soldiers from coming too close. It was rescued by the arrival of the rest of the victorious fleet, and the Carthaginians suffered heavily, being caught between the two forces. Hamilcar lost thirty ships sunk and sixty-four captured, the Romans twenty-four, and the way to Africa was open.[25]

The Romans landed at Aspis on the east of the Cap Bon peninsula; from a base in this area they could cut off Carthage from her richest dependencies. The invaders soon amassed a large amount of plunder from the fertile estates, including 20,000 slaves. But the summer was far advanced and the senate advised Regulus to winter in Africa with forty ships, 15,000 foot, and 5,000 cavalry, while Vulso returned to Italy with the rest. It was obviously felt that the difficulty of supplying a larger force through the winter, when in practice the Mediterranean was closed to ancient shipping, was too great.

At Carthage measures were put into effect for the defence of the city. The survivors of the fleet had sailed home immediately after their defeat; two generals, Hasdrubal son of Hanno, and Bostar, were elected, and they were joined by Hamilcar, who was withdrawn from Sicily with 5,000 foot-soldiers and 500 horse. When Regulus pursued his plundering activities as far as the fort of Adys (Hr Oudna) only twenty-five miles from Tunis, a Carthaginian army advanced to its relief. The

Possible portrait of Hannibal

Carthaginian
jewellery

generals were reluctant to face the formidable Roman infantry on level ground, in spite of their superiority in cavalry and elephants, but this caution did not save them; the force was dislodged with heavy loss from the high position it had taken up. Regulus then seized Tunis, as Agathocles had done half a century before in a campaign which was doubtless an object of study by the Roman staff.

At this point there were discussions about the possibility of peace, probably initiated by the Carthaginians. Our authorities are unanimous that the terms offered by Regulus were so harsh as to be impossible for Carthage to accept. The likelihood is that Regulus and his advisers, brought up in a tradition in which the Romans generally demanded at least a technical surrender before concluding peace, tried to treat a major power as if she were some small Italian community. The Carthaginian position was serious, but by no means hopeless to any who considered the ultimate fate of Agathocles' expedition. There were revolts among the Numidian allies, but Regulus, who emerges from our accounts as an over-confident and unimaginative commander, made little use of what could have been an important source of cavalry reinforcement.

Polybius argued that the Carthaginian failure up to this point had been due to the incompetence of their generals, but since this is one of the few occasions in this period on which we do not hear of the punishment of the unsuccessful commanders, it may be that there were reasonable excuses for them. In any case Polybius' criticism was probably intended to enhance the credit of the Greeks, for at this moment there arrived at Carthage a band of Spartan mercenaries under their leader Xanthippus. This officer had been brought up in the stern Spartan way of life, which still survived in spite of the decline of Sparta as a major power. He inspired both the Carthaginian leaders and their soldiers, not so much by any original ideas as by this confident bearing and his assertion that if they would only make full use of their superiority in cavalry and elephants they could defeat the Roman legions.

After spending some time in training and drilling his heterogeneous force, Xanthippus marched out with at least 12,000 foot, 4,000 horse, and 100 elephants. The numbers may have been a good deal more, but hardly greater than those of Regulus, and perhaps two-thirds were Carthaginian citizens. Regulus accepted the challenge on level ground, as Xanthippus had planned. The Spartan placed his elephants in a line in front of his infantry, with cavalry on the wings. Regulus showed his incompetence by keeping his infantry in their usual close order, instead of spreading them out to avoid the charge of the elephants. The result was that though his left somehow escaped serious loss from the elephants, and pressed the Carthaginian right, his own right was massacred by the charging animals and the Carthaginian infantry which was following up. Xanthippus' cavalry soon drove their opponents from the field on both wings, and then returned to complete the destruction of the Roman infantry; Regulus and 500 men were taken prisoner; 3,000 escaped to Aspis, but all the rest were killed.

Such was the complete failure of the first Roman venture in Africa. There later grew up a legend that Regulus was sent to Rome to negotiate, and that having refused to advise the senate to make peace, he returned in accordance with his parole to suffer torture and death. In fact he died in captivity, and the legend was invented to cover up the fact that his own family had ill-treated Carthaginian prisoners entrusted to them.[26]

The battle, whose site must have been somewhere between Carthage and Tunis, took place early in 255. In the same year there was a remarkable double reversal of fortune at sea. The Carthaginians, in spite of their preoccupation with the presence of Regulus at the walls of the city, had made great efforts to rebuild their fleet and were able to put to sea with 200 ships. The news of the disaster to Regulus reached Rome before the departure of a fleet with reinforcements, but it sailed to Africa just the same, to pick up the survivors. The Carthaginians met this fleet, which amounted to 210 ships, off Cap Bon. But many of their rowers were untrained, and no less than 114 ships were captured by being driven aground. After picking up the survivors, the Romans sailed back to Sicily.

As they were proceeding east along the Sicilian coast, a gale from the south blew up when they were off Camarina, and drove a greater part of the fleet on to the rocks. Only eighty of the 264 ships which the Roman fleet now had—including those that had wintered in Africa and those captured from the Carthaginians—weathered the storm, and the number of men drowned may have amounted to 25,000 soldiers and 70,000 rowers. The latter figure would include a number of Carthaginians, if they were forced to row the ships. This was the greatest disaster that had ever happened at sea, to Polybius' knowledge, and the losses in manpower affected both Rome and her allies. It is remarkable that the consuls were allowed to hold a triumphal procession for their naval victory of Cap Bon, and the disaster must have been attributed to an 'act of God' rather than to incompetence, of which in this case there is in fact no sign.

The Carthaginians had thus warded off the immediate threat, and now faced the Romans' alternative plan of a reduction of the Sicilian towns one by one. The determination of the Romans was never so well revealed as by their building another 140 ships in the winter of 255–254. Carthage was not able to compete with this effort, no doubt because of her losses in manpower in 255, and also had to use most of her available troops to restore her position among the Numidians. She was unable to prevent the Roman capture of Panormus in a combined sea and land operation; there is actually some evidence that a part of the population of the place, probably the wealthy, welcomed the Romans. Five other coastal towns were inspired by the presence of the Roman fleet to expel their Carthaginian garrisons. However, her position in the island was preserved by Roman negligence and lack of a firm conception of the immediate strategic necessity in Sicily; in 253 the Roman fleet, after an unsuccessful attempt at a surprise assault on Lilybaeum, raided the east coast of Tunisia, a venture which could hardly have more than a nuisance value. On the way home, the consuls decided to sail direct from Panormus to Rome instead of coasting as was usual, and the fleet was caught on the high sea in a gale; 150 ships were lost with their crews.

Both sides were now reduced to the same level of exhaustion, and only limited operations occurred in the next two years. The most significant feature was that Hasdrubal was able to proceed to Lilybaeum with some reinforcements, and it must have been the hope of the Carthaginians that peace might be reached on the basis of the *status quo*. They themselves were prevented by shortage of money and men from again enlarging their fleet, while the Romans had to take account of public opinion throughout Italy, which was shaken by the tremendous losses at sea. But in desperation at the lack of progress in Sicily, they decided to venture once more on a naval operation in 250, bringing their fleet up to a strength of 120, and electing as consuls C. Atilius Regulus, who had won a minor engagement at sea in 257, and Manlius Vulso, the victor of Cape Ecnomus.

Before its departure from Rome, news arrived of a success in Sicily; Hasdrubal in some confidence had marched up to the walls of Panormus, which was now the Roman base in the west of the island. There he was enticed up to a system of trenches which the Romans had dug near the wall, and his elephants, which were leading, were driven back by a shower of missiles, to spread confusion among their own men. In the Roman victory which followed, 20,000 out of 30,000 mercenaries are said to have been lost by the Carthaginians, and certainly the entire force of elephants was killed or captured, later to be slaughtered in the circus at Rome. Hasdrubal was recalled to Carthage and executed, and the Romans now sent out their fleet in much greater confidence, to take part in the investment of Lilybaeum.

For Carthage, retention of this base was essential if she were to remain in Sicily at all. It had extremely strong defences on the landward side; outside the wall itself was a ditch ninety feet wide and sixty deep. The approach by sea was also difficult to those who had no knowledge of the shoals. The garrison, mostly Greek and Celtic mercenaries, was reduced to only 7,000 foot and 700 horse by the defeat of Hasdrubal, and some of these were of doubtful loyalty; a movement to betray the place to the Romans was only prevented by a Greek officer called Alexon. However, the commander, Himilco, resisted fiercely, and the prospects of the garrison were enhanced when fifty ships with 10,000 soldiers on board ran the Roman blockade under the command of Hannibal, the son of the Hamilcar who had been defeated at Ecnomus.

The besieging force was probably double the total number of the defenders; they tried every method of siege warfare which they had learnt in Sicily, but the Carthaginians had an answer to all of them, and were constantly encouraged by the exploits of some of their sailors, who kept communications open with the outside. The Romans, besides the heavy losses suffered in the siege wars, were further weakened by epidemics during the winter. Thus when the consuls for 249 arrived, the position was by no means favourable, particularly as it was probably known that Carthage had prepared a considerable naval reinforcement. This was destined for Drepana, a naval station some twenty-five miles north of Lilybaeum, which the Carthaginians were now using as their main base. They already had a fleet there, under a general named Adherbal, but it was presumably outnumbered by the Roman force blockading Lilybaeum.

One of the consuls, P. Claudius Pulcher, the son of the Claudius who had been consul when the war began, determined to attack Drepana before reinforcements arrived, his plan being to sail directly into the harbour there and destroy the Carthaginian fleet at anchor or beached. Adherbal, however, was able to get his ships under way, and sailed out of the harbour by the other of its two entrances. This gave him a dominating position, as he was able to draw his fleet up facing the shore while the Romans were putting about in a confined space.

Polybius describes the battle as follows:

The Carthaginian ships were faster than those of the Romans owing to their superior construction and the skill of their rowers, and their position was favourable, as they had developed their line in the open sea. If any found themselves hard pressed, they could use their speed to retreat to open water and then turn on their pursuers and take them in the rear or on the flank; in such a situation, the Roman ships had to turn about also, and getting into difficulties because of their weight and the poor oarsmanship of their crews, were repeatedly rammed, and many were sunk. Again, the Carthaginian ships could easily sail to the assistance of each other in open water astern of their own line. By contrast, no Roman ship could retire backwards, as they were too close to the land, and those who were hard pressed either ran aground by the stern or made for the shore. To sail through the Carthaginian line and take in the rear enemy ships already engaged (one of the most effective manoeuvres in naval warfare) was impossible, owing to the weight of the ships and the inexperience of the crews. They could not give each other help from the rear, because they were so hemmed in to the shore . . . Such was the difficult position of the Romans in the battle; some of the ships grounded in the shallow water, and others ran ashore. The consul, seeing what was happening, slipped out to the left along the coast and escaped with about thirty ships.

In fact few of the Roman ships appear to have been sunk, but ninety-three were captured. The only consolation for the Romans was that a fair number of men escaped ashore and got back to Lilybaeum. A notable point was that Claudius was one of the mere handful of defeated generals throughout the history of Roman warfare who was put on trial for negligence; he was heavily fined. He was perhaps a victim of popular outcry, because the Claudii were generally regarded as the most arrogant of Roman aristocratic families; there was nothing inherently rash or negligent in his plan, since up to this point the Roman had no great cause to fear Carthaginian seamanship.

The arrival of the expected reinforcements under Carthalo—seventy ships—completed the domination of Carthage in the western Sicilian waters. A number of Roman transports were taken off Panormus and a few warships seized or destroyed near Lilybaeum. Carthalo then sailed along the south coast of the island, to intercept supplies that were being sent by the Romans for the relief of their forces outside Lilybaeum.

The other Roman consul, Iunius Pullus, seems to have had only sixty warships at his disposal, though there may have been another sixty smaller ships levied from the allies, so unless he had ordered the convoy to sail from Messana before he had heard of the defeat at Drepana, his action was extremely rash. Carthalo, with 100 ships, intercepted the convoy off Gela, but the Romans were able to put into a roadstead off Phintias (Licata). Catapults erected on shore prevented Carthalo from closing, and he anchored in the River Himeras till the Romans should venture to sea again. While there, he was informed of the approach of another Roman fleet from the east; this was the rest of Iunius' force, under the consul himself. He put to sea, and Iunius, refusing battle, anchored immediately off a rocky shore near Camarina. The place was in fact so dangerous that Carthalo decided not to engage, and patrolled between the two groups of Romans. Finally he was advised that bad weather was approaching, probably from the south. With some difficulty he rounded Cape Pachynus, but both sections of the Roman fleet, caught on an exposed and rocky coast, were dashed to pieces.

A census of Roman citizens (adult males) taken in 247 showed that in the preceding twenty years the number had decreased by 50,000, some seventeen per cent; many allied states must have suffered as much. Even had the populace been willing to tolerate yet another naval adventure, it was impossible to find the money. In such a situation, if Carthage had pressed her advantage she might have been able to procure a reasonable peace. Yet apart from supplying the garrisons in Sicily and making raids on the Italian coast, the fleet was not used and in fact seems to have been laid up. The explanation for this seems partly to be that extensive operations were undertaken in Africa under Hanno, surnamed 'the Great', who extended Carthaginian territory as far as Theveste, and that Carthage could not now afford to keep a large fleet and a large army going at once.

This Hanno is known to have been an enemy of another Carthaginian who now came to the fore, Hamilcar Barca, the father of the great Hannibal. Hamilcar was sent to Sicily in 247, was entirely successful in maintaining the Carthaginian position in the west, and can hardly be said to have lacked support from his government, even if the Carthaginian senate was divided between supporters of the two men. Whether there was a division of interests between Hanno and his supporters, as representing a 'landed interest', and Hamilcar as the leader of mercantile imperialists, may be doubted. Arguments could be found to justify the laying up of the fleet, such as that the Romans would ultimately tire of a useless blockade of the Sicilian bases, and that no force large enough to conquer could be landed and maintained in Italy even if the fleet were retained. Against this may be set the failure of a tentative approach for peace in 248, and more certainly the renewal of Hiero's treaty with Rome in the same year; the Syracusan was convinced that Rome would never make peace from weakness. In the long run, therefore, the Carthaginians were at fault in trying to win the war 'on the cheap' by a holding operation, and in not realizing that this would never suffice to reduce the will of the Romans, the quality of which ought by now to have been evident. Above all, even granted that vigorous use of the fleet was impossible for reasons of manpower or finance, or strategically useless, it was criminal negligence not to keep it actually in being.

It was Hamilcar's success in defending Lilybaeum and Drepana that led Rome once more to build a fleet, in order to try to reduce them by blockade. To provide the money, the wealthiest of the Romans made loans of substantial parts of their fortunes. This was much praised in antiquity, but the fact remains that it was not a capital levy but a loan, to be repaid in the event of victory.

In the winter of 243–242, 200 ships were built on the model of a Carthaginian quinquereme captured in 250, and were thus more seaworthy than the vessels of the earlier fleets. The effort took Carthage by surprise, and when this fleet arrived off Drepana in the summer of 242, there was not a single Carthaginian ship there. It took eight months for their fleet to be reactivated, and when it put to sea it was undermanned, the crews were out of practice, and it was burdened with supplies for the garrisons, who by now were running short. It got safely to the Aegates Islands, and from there its commander Hanno (not 'the Great') determined on a dash to Drepana with a westerly wind, in the hope that the Roman consul, Lutatius Catulus, would never oppose him in the teeth of a strong head wind. But Catulus had spent the winter in continued training of his oarsmen, and drew up his ships in spite of the heavy sea. Outnumbered, undermanned, and deficient in training, the Carthaginians lost seventy ships taken and fifty sunk, and the remainder (about fifty) escaped owing to a sudden change of wind.

So with dramatic speed the war was over, for without a fleet it was impossible to save the last Carthaginian strongholds in Sicily, the retention of which had been the cause of her determination to continue the war. Hamilcar Barca was given the task of concluding a peace on the best terms he could get, and as a result of his determined attitude, and the good sense of Catulus, he succeeded very well. The first draft stated that Carthage should evacuate Sicily, give up all her prisoners without ransom, and not attack the Syracusans or their allies; in addition Carthage had to pay 2,200 talents of silver in instalments over twenty years. These terms were not accepted at Rome, but a commission of ten did not impose anything particularly severe; Lipara and the Aegates Islands were to go to Rome, an additional 1,000 talents were to be paid at once, and the term of payment for the indemnity was reduced to ten years. Further clauses guaranteed the allies of each side against attack by the other, and prohibited each side from detaching the other's allies from their allegiance and from raising troops in the other's territory.

Later writers naturally concentrated their attention on the persistence of the Romans in overcoming their lack of experience at sea and carrying on in spite of the terrible losses in men, which were far greater than those of Carthage, even if subjects and mercenary losses are included.

Polybius stressed the magnitude of the efforts of both sides in comparison with well-known campaigns by Hellenistic monarchs. It is certainly easier to comprehend the determination of Carthage than that of Rome; the retention of Sicily had been a cornerstone of her policy for so long that it had become second nature to regard it as a matter of life and death. It is not sufficient to observe that Carthage survived its loss a long time; in fact it was the challenge presented by its loss, and, at least as important, the loss of Sardinia which was an inevitable consequence, that forced the more intelligent Carthaginian leaders to look elsewhere for expansion. The mercantile oligarchy had been content to exploit its traditional sphere of interest for over two centuries, with very few and short periods of more adventurist policy; and the conquest of the rugged and warlike Spaniards only appeared practicable or profitable when it became essential.

On the other hand, the Roman will to win, regardless of losses, in a war which was basically of little concern to her security might suggest that during it (if not before) the Romans developed an inordinate lust for territory. This is not the case; the evidence for consistent exploitation, even for proper administration, of her Sicilian conquest is negligible for the period before the end of the war with Hannibal, and it was the middle of the second century before deliberate plans of conquest can be attributed to Roman leaders. In point of fact the Roman will to win was at least in part irrational; it became stronger, not weaker, with the realization of the power of her enemy and the successive disasters which befell one attempt after another to reach a decision. One can rationalize this determination, as the Romans themselves perhaps did, by describing the war as a test of the Italian system they had created; it is true that in the twenty-four years of war there are remarkably few records of anti-Roman movements in Italy, but it could be argued that a total victory was necessary unless allied belief in Roman invincibility —an important and often understressed element in Roman success— was to be shaken. Essentially, however, the Romans not merely failed to recognize the possibility of defeat; they even scorned to admit a draw.

As for the war itself, the Roman legionaries and their Italian allies had by no means proved themselves invincible in the field against heterogeneous but experienced mercenary forces. The lack of discipline and loyalty among the latter was sometimes matched by a decline in the morale of the Italian citizen levies, called away from their homes and farms year after year with small result. On the other hand, the Carthaginian generals, who were allowed an indefinite length of command (so long as they were not defeated), failed to make use of the experience they should thus have acquired and to assert a superiority over the annually-changing Roman commanders.

It is notable that the Romans obtained no spontaneous help from the Siceliots, in spite of the long history of war between Greeks and Carthaginians in the island; help given to either side was determined by calculation, not sentiment. The Romans undoubtedly lost support by their alliance with the Mamertines and their ruthlessness to captured cities. In point of fact their behaviour was only slightly worse than that of the Greeks themselves when fighting each other, but the Greeks, humanly enough, resented these horrors more when they were committed by non-Greeks. Past Carthaginian atrocities were forgotten with time, as is usual, as also their opposition to Pyrrhus' (temporary) alliance with the Mamertines. To many Siceliots—and Greeks from the east such as Xanthippus and Alexon—Carthage was a state of a similar sort to their own, while the Italians (even the Romans, for all their protestations) were not.

The most serious aspect of the defeat from Carthage's point of view was the fact that in spite of her centuries-long tradition of sea power, her fleet had won only a single major victory over the Romans. This was not due entirely to the '*corvus*', which seems to have disappeared after Ecnomus; but the Romans continued to concentrate on boarding tactics, and the Carthaginians never found an effective answer to this. The fact is that the heavy galleys (quadriremes and quinqueremes) were unwieldy and slow, making five miles an hour at the most, and made experience of sea warfare of little value. The Italians learned to handle the ships well, and the great losses were due to the commanders' general ignorance of weather and sea conditions, not to the inability of their crews. The resources of the Romans in manpower also told in the long run, as their persistence in the face of the terrible losses shows.

The defeat at sea had a profound effect on the military thinking of the best minds in Carthage, as will be shown. It came to be argued that Carthage had as good a chance on land as on sea, and that in any case the dogged resistance of the Romans showed that in a future war the aim must be to destroy her in Italy itself.

8

Hannibal[1]

THE long war with Rome was no sooner over than another disaster fell on Carthage; this was the revolt of the mercenaries and Numidians generally called the Mercenary War. It is described in detail by Polybius and Diodorus Siculus, who both used a monograph on the subject favourable to the most important Carthaginian general involved,[2] Hamilcar Barca. For Polybius it was of interest as being a classic example of a 'truceless war', that is one in which all the normal usages of war were forgotten and which continued until the total destruction of one side. His account justifies his claim that in inhuman cruelty it far excelled all other conflicts he knew of. It forms the basis for Flaubert's *Salammbô*, a sinister masterpiece of imagination not to be compared with more pedestrian works of historical fiction far better briefed on the archaeological and religious backgrounds.

When the negotiations with Rome had been completed, Hamilcar Barca transferred his troops from Eryx to Lilybaeum and handed them over to the garrison commander Gisgo; now that Sicily was being given up, his command was due to end, but his rapid recall was perhaps a concession to Rome, of whom he had been so vigorous an enemy.

Gisgo sent the mercenaries in batches to Carthage, where they were to be paid the arrears due to them, and discharged. The authorities, however, kept them waiting about, in the hope that they would be content with less than the full amount in their impatience to get home. As more and more arrived and began to create disturbances, they were sent to Sicca, over a hundred miles south-west of Carthage, for a further period of waiting. They were given a gold piece per man on account, and were obliged to take their families and baggage with them, though these had normally been allowed to remain at Carthage. The mercenaries recalled the lavish promises made to them at critical times in Sicily, and so far from abating their demands, increased them.

The man now in the ascendant at Carthage was Hanno, the long-standing opponent of Hamilcar Barca; he had no intention of redeeming the promises of his rival, and tried in person to persuade the mercenaries to accept the authorities' offer. He made little impression upon them, partly because many cannot have understood him; although more than half were Libyans who doubtless had some knowledge of Punic, there were Iberians, Celts, Ligurians, Balearic islanders, and half-breed Greeks. They would have listened more willingly to a general who had served in Sicily, and the Libyan element was particularly hostile because Hanno had been notorious for his rigorous exaction of taxes from their people during the war. It seems that Carthage had substituted a payment in silver or foodstuffs for the earlier compulsory service of the Libyans, who at this date certainly appear as mercenaries, but that this was regarded as oppressive rather than generous. In a mutinous and threatening frame of mind, the whole force left Sicca and camped outside Tunis.

The Carthaginian government was terrorized by this move into agreeing to their demands and to some further ones which were added; Gisgo was despatched with the money, which was paid to the mercenaries by nations, though there was a delay in the payment for horses lost in the war—an outrageous demand by the soldiers, since the horses were provided by Carthage—and for rations in kind not received.

A prominent member of the more mutinous section, an escaped slave of Oscan origin named Spendius, continued to agitate against the Carthaginians, and he was supported by a Libyan soldier called Matho. They claimed that after paying off and sending home the soldiers of other nations the Carthaginians intended to wreak vengeance on the

Libyans, who would be at their mercy. More riotous meetings were held at which Spendius and Matho were elected generals, those who were lukewarm stoned to death, and Gisgo and his entourage arrested. This was the signal for open conflict, and when Matho sent messengers to rouse the Libyan communities there was an enthusiastic response. Some 20,000 volunteers joined the mercenaries, and sufficient supplies of silver and food were sent to support a long war. Spendius undertook the siege of Utica, Matho that of Hippo Acra, while the Carthaginians themselves were kept within their walls by a force left at Tunis.

In this crisis, Hanno was appointed to the generalship, and made good progress during the winter in equipping ships and in arming and training fresh mercenaries and citizen troops. In the spring of 240 he led a force of 15,000 men and 100 elephants to Utica, but failed to relieve it, after which Hamilcar Barca was recalled to power to bring his experience to bear. He was given 10,000 men, mostly cavalry, and seventy elephants, and met Spendius at the only bridge over the River Bagradas. Spendius lost 6,000 dead and 2,000 prisoners, out of 15,000, but was able to prevent Hamilcar in his turn from relieving Utica. Later he followed him in the direction of Hippo Acra, avoiding the plains, in which the superiority of Hamilcar's cavalry was manifest. After receiving reinforcements, however, he offered battled again; in this engagement Hamilcar was again successful, largely through the assistance of a Numidian chieftain, Navaras, who brought over 2,000 of his tribe, and was then betrothed to Hamilcar's daughter as a reward. The prisoners were treated leniently; they could enrol in his army or go home, on pain of punishment if captured again fighting against Carthage.

Matho and Spendius, and another leading mercenary, a Gallic chief named Antaritus, were alarmed that this treatment would weaken the solidarity of their men, and sought to involve them all in a crime which would make any hope of pardon by Carthage impossible. They alleged that Hamilcar's leniency was a trick to get everyone into his power and then punish them all. Antaritus, who spoke Punic, demanded that only those who were most violently hostile to the Carthaginians should be regarded as trustworthy. He proposed that all Carthaginian prisoners should be tortured and killed, and after a few who had opposed this had been stoned to death, Gisgo and 700 prisoners had their hands cut off and legs broken, and were mutilated and thrown alive into a trench. The soldiers then bound themselves by an oath to treat future prisoners and ambassadors in the same way.

Hamilcar's reaction was to throw his prisoners to the elephants to be trampled to death. At this point the dual command of the Carthaginian troops appeared to be ridiculous, but when Hanno and Hamilcar met they again quarrelled and were incapable of carrying out decisive action. The senate then decided to entrust one of the two with the supreme command, and left the choice to the army. The result was a vote in favour of Hamilcar.

This was the turning-point in the war, in spite of the loss of a fleet bringing supplies from Emporia, and the surrender of Utica and Hippo to the rebels. Spendius and Matho proceeded to invest Carthage from the land, but the city was able to import its requirements from Italy; meanwhile Hamilcar and Navaras scoured the interior and gradually reduced the besiegers to such a state that they had to desist. Spendius resorted to his former tactics of avoiding battle on low ground and trying to outmanoeuvre Hamilcar in hilly territory, but was no match for the experienced general. He was finally besieged in a position in which he could not risk a battle; the mercenaries were reduced to cannibalism eating first the prisoners and then the slaves.

According to Polybius, ten leaders, including Spendius, realizing they were in danger because of their men's extremity, went to Hamilcar to discuss terms. They agreed that he should choose any ten men as prisoners and let the rest go; and Hamilcar at once chose the ten envoys. The Libyans thought there had been treachery when they heard of the leaders' arrest, and rushed to arms, but Hamilcar surrounded them, and the entire force, now leaderless, was wiped out. It would seem likely that sharp practice by Hamilcar at the expense of the Libyans has been glossed over in Polybius' pro-Barcid source.

Hamilcar then proceeded to invest the surviving mercenaries at Tunis; Spendius and the other prisoners were crucified in full view of their former colleagues, but this was soon avenged when Matho captured Hamilcar's second in command and crucified him in the same place. Hanno's stock rose at this setback to his rival, and after a public reconciliation arranged by the senate, he was again associated in the command. The end came when Matho, after being forced out of Tunis, was defeated near Leptis (Minor). Utica and Hippo Acra, which after the surrender to the rebels had been loyal to their cause, held out for some time and were apparently not treated with excessive severity when they finally submitted.

The war ended in 237, and the Carthaginian conduct, however much it was provoked by the initial decision of the mercenaries, was added to other incidents in their history to make up the traditional Roman picture of them as a people particularly prone to cruelty. Although

we do not hear of the participation of slaves, the enthusiastic participation of the Libyans, whose position was obviously very depressed,
gave the war the appearance of a social conflict such as became not
infrequent in the Hellenistic world in the next century. The rebels were
better organized than the account of Polybius implies, as is shown by
their coinage; they used Carthaginian coins at first but soon struck
their own. Many of them show the word LIBYON , 'of the Libyans',
in Greek, which indicates the number of Greek or Italiot mercenaries.
But it is significant that the name appears at all; Carthage herself never
put her own name on her coinage in Africa. The ethnic nature of the
revolt was thus emphasized.[3]

This disaster was accompanied by an act of high-handed aggression
by the Romans. At an early stage in the revolt, the mercenaries who
formed the garrison of Sardinia were infected with the mutinous spirit,
killing their Carthaginian commander. When a fresh force was sent,
it went over to the mutineers, and most of the Carthaginians on the
island were massacred. After it appeared that the rebel cause in Africa
was in decline, the Sardinian group appealed to Rome to take over the
island. This appeal was rejected; for one thing, to accept it would have
been a breach of the late peace treaty, but more important was the
implacable opposition the Romans always showed to movements of
popular unrest and anarchy. The senate's sympathy with its opposite
numbers in Carthage was shown in another way: Carthage had arrested
500 Italian merchants who had been supplying the rebels; they were
released on Roman representations, but at the same time Rome sent
back all Carthaginian prisoners who had not been ransomed, forbade
Italians to supply the rebels, and rejected an offer by Utica to put
herself under Roman protection.

This correct attitude makes it all the more extraordinary that within
two years at the most there was a complete reversal of policy. The
mercenaries, now under heavy pressure from native Sardinians, again
appealed to Rome, and this time an expedition was sent to take over
(238–237). On hearing this, Carthage informed Rome that Sardinia
was still regarded as Carthaginian territory and it was intended to recover it. The Romans called the preparations which Carthage was
making a hostile act, and sent an ultimatum demanding the surrender
of all rights to Sardinia and an indemnity of 1,200 talents. To avoid
war, Carthage accepted these demands, which were incorporated in
the treaty of 241. Polybius, in one of the few places in which he ever
criticized Rome, called this an act without reasonable pretext and contrary to all justice; later Roman efforts to justify their action were

tendentious in the extreme.[4] We may surmise that since the end of the Punic War opinion had been growing that Rome had got very little out of all her efforts; Sardinia could have been acquired in 241, but the compulsive desire for peace had prevented any demand which might have stimulated further Carthaginian resistance. Now the chance to make the Tyrrhenian Sea exclusively Roman had come and was too good to be missed, whatever the rights of the case; no doubt arguments based on the proximity of the island to Rome figured largely.

The seizure of Sardinia and the outrageous claim for an indemnity nipped in the bud the possibilities of a reconciliation between the powers, which certainly existed when Rome was acting correctly, and stifled any opposition to a great venture which was begun immediately after by Hamilcar Barca, the creation of an empire in Spain. The motives for this policy, which later appeared to lead directly to the second war with Rome, were discussed by ancient historians.

Polybius[5] says clearly that Hamilcar was determined from the start on a war of revenge against Rome and conquered Spain to get the resources for it. A slightly different view attributed to the Barcid family the ambition of building a 'private empire' in Spain, from which Carthage itself could be effectively dominated.[6] The main Roman tradition followed the views of Carthaginian opponents of the Barcids, who were naturally eager to throw the entire responsibility for another war on the family of Hannibal, and held that the conquest of Spain was undertaken without the consent of the government at Carthage. The last view is certainly wrong, though Hamilcar was opposed by Hanno, who perhaps wished to concentrate on a purely African policy.[7] The unlikelihood of a deep-seated division between a landed interest and wealthy merchants has already been mentioned, though at this date the merchants with interests in the west must have been weakened by the loss of Sicily and Sardinia. On the other hand, they will have looked for new markets, and the rapid success of the policy must soon have won over any waverers. It must be stressed that there is no evidence for the view that any of the Barcids lacked support from the senate as a whole. The hypothetical question might be put whether Hanno's view was not the better one for Carthage. It is perhaps the case that the Numidians and Mauretanians could have been subdued as easily as the Iberians, and that there was less chance of a collision with Rome; but there was no mineral wealth as there was in Spain. Above all, it must now have appeared that the Romans were capable of anything, and that a source of money and men to meet a future threat was essential.

In 237 (after clearing up the remnants of the revolt in Numidia, in
company with Hanno) Hamilcar was designated sole general. His chief
assistant was his son-in-law Hasdrubal, who is outstanding among Carthaginian politicians known to us as being opposed to the aristocracy and
having mass support among the ordinary citizens.[8] It does not appear
that any changes were made in the constitution under his influence,
but no doubt such popular rights as existed were fully exercised. Such
a combination of general and popular leader was a feature of the
Roman republic in its last stage, and there were sufficient parallels with
Greek cities to lend support to the view of the Barcids as having
tyrannical ambitions.

Soon after his appointment, Hamilcar crossed to Gades and began
to restore the position in the limited coastal area which Carthage had
previously held. He went on subsequently to a deliberate policy of
conquest in the south and east of the Iberian peninsula. There was much
hard fighting, and victories are known over the Turdetani (the successors of the earlier Tartessians), the Iberians of the east coast, and Celts
in the service of other tribes. The limit of his advance was the town he
founded at Acra Leuce (Alicante), and he no doubt brought under
control the silver mines of the Sierra Morena and those near Cartagena;
only a few years later Hannibal drew 300 talents a year from one mine.
Further, he formed an army of picked men from subjugated and allied
tribes, well paid and loyal to himself personally, to replace the sort of
armies which had lately done so much damage to Carthage.[9]

There was another power in the west with interests in Spain which
had profited from the eclipse of the Carthaginian navy. This was
Massilia, an old friend of Rome owing to their common danger from
the Gauls. On the Massilians' instigation, it appears, Rome sent an embassy to Hamilcar in 231 to ask him his intentions. His reply was that
he was fighting in Spain to obtain the money with which Carthage
could pay off her indemnity to Rome. This was the sort of reply the
Romans could appreciate, and they allowed themselves to believe it.
Two years later he met a heroic death in a retreat from the siege of
Elice (Elche) while saving the lives of his son and staff.

He was succeeded as general by Hasdrubal—his eldest son Hannibal
was still too young to be considered—probably on the nomination of
the Carthaginians serving in the army. Loyal to their government
though the Barcids undoubtedly were, the succession of Hasdrubal to
the command indicated the personal character of their rule in Spain.
This was further emphasized by Hasdrubal. His first wife had died,
and he now married the daughter of an Iberian chieftain; he was

Carthaginian jewellery

Amulets of glass paste

subsequently recognized as their overlord by many Iberian tribes. It was true that the Carthaginian leaders (unlike their Roman counterparts) sometimes married foreigners—as early as the sixth century, the mother of the Hamilcar defeated at Himera was a Syracusan. But evidence of the quasi-monarchical position held by the Barcids in Spain is also provided by the coinage they issued there. The coins are thoroughly Hellenistic in style, and whereas Carthaginian coinage issued in Africa and Sicily used a restricted range of impersonal types referring almost exclusively to Carthage and her protecting deities, Barcid coinage is varied and had explicit references to Hasdrubal and Hannibal; both appear to have served as portraits for representations of Melkart, and the coins are reminiscent of the contemporary issues by the kings of Syracuse and of Syria.[10]

Hasdrubal preferred, or was now able from a position of strength, to use diplomatic rather than military methods to consolidate the Carthaginian position. This did not, however, mean any neglect of the army, which was brought up to a strength of 50,000 infantry, 6,000 cavalry, and 200 elephants. He saw disadvantages in the site of Acra Leuce, and founded a new city which became the capital of Carthaginian Spain. This was the modern Cartagena, which derives its name from the fact that Hasdrubal named it after his own city; to the Romans it was Carthago Nova, New Carthage.

About 226–225 the Romans again became concerned about the position of Spain. At this moment Italy was menaced by an invasion of the Gauls, and the Romans wanted to prevent the Carthaginian Empire in Spain reaching the Pyrenees and Gaul. They obtained an undertaking from Hasdrubal that he would not cross the River Ebro in arms. This was satisfactory for Rome, the more so since it protected Massilia's colonies north of the Ebro. The undertaking was presumably not felt to be limiting by Hasdrubal, as his territory was as yet nowhere near the Ebro, but the question arises whether he received any *quid pro quo*. Our sources say nothing about this, but it is often assumed that Rome recognized the right of Carthage to conquests as far as the Ebro. It is perhaps better to accept the silence of our authorities, and say that Carthaginian rights as far as the Ebro were only admitted by implication. As will be seen, this agreement played a part in the origins of the second Punic War.

After governing Spain for eight years, Hasdrubal was assassinated by a Celt in 221. Hannibal was now about twenty-five years old and had been in Spain ever since his father's crossing to Gades; he was therefore the obvious person to be chosen by the army to succeed.[11]

It need hardly be said that though we know more about him than about any other Carthaginian, there are plenty of difficulties in arriving at a just estimate of his career. He of all men came nearest to destroying Rome, and the tradition, reflecting the fear of the Romans in their worst moments, attributes to him alone the war and its disasters. Like Hasdrubal, he was married to an Iberian, and was fully identified with his family's policy in Spain. His genius being primarily though not exclusively military, he reopened the campaigns which had marked his father's generalship. Within the short space of two years, he had brought under control a large part of central Spain as far as the River Douro; but when he returned to New Carthage for the winter of 220–219 he found waiting for him an embassy from Rome with a grave message concerning the town of Saguntum.[12]

We here approach the question of the responsibility for the war which was soon to break out, the difficulty being not so much to distinguish basic from proximate causes as to distinguish both these from the causes which later Roman tradition alleged when seeking to justify Roman action to a very different and critical public.

Saguntum was a small town on the Mediterranean coast south of the Ebro. At some date, probably in the generalship of Hasdrubal, it became a 'friend' of Rome, that is a state which the Romans felt an obligation to protect even if, as is quite possible, no actual treaty of alliance was signed.[13] About 221, the party in the town favourable to them had to be established by Roman 'mediation', and several of those who supported the Carthaginians were executed. In addition the town became involved in hostilities with a pro-Carthaginian tribe, the Torpoletae. The Saguntines had frequently told the Romans about the growth of Carthaginian power, but nothing had been done, as the senate presumably realized that the Saguntines were exaggerating the threat to themselves. At last, however, it was decided to send a warning to Hannibal not to harm Saguntum, which, it was emphasized, was under Roman protection.[14]

It is not known whether Rome's friendship with Saguntum dated from before or after the Ebro agreement; in either case it introduced an awkward element into the situation, because it was inevitable that the Carthaginians would claim a free hand south of the river even if this was not specified in the agreement; if you agree not to go beyond a point, you presumably expect freedom of action up to it. If it came before the Ebro treaty, Carthage could justifiably consider that it was annulled by the implications of the treaty; if it came after, the Romans could be held guilty of most provocative action.

Hannibal's reply that he considered the Roman intervention at Saguntum in 221 a breach of faith which could not be ignored is perhaps an indication that the former alternative is the more likely, the Romans having correctly observed the implication of the treaty up to that date. He went on to say that it was the Carthaginian practice to aid those who were unjustly treated—i.e. the Torpoletae. However, before taking any action he sent to Carthage for instructions, no doubt making clear his own view, and though his policy was attacked by Hanno he was given a free hand. The Roman embassy went on to deliver their warning at Carthage, where they were presumably told the matter was in Hannibal's hands.[15]

The later Romans naturally sought to portray the attack on Saguntum which Hannibal eventually made to be a breach of treaty, but realized they were on shaky ground. As a result, it was alleged that there was a special clause in the Ebro treaty which guaranteed the independence of Saguntum, or, even more fantastic, that Saguntum lay north of the Ebro! The treaty of 241 was brought into question; the clause guaranteeing the independence of the allies of both sides was held by the Romans to include states which became allies after the signing of the treaty, when in fact the states concerned were those listed in an appendix to the treaty.[16] In point of fact legality was of decreasing importance in determining Roman policy, though it had to be stressed for the record. Saguntum was intended to be a thorn in the side of the Carthaginians if it was left alone; but if Hannibal took up the challenge Rome might back up her warning, for precisely the same reason as she had assisted the Mamertines, namely the obligation to help small states who claimed her friendship, regardless of other considerations.

Legality was on the side of Hannibal, but legal rights are not always asserted. Leaving aside the question of treaty-breaking, the earliest Roman view of Hannibal's motive in going to war was that he shared Hasdrubal's lust for power, the implication being that both favoured a war policy to further their political ambitions.[17] In fact, Hasdrubal was the least warlike of the Barcid family. More deeply rooted was the view that Hamilcar lived only for revenge on Rome, particularly after the seizure of Sardinia, and that he ordered Hannibal when he was only nine years of age to swear never to be a friend of Rome, an oath which dominated Hannibal's thinking. It is certainly not sufficient to say in reply that these are not motives worthy of a statesman such as Hannibal obviously was; it is too favourable a view of a number of statesmen of antiquity, which denies them the prejudices, even the irresponsibilities, of the moderns. Hannibal's oath fits in very well with the sombre fanaticism of Carthaginian religion.[18] But hatred for Rome was not the same as a plan for a war of revenge from the start; what the Barcids did was prepare their city for a war which, following the Roman aggression in the Sardinian affair, they must have considered almost inevitable.

With the picture of Roman policy in the past—expansive, hypocritical, and untrustworthy—which he must have been brought up with, it is easier to see why Hannibal at Saguntum decided 'now' not 'later'. The consequences of a Roman enclave within the limits of the Spanish empire would have been disastrous; the Roman policy of expansion by protecting smaller states would have been applied in the Carthaginian territory, and at any moment some disgruntled tribal chief might turn to the Romans for 'friendship'. Hannibal and his advisers could easily predict the collapse of the still unconsolidated empire they had won, if they gave way to the Roman warning. This fear was justified; Roman policy at this period and in the next century was consistently designed to weaken powerful rivals, and the weakness once induced was only the prelude to subjection. Besides these sensible calculations, we must not forget one last personal aspect. Hannibal was in the prime of young manhood, with a justifiable confidence in himself and a superb military machine built up over the years; such a man will not hesitate and say '. . . if we should fail—'

There was a new generation of Carthaginians who could hope for a reversal of the decision of the first Punic War; twenty-one years had elapsed since the peace of Catulus in 241; almost the same period which separated Hitler's war from the Treaty of Versailles.

So, early in 219 Hannibal advanced to the siege of Saguntum and the Romans were forced to consider whether they should take action.

It is immediately noticeable that they made no effort to help their friend throughout its desperate eight-months-long resistance. It is true that both consuls were absent in Illyria, but this would not have hampered a united senate. The fact is that the warning had been at least partly bluff, and now the bluff had been called there was opposition to war. Those of this opinion were led by a respected senator, Quintus Fabius Maximus, and Rome's uncertain right was certainly emphasized by them. The party in favour of going to war, headed by the Cornelian family, will have argued the traditional Roman policy of helping injured friends and the loss of prestige if this policy was not maintained. The decision for war had been taken when news reached Rome in April or May of 218 that Hannibal had anticipated the result of the debate

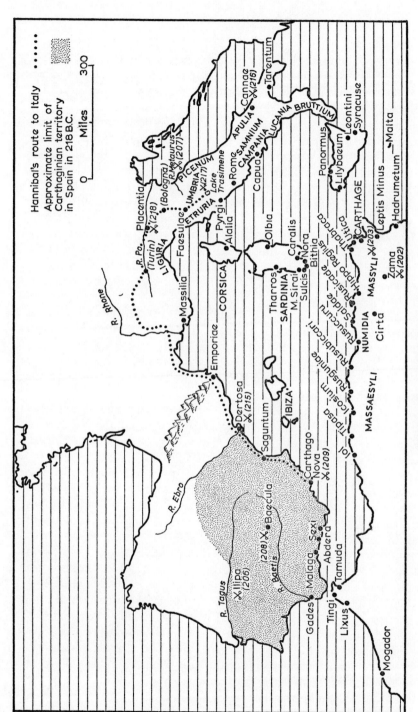

THE WESTERN MEDITERRANEAN

Hannibal's route to Italy ·········

Approximate limit of Carthaginian territory in Spain in 218 B.C.

0   Miles   300

R. Rhone

R. Po
Placentia
(Turin)×(218)
LIGURIA
Faesulae
Bologna)
UMBRIAN
ETRURIA
Pyrgi
Alalia
R. Metaurus ×(207)
PICENUM
Rome
Lake Trasimene ×(217)
SAMNIUM
CAMPANIA
Capua
APULIA
Cannae ×(216)
Tarentum
LUCANIA
BRUTTIUM
Leontini
Syracuse
Lilybaeum
Panormus
Malta
Hadrumetum
Leptis Minus
MASSYLI ×(203)
Zama ×(202)
CARTHAGE
Utica
Thapsca
Hippo Regius
Bithia
Nora
Caralis
Olbia
Tharros
M. Sirai
Sulcis
SARDINIA
CORSICA
Massilia
Emporiae
Rusicade
Saldae
Rusiccari
Icosium
Iomnium
Tipasa
Iol
NUMIDIA
Cirta
MASSAESYLI
Dertosa ×(215)
IBIZA
Saguntum
Carthago Nova ×(209)
R. Ebro
R. Tagus
×Ilipa (206)
Baecula (208)×
R. Baetis
Malaga
Sexi
Abdara
Gades
Tingi
Tamuda
Lixus
Mogador

and crossed the Ebro. This merely gave the embassy sent to Carthage, with an ultimatum to disown Hannibal, an extra argument, and was not the decisive factor. It need hardly be said that the ultimatum was rejected.[19]

The Barcids had a war plan for just such an occasion. It was based on the correct estimate that Rome could only be defeated through the destruction of her armed forces in Italy; no amount of victories on the periphery was a substitute for this. The ill-success of the fleet in the first Punic War, and probably also the excessive strain which maintaining both a huge army and a fleet at once would have imposed on Carthage, also influenced them in their thinking. They accordingly concentrated their efforts on their soldiers, particularly cavalry, at the expense of the fleet, even though this made it necessary to attempt the invasion of Italy by land. Further, the invasion had to be timed to prevent a Roman invasion of Africa, which it was expected would be the first counter-move.

This was why Hannibal was in a hurry in 218, and even then he was delayed by the height of the rivers in spring flood. He left his headquarters with about 40,000 men, and after crossing the Pyrenees and defeating tribes friendly to Massilia, reached the Rhône some distance above its mouth in late August. There he was opposed by a hostile tribe of Gauls, but forced a crossing, probably in the region of Avignon, his chief difficulty being the transport of his elephants on specially constructed rafts. Only three days later one of the consuls, Publius Cornelius Scipio, arrived; by such a narrow margin was a major battle missed, before Hannibal ever got to the Alps.

It was only at this point that Scipio realized that Hannibal was making for Italy, not Massilia as had been supposed. He then made a very important decision, sending his brother Cnaeus with two legions to Spain, while he himself returned to Italy. There was an obvious risk in this, but he had grasped the fact that there was a possibility of cutting Hannibal off from Spain. It is true that these legions were soon to be desperately needed in Italy, but Scipio could not foresee the military genius of Hannibal and the defeats he would inflict on Rome.

Hannibal's crossing of the Alps was an object of admiration in antiquity, though as Polybius observed it had frequently been done by Gallic tribes. The point was that it was the first crossing by the army of a civilized power. The pass he used cannot be identified with certainty; he entered the mountains up the valley of the Isère and descended into Italy not far from Turin, so the Mt Genèvre is a possibility. At the summit of the pass he was held up by the first snows of winter, which puts the date in late September, and his troops, used to a far warmer climate, suffered greatly. Many horses and almost all the elephants died, and when after eighteen days he descended into Italy, his army numbered no more than 20,000 foot and 6,000 horse. However, only one Gallic tribe in the north of Italy, the Taurini, failed to welcome him and within a short space of time he had 14,000 fresh volunteers.

After resting his men, Hannibal advanced eastwards along the Po valley towards Placentia, where Scipio was waiting with 20,000 men. The Roman was worsted in a cavalry engagement, after which he refused battle until the arrival of his colleague Sempronius, whose projected invasion of Africa had been cancelled, as Hannibal had hoped it would be, on the news of the arrival of the Carthaginians in Italy. Sempronius was in favour of an attack on Hannibal as soon as possible, since his strength was increasing every day, but Scipio advised further delay, on the grounds that Hannibal's Gallic support would melt away in a winter of inactivity.

Sempronius' view won the day, as Scipio was incapacitated owing to a wound, but Hannibal's tactical handling of the situation forced him into attacking across the River Trebia in the worst possible conditions in the cold of a December morning. His cavalry broke the Roman wings and destroyed the rear formation, and only the Roman centre got through and returned to Placentia. About two-thirds of the Roman force was destroyed, while Hannibal's own losses were mostly Gauls. He kept his Roman prisoners under harsh conditions, but released all the Italians without ransom, saying that if they were wise they would join him, since his first aim was to liberate the Italians and restore the cities and lands of which they had been deprived by the Romans. By this diplomatic move Hannibal hoped to disrupt Rome's Italian confederacy, which provided about half the strength of the Roman army, and in fact the whole issue in Italy really hung on the attitude of the Italians to the invasion.

Hannibal wintered at Bononia, while Rome recruited fresh armies, and in the spring he crossed the Apennines by the pass of Collina and the middle reaches of the Arno, where he lost the sight of an eye from a chill taken crossing a stretch of marshes. After resting at Faesulum, he tried to entice the new consul Flaminius to fight by plundering the region of Arretium where he was stationed. The consul was outnumbered, and declined; he proceeded to dog the Carthaginian's footsteps. Hannibal knew that Flaminius was a man of only moderate military ability, who had been elected against fierce aristocratic opposition because of his great popularity amongst the mass of the Romans, and set a trap for him on the northern shore of Lake Trasimene. Here the road ran through a narrow defile between the shore of the lake and some hills, and Hannibal stationed his men on the latter. Flaminius' army of 25,000 entered the defile without detecting the presence of the Carthaginians, and was completely trapped: 15,000 were killed and most of the rest taken. Again the Italians were sent home, to spread the propaganda version of Hannibal's invasion. He then marched to Picenum on the Adriatic, and south to Apulia; in all these parts was fertile land which his troops could plunder at will, and on Roman territory at least he acted with great ruthlessness, but there was still no sign of a general movement of revolt against Rome.

Hannibal now had to face a different Roman tactic, introduced by the elderly Quintus Fabius Maximus. Fabius had been appointed 'dictator', the Latin designation of an office of supreme power held only for six months, which was resorted to in times of crisis. He raised two new legions to which were joined those of Flaminius' colleague Servilius; with this force he watched Hannibal's activity but refused battle, in the hope that sooner or later Hannibal would be forced to fight in a disadvantageous tactical position. The danger in this was that the allies might begin to doubt Rome's invincibility, particularly when Hannibal marched east across the Apennines and devastated yet another fertile region of Italy, Campania. However, he failed to take any fortified town and returned to Apulia for the winter.

At the crossing of the Volturnus near Teanum, Fabius saw a good position to force a battle, but Hannibal avoided it by one of his most remarkable stratagems. One night a herd of bullocks with lighted faggots tied to their horns was driven towards Fabius' camp; the posts on the pass by which Hannibal had to proceed were confused by what was happening and left to engage the small force accompanying the decoy, while Fabius himself stood fast in camp, unwilling to risk a night battle. In the confusion Hannibal's main force with all its booty crossed the Volturnus unopposed.

During the winter Fabius' term came to an end, and popular opinion at Rome became very dissatisfied with the lack of resistance to Hannibal's devastations; one of the two consuls for 216, Caius Terentius Varro, was elected against the opposition of the aristocracy. The senate gave way to popular pressure, and the consuls were given permission to engage Hannibal if they wished. Hannibal, who no doubt knew of the turn of opinion in Rome, seized the Roman base of Cannae on the River Aufidus, in an area of flat country entirely suitable for his cavalry. His army now amounted to 40,000 infantry and about 10,000 cavalry,

and since we do not hear of any reinforcements reaching him from
Africa, some half must have been Gauls. The new consuls went out in
late summer with the traditional two legions each, making a force
which was about equal to Hannibal's in infantry but most inferior in
cavalry.

It is unfortunate that no certainty can be reached about the site of
the battle that took place near Cannae early in August; one of the
paradoxes of Roman historical writing is its indifference to the details
and technicalities of war, in spite of the recognition by all authors that
Rome's distinguishing feature was her military prowess. The battle
was probably fought on the south bank of the river.

Hannibal knew the strength of the massive thrust of the Roman
legions, and reckoned to counteract it by arranging his line in crescent
shape; the front was of Gallic and Spanish infantry, and on either side
but to the rear were his African troops. Each flank was extended by the
numerous cavalry contingents. The aim was for the cavalry to get
round to the rear of the Roman line while it was pressing back the
centre; it would then be encircled as the African troops attacked the
Roman flanks. The two essential points were the succes of the Gallic
and Spanish cavalry, and the ability of the infantry of the same peoples
to withstand the shock of the Roman charge and retreat without breaking. Hannibal could rightly have more confidence in the success of the
cavalry; to do everything to hold his centre together, Hannibal
stationed himself and his younger brother Mago in this sector.

The plan was as successful as he could have hoped, the Romans being
entirely surrounded and cut to pieces. They lost 25,000 killed and
10,000 captured; only the consul Varro escaped, with perhaps 15,000.
Hannibal lost only 5,700 of whom 4,000 were Gauls. It is probable
that Hannibal deliberately risked his Gallic allies in places where
casualties were likely to be heaviest, in order to preserve the Africans
and Spaniards who were his élite troops, but it is remarkable that
under Hannibal's leadership the Gauls showed qualities of steadiness
under pressure which they very rarely did when fighting in their native
fashion.

Cannae was Rome's greatest military disaster, and Hannibal could
now at last hope for some defections in Italy. He is said to have been
urged by one of his officers to march on Rome at once, but his inability
later to capture many small places shows that he was quite correct in
ignoring such advice. He was in fact joined by many of the Samnite
tribes, who had in earlier days been the most vigorous opponents of
Rome, by the Lucanians and Bruttians, and by some Apulian cities

such as Arpi. Most important of all, Capua deserted Rome, on the arrival of Hannibal in Campania after the battle. Capua was the most important city in Italy next to Rome, whom she actually surpassed in wealth and culture owing to her contact with the Greek world. Unlike many of the communities which joined Hannibal, Capua had Roman citizenship without the vote, but the burden of military service and resentment at her lower status had turned the people hostile to Rome; the latter's policy here and elsewhere had supported and been supported by the local aristocracy, so the defection to Hannibal was marked by a social revolution.

But, with the exception of a few smaller Campanian towns, this was the limit of the movement in favour of Hannibal for the moment. The heart of Rome's confederation, Latins, Umbrians, Sabines, and Picentines remained loyal, and Hannibal must have realized now if not before the formidable nature of his task; it was evidently much easier to defeat Rome in the field than to destroy her political domination. It is true that Roman propaganda enthusiastically dilated upon the barbarous nature of the invaders, who, it was said, could hardly be considered human beings at all, but this would have had little effect if it had fallen on unwilling ears. Two positive feelings worked in favour of Rome; the first was a recognition of the generally liberal treatment her allies had received, the second a sense that Rome had been a worthy leader of the Italian peoples against the ferocious attacks of the Gauls in the previous generations—and these Gauls were now allies of Hannibal.

Yet if at this distance we can see that even on the morrow of Cannae there were limitations to Hannibal's success (and more will be mentioned), it can hardly have appeared so at Rome. To survive the defeat and the desertions of the allies, there was needed a common will among the citizens and clear thinking in the leadership. At first there was an outburst of popular superstition not unlike that which had occurred at Carthage after the victories of Agathocles: it was discovered that two of the Vestal Virgins were no longer such, and one was buried alive, the usual punishment for a Vestal's breach of her vows; the other committed suicide. The Sacred Books, which were supposed to contain divine instructions on how to act in a crisis, were consulted, and an embassy sent to discover the views of the oracle at Delphi; finally the populace demanded human sacrifice, and two Gauls and two Greeks were buried alive. After the appeasement of this outbreak, however, that fierce determination which had marked the Romans in the worst days of the first Punic War returned. As for the direction of the war, the voters from now on regularly chose candidates who had the support of the senate, since two of the consuls who had been chosen against its wishes were at least partly responsible for the defeats at Trasimene and Cannae. Tremendous efforts were demanded of themselves and the allies; the war-tax was doubled in 215, by 212 there were twenty-five legions in the field, and all the while a fleet of 200 ships with 50,000 rowers was kept in being.

The strategy adopted by the senate was that of Fabius Maximus; avoid battle in the open and wear Hannibal down by a process of exhaustion. With the manpower available, it was possible for one army to dog the Carthaginian wherever he went, while others attacked those of his allies he could not protect or prevented the defection of further members of the confederacy. Hannibal essentially had no answer to this except a ruthless devastation of Italian territory in an effort to break the will of Rome and her allies (and to supply his own troops); so severe was the destruction that its effect on parts of Italy was permanent. Furthermore, the crucial decision was taken not to withdraw the Scipios from Spain, and consequently Carthaginian reinforcements had to be diverted there from Italy.

Hannibal's problem in fact was one of manpower. As far as we know the agreements his Italian friends made with him, it is clear that he was bound by his own propaganda to treat them even more generously than Rome had done, particularly as regards military service. In the treaty with Capua, full autonomy was guaranteed and none of its people could be forced to undertake military or other service. Thus while he could use these allies to obtain strongpoints or winter quarters, he could get only voluntary help, and in fact what he got was negligible: his allies were willing enough to throw off Rome's rule, but not to do anything to protect their further independence. This fact was a very critical one for Hannibal, because things were not going well in Spain, from which he had expected to receive continual reinforcements. It will be recalled that Cnaeus Scipio had been sent on there by his brother when Hannibal's intention to invade Italy became clear.

In the family of the Scipios we have the Roman counterpart of the Barcids, both in talent and in appreciation of the importance of Spain. From 218 to 206 one or more members of the family upheld the Roman cause in Spain, with the initial aim of preventing Hannibal from getting reinforcements, but later also with the intention of driving the Carthaginians from it entirely and so preventing a recurrence of the Carthaginian threat. In the first year's operations, Scipio had landed at Emporiae (Ampurias) and then moved to Tarraco, defeating the general Hanno, whom Hannibal had left behind to complete the conquest of the area north of the Ebro. In 217, Hasdrubal Barca, a brother of Hannibal, advanced with a fleet and army to the Ebro from the base at Cartagena. Scipio, though he only had thirty-five ships against Hasdrubal's forty, ordered an immediate attack off the mouth of the Ebro. The Carthaginians, whose confidence in their fleet was small, chose a position near the shore to which they might escape if worsted, and the greater part of the fleet was destroyed, the Romans being greatly helped by the seamanship of their allies from Massilia. This gave the Romans command of the sea on the Spanish coast, and Cnaeus Scipio, now reinforced by his brother Publius and fresh troops, was able to cross the Ebro.

Most of the rest of this year and 216 were spent in consolidating the position in northern Spain and in undermining the loyalty of the tribes south of the river. Hasdrubal received reinforcements from Carthage and had to deal with revolts of tribes as far south as the mouth of the Guadalquivir, and was quite unable to send any reinforcements to Italy. In 215, reinforced again from Carthage, he made another effort to repel the invasion of Spain; the two armies, each of about 25,000 men, met opposite Dertosa (Tortosa) on the south bank of the Ebro. Hasdrubal tried the plan which had been so successfully used by his brother at Cannae, but on this occasion his Spanish troops in the centre broke and his army was routed, with heavy losses to the best African troops. This was a serious blow to Carthage; had the battle been won, Hasdrubal could have gone on to Italy if required, while in the event reinforcements which it had been planned to send to Hannibal by sea had to be diverted to Spain to prevent any further losses.

At the moment, however, Hannibal was not insistent on getting reinforcements; an attack was even launched on Sardinia, but before the army sent there could join the disaffected islanders the latter were defeated, after which the Carthaginians in their turn were driven from the island. Meanwhile Hannibal, with that farseeing statesmanship which marked him out from most of his fellow countrymen, was seeking to complete the encirclement of Rome by an alliance with Philip V of Macedon. This energetic and unscrupulous ruler had a grievance against the Romans for their intervention in Illyria a few years before to suppress piracy in the Adriatic.

The alliance provided that the two powers were to wage war against Rome together and remain allies afterwards; in any peace with Rome, the latter was to give up her possessions in the eastern Adriatic. There was a provision by which Philip agreed to send troops to Italy if Hannibal requested it. In point of fact it transpired that the two sides were more united in their opposition to Rome than in anything else. Hannibal can never have wanted to see Macedonian troops in Italy, which would almost certainly have led to Philip's intervening in the Greek states; nor for that matter can Philip have been particularly keen to see a total Carthaginian victory in the west. The Romans learnt of the alliance when they captured Philip's representatives, and sent a fleet and a small army to Greece to build a coalition of anti-Macedonian states, of which there were a number. Desultory warfare continued against Macedonia until 205, with little or no effect on the ultimate result of the struggle with Carthage. The latter entirely failed to make use of her ally; Philip could make no headway against the coalition without a fleet, and he waited in vain for Carthaginian help in this sphere. So the retreat from the sea, which had already cost so much in Spain, had further serious results.

In this treaty with Philip the survival of Rome in the event of a Carthaginian victory is envisaged, and this brings us to the question of Hannibal's war aims at this date. Many ancient writers attributed to Hannibal the intention of destroying Rome entirely, and they have some modern followers. The treaty cannot be taken as conclusive evidence to the contrary, because, as has been said, a total victory for Carthage would not have been altogether pleasing to Philip, and Hannibal's diplomacy required that notice be taken of this feeling; it is, however, probable that Hannibal did not think in terms of doing to Rome what the Romans later did to Carthage—an action about which the Romans' bad conscience helped to further the notion of Hannibal's destructive intentions—but of reducing her will to continue the fight and forcing her to make peace by destroying the confederacy. But he must have realized that this was the same in the long run as destroying Rome; she could not survive as an independent state among Gauls, Samnites, Campanians, Lucanians, and others who would regain their independence; one or other of them would see to it that their former ruler never revived. Hannibal is actually recorded as having held out to Capua the prospect of becoming the leading state in Italy.

The situation would have been in some ways similar to that which actually occurred in Africa after the defeat of Carthage; she was reduced to impotence, and her destruction by Rome in 146 only anticipated her absorption into the Numidian kingdom. But while a Carthaginian victory would have brought her supremacy in the western Mediterranean, it is clear that it would not have brought about a similar imperial result as that which followed the Roman. Carthage could never have controlled Italy in the same way as Rome had done, but her victory would have given her security in Africa and Spain and vast wealth to be acquired from the extension of her trading monopolies to the whole of the western Mediterranean.

At the same time that Hannibal was making the alliance with Philip, a circumstance favourable to him occurred in Sicily. The elderly King Hiero died, after almost fifty years of faithful friendship with Rome during which Syracuse had enjoyed great prosperity. But there was a party in the city which was favourable to Carthage from resentment at the dominance of Rome in Sicily. This party had actually won the secret support of Hiero's son and heir, when he predeceased his father by a few months. The final successor was Hiero's grandson Hieronymus, an arrogant youth of fifteen who was soon won over by the leaders of the Carthaginian party, and Hannibal sent two agents of mixed Carthaginian and Greek blood to arrange an alliance.

However, in 214, when Hieronymus was about to begin the attack on towns garrisoned by the Romans, he was assassinated; a burst of anti-monarchial feeling united the masses of the people and those who were opposed to the friends of Carthage, and after the massacre of the rest of the royal house, envoys were sent to arrange a new treaty with Rome. A rapid revulsion of feeling then occurred, and it soon appeared that the majority were really in favour of the Carthaginians though not necessarily for war with Rome; Hannibal's two agents, Hippocrates and Epicydes, were elected generals and went to the help of Leontini, which feared a Roman attack. At this point the consul Marcellus warned the Syracusans that the peace had been broken, and demanded that Hippocrates and Epicydes be sent away from Sicily. The two, perhaps doubtful of the support they might expect, threw themselves into Leontini. When in the spring of 213 it was taken by assault, they escaped and opportunely met a Syracusan force marching to its aid. They inflamed the soldiers with an account of the Roman atrocities, which included the scourging and beheading of 2,000 Carthaginian sympathizers. The Syracusans at once returned to do the same to the pro-Roman party in their city and prepare for a defence.

It was fortunate for Rome that the revolt in Sicily occurred some time after the initial shock of Cannae, and when it had become possible to bring the forces in Sicily up to a strength of four legions. The siege of Syracuse was chiefly notable for the machines devised by the mathematician and engineer Archimedes, which greatly assisted the defenders. Carthage made great efforts to assist their new allies, and an army of 25,000 foot-soldiers was put into the island and took Agrigentum, but the fleet of fifty ships was outnumbered by the Romans by two to one and was unable to relieve Syracuse itself. The rest of the year passed with Himilco, the Carthaginian general, unable to attack Marcellus' superior force outside Syracuse; and in 212 the latter succeeded where so many Carthaginians had failed. He got possession of the Epipolae and the outlying suburbs at a moment when the garrison's watchfulness was relaxed, and pressed the siege of the rest of the city. However, determined resistance was continued, and a full assault could not be made while the Carthaginian army was only a few miles away. Twice substantial fleets slipped into the Great Harbour with help for the defenders.

The situation was changed by an epidemic which swept through the Carthaginian camp, just as it had done on previous occasions when they were attacking Syracuse; the Romans also suffered, but not so severely, because of their greater attention to hygiene. The fall of Syracuse in the spring of 211 was made certain by the decline in the morale of the Carthaginian fleet; 130 ships were sent with a large supply convoy, but when the Romans, who only had a hundred, came out to fight, the admiral ordered the convoy back to Africa and made for Tarentum with the warships, leaving Syracuse to its fate. This was the largest effort at sea made by Carthage, and its ignominious failure underlines the weakness they now had in this field. Syracuse, the richest and most civilized city the Romans had yet taken, was sacked: in spite of widespread destruction, the loot in the form of artistic treasures brought back to Rome was so enormous that it was a major factor in the Hellenization of Roman taste.

The year 211 had two other significant events. For five years the 'Fabian' policy had been pursued in Italy, and in spite of the defection to Hannibal of most of the Italiots in 213, his position had not improved and he was more or less confined to south Italy. Whenever he went beyond the area solidly held, he found it difficult to feed his troops, as the Romans continually scoured the countryside destroying crops or bringing them within the walls of fortified cities.

In 212 the siege of Capua was undertaken by no less than six legions, who were protected by a line of entrenchments from a relieving attack by Hannibal. The strength of defensive works of this period, already demonstrated at Syracuse, was shown again at Capua, since the Romans, in spite of their numbers, simply waited until the city was obliged to surrender in 211 from lack of food. Hannibal tried to force them to divert some forces by marching up to the walls of Rome, which had not been visited by an attack for nearly two centuries; but this failed, as the senate refused to be panicked, knowing that the defences were far too strong to be breached by a force the size of Hannibal's without siege engines.

However, there was some compensation for the loss of Syracuse and Capua in a victory in Spain. The Scipio brothers had not advanced far after the battle near Dertosa in 215; their army was small, and it appeared more desirable to win over Spanish tribes by diplomacy than by force. In 212, after the town of Saguntum had been captured, it seemed possible to advance down the coast road from this new base, and Publius Scipio was even able to winter at Castulo, on the upper reaches of the Baetis. In 211, however, considerable Carthaginian reinforcements were sent to Spain, after the suppression of the revolt of a Numidian chief named Syphax. Hannibal's two brothers, Mago and Hasdrubal, commanded divisions of the army, and there was a third under another Hasdrubal, son of Gisgo, who had been in Spain since 214, when Hasdrubal Barca had been brought back to Africa to deal with Syphax. The two Scipios were operating separately, and cut off from each other, deserted by most of their new Spanish allies on the approach of a Carthaginian army, they were both defeated and killed, Publius by Hasdrubal son of Gisgo, Cnaeus by the combined Carthaginian forces. Rome now lost all that had been gained south of the Ebro, and even that line was held with difficulty; what saved the position was the fact that the Carthaginian generals neglected to co-operate with each other and so lost their chance of driving the Romans completely out of Spain.

Both sides were now suffering from war-weariness, and operations were limited for a time. It was found possible at Rome to reduce the number of legions in 210, but as a result of the decreasing pressure twelve out of the thirty Latin colonies refused to send their contingents to the army. This was not so serious as defection to Hannibal, but if the feeling had spread would have had disastrous results on the Roman position. What was needed was a series of victories which would give some prospect of an end to the war in Italy; no doubt the Roman will was as strong as Hannibal's, but this was not the case with the allies as the destruction went on year after year with increasing ruthlessness by both sides.

It was at this point that there came into prominence Publius Cornelius Scipio, later surnamed Africanus, the son of the Publius Scipio who had been killed in Spain.[20] He was only twenty-five years of age— almost the same age as Hannibal had been when he succeeded to the

Cuirass of Campanian provenance, third century

Sanctuary at Cappidazzu, Motya

command in Spain, and too young under Roman constitutional practice to hold a command; however, his qualities of leadership were widely known, and popular enthusiasm combined with the political influence of the family, of which he was now the head, to force his dispatch with a new army to Spain late in 210. Scipio was outstanding among Roman generals, who (with the other notable exception of Caesar) were content to work within the traditional framework of an admittedly successful military tradition. His genius was marked by the intense preparation which he put into every operation and the enthusiasm with which he inspired his officers and men; he was able to impart this because of his own self-confidence, which was derived from a sense of direct communion with the gods in frequent prayers. Such a combination of the practical and the religious is rare enough, and was unique among Roman generals (though not in military history in general).

On his arrival in Spain he learnt that the Carthaginian army was divided. Mago was near Gibraltar, Hasdrubal Barca in central Spain, and the other Hasdrubal near the mouth of the Tagus. This dispersion was due to more than differences among the commanders; Carthaginian power had to be consolidated again if possible, and Hasdrubal Barca was enlisting picked Celtiberians to take to Italy. This left Carthago Nova with only its garrison, but it can hardly have been expected that a Roman general would make such a hazardous move as an attack on this powerful fortress several hundred miles from the Roman base. This, however, was what Scipio did. By forced marches from the Ebro, he arrived at the fortress before the Carthaginians moved, and took it by storm on the second day. Carthage was thus deprived of half her Spanish silver mines and an immense quantity of treasure, arms, and the hostages needed to keep the fickle tribes loyal, while Scipio now had a secure base from which to attack the rest of southern Spain. Scipio's liberal treatment of the citizens contrasts with that of Marcellus at Syracuse; they were allowed their freedom, and even the slaves in the arsenal and docks were promised liberation at the end of the war if they worked hard; others were used as rowers on captured ships, with which Scipio doubled his fleet.

None of the Carthaginian commanders made any move during the year. The explanation is at least in part that the liberal attitude of Scipio to the hostages, who were sent home, began to affect the loyalty of many tribes to the Barcids; it must be stressed that Barcid rule in Spain was largely a personal one backed up by force and had no deep roots. Hence the presence of divisions of the army in various parts of Spain continued to be necessary; further, the demands made on the tribes

14

continued to be harsh and overbearing, and contrasted unfavourably with Scipio's generosity, so there were continued desertions. There is also evidence that the commanders were still at loggerheads. Consequently, when Scipio advanced towards the Baetis valley in 208, Hasdrubal Barca had to decide whether to oppose him with inferior forces or make for Italy straight away. He courageously chose the former alternative, though taking up a position which allowed him the chance of retreat if he were defeated.

The battle took place near Baecula, and as soon as Hasdrubal saw that he was being outflanked by the more numerous Roman army he disengaged. His losses amounted to about a third of his 25,000 men, but with the rest he set out on the long march to Italy, crossing the Pyrenees on the Atlantic side to avoid the tribes friendly to Rome on the Mediterranean. This exploit, though less famous than that of Hannibal, was at least as great an achievement. Scipio was forced to let him go, since pursuit would have involved great difficulties of supply, nor could he leave Spain with a substantial Carthaginian force still in it, even if his instructions had permitted this.

For the rest of this year and the next, Hasdrubal son of Gisgo, who now commanded in Spain, applied the tactic which Fabius had used in Italy; he refused battle in the open and used his troops to garrison the more important towns in the valley of the Baetis and elsewhere in southern Spain. With further reinforcements from Africa he had perhaps 40,000 men, though some of these were lost in an expedition to raise more troops among the Celtiberians. It was probably after hearing that Hasdrubal Barca's march had been in vain and that he had been defeated in northern Italy that he decided to risk battle; it was to be expected that Scipio would attack the garrisoned cities one by one, and no doubt successfully, so that the result would in the end be the same as defeat in battle—the loss of the empire in Spain. On the other hand, if Scipio was defeated another attempt could be made to get help to Hannibal in his increasingly difficult position. Accordingly when Scipio left his winter quarters early in spring (206) and marched south down the valley of the Baetis, Hasdrubal went out to meet him at Ilipa, the modern Alcala del Rio, a few miles north of Seville. At this point Scipio had 45,000 foot-soldiers (of whom no more than 25,000 were Romans) and 3,000 horse, but Hasdrubal's strength had also increased and amounted to at least 50,000 infantry and 5,000 cavalry.

The battle which followed was a classic example of a victory by smaller forces over larger. Several days passed, in which the opposing armies were drawn up but did not engage; on each of these Scipio arranged his troops with the Romans in the centre facing Hasdrubal's African soldiers, his élite corps; on the wings the Spanish allies of each side faced each other, the Carthaginian line having the elephants in front. Hasdrubal accordingly believed a straightforward static engagement would ensue, in which his numbers would tell. However, Scipio the next morning sent skirmishers to attack the Carthaginian outposts, and marching out with his main force compelled Hasdrubal to draw up his line in a hurry, before the usual morning meal had been taken. Hasdrubal arranged his troops as on previous occasions, and discovered too late that Scipio now had his Spanish troops in the centre and the Romans on the wings; it was obvious that he was going to attempt an encircling movement with these experienced troops. Hasdrubal's cavalry were rendered ineffective by a stampede of his elephants as they were attacked by Scipio's cavalry and light armed troops, and were not able to take the important part they usually did in Carthaginian tactics. Scipio's outflanking movement (which involved wheeling both his wings outwards) was hazardous, as it left his Spanish centre liable to assault by Hasdrubal's African troops; but, for whatever reason, this never took place. The Spaniards on the wings resisted fiercely but finally were dispersed.

Hasdrubal was able to extricate a large proportion of his army, including the Africans, but as the Spanish troops began to desert his cause he was forced to attempt a retreat to the coast, harassed all the way by Scipio. Ultimately he himself escaped by ship from Gades, but most of the army was forced to surrender. Mago continued with the defence of Gades, in which there was a substantial element which wanted to surrender to the Romans; he made an attempt at a surprise attack on Cartagena, which failed, and when he returned he found that the people of Gades would not let him into the city. Following instructions, he then sailed towards Italy in a further attempt to bring help to Hannibal.

Scipio returned to Rome in late 206 and was elected one of the consuls for the ensuing year; more than this, he made it clear that it was his intention, if the senate agreed, to invade Africa even if Hannibal still remained in Italy. There was opposition to this proposal, led by Fabius Maximus and his friends. This group wished to get Hannibal out of Italy before any hazardous overseas projects were undertaken. Rome now had a general able to meet Hannibal in the field, and it seemed that the thing to do was to meet him in Italy; if he were defeated, Italy could then return as quickly as possible to the task of repairing the tremendous damage that had been caused. This was not the idea of Scipio, who saw that if Hannibal left Italy, war-weariness would make the people demand peace, and thus Carthage would be left in a position no worse than at the end of the first Punic War. Filled with a vision of Rome as the master of the western Mediterranean, he wished to defeat Carthage in Africa and so bring her to her knees, reducing her to a status of a dependant. The aura of success which surrounded Scipio, and the prospects of inflicting upon the Carthaginians some of the sufferings which Italy had endured at their hands, won him the support of the mass of the citizens, and the senate agreed to his plan.

There is a possibility that Hannibal was ready to make peace in 205, and that senators of Fabius' way of thinking would have been prepared to consider it. Scipio later said that if Hannibal had evacuated Italy before the invasion of Africa, peace could have been secured. Hannibal's position was indeed grievous; after all the hopes of the early years, he was now confined to a small part of southern Italy. The major effort which had been made to help him, the expedition of his brother Hasdrubal, who reached Italy in 207, had failed, with the destruction of the entire force and the death of Hasdrubal himself in a battle on the river Metaurus. Now Spain had gone, and this meant not only that he could not be reinforced except by sea, but that, as Carthage's chief source of revenue had been lost, any help at all would be on a small scale.

In 205 two attempts were made by Carthage to keep up the pressure in Italy and prevent the invasion of Africa. Mago, who had won a base for his fleet on Minorca at Mahon, which still bears his name, made a descent on the coast of Liguria with 14,000 men later reinforced from Carthage with another 6,000. He was unable to march south, however, because the Gauls, who had suffered heavy losses at the River Metaurus, refused to send him help. A major effort to get supplies direct to Hannibal by sea failed when a fleet of a hundred transports was driven off-course by a storm in the direction of Sardinia, where the Romans captured sixty ships and sank twenty. Yet no open diplomatic moves were made to avert the invasion.

In Africa, when the Roman attack was imminent, the attitude of Numidian tribes was important. Syphax, the chief of the Masaesyli, who were the largest Numidian tribe, and who inhabited the territory from the River Ampsaga in the east to the Mulucha in the west, had defected from the Carthaginian alliance in 213 but was reconciled about 208, the new alliance being sealed by his marriage to Sophoniba, daughter of Hasdrubal, son of Gisgo. But tribal jealousies, or the antagonism of their chiefs, had plenty of scope at the time of Carthage's crisis. The chief of the Massyli, who lay between Syphax' territory and that controlled directly by Carthage, had been on bad terms with Carthage till the defection of Syphax, when the quarrel was made up. One of his sons, Masinissa, then rendered loyal service to the Carthaginians in Spain, particularly on the occasion of the victory over P. Scipio. After the Roman victory at Ilipa, however, Masinissa was able to make his peace with the Romans. He returned to Africa where the chieftainship of his tribe was in dispute, his father having died. He was unsuccessful, but survived with a small band of followers ready to join the Romans when they came to Africa.

In the spring of 204 Scipio landed his army of 25,000 men at Cape Farina without interference, and pressed on to attack Utica. The city held out until the approach of Hasdrubal and Syphax; the size of their respective forces is not known, but altogether it perhaps amounted to 30,000 infantry and 5,000 cavalry. In any case it was large enough to force Scipio to desist and to retreat to a rocky peninsula a few miles east of Utica, where he encamped for the winter. So Carthage seemed easily to have survived the first year of the invasion, though Scipio's lack of success and unwillingness to engage was probably due solely to his inferiority in numbers, especially cavalry.

During the winter we find Syphax acting as an intermediary in peace negotiations between the two generals; the chief proposal was that after the evacuation of Italy by Hannibal and Mago, and of Africa by Scipio, peace should be made on the basis of the *status quo*. Such terms were the best that Carthage could hope for now, and might have been supported by a Fabius, but Scipio had not come to Africa for such a small return. He kept negotiations going, so that his officers in the guise of envoys could learn about the dispositions of the Carthaginians' camps, a stratagem which would have been denounced as typical Punic treachery if it had been used by Hannibal. One night in the spring of 203 Scipio sent out troops to set fire to the camp of Syphax, in which the huts were of timber and reeds. The Numidians, believing the fire was accidental, rushed out of the camp, where the main Roman forces were waiting for them; a similar attack was made on the Carthaginian camp. A large part of the combined army was burned to death or killed in flight, though not as many as our sources imply, since a month later Hasdrubal again had some 20,000 men. Masinissa played a major part in this success and was increasingly influential in Scipio's council.

The will to resist in Carthage was by no means crushed; proposals to treat for peace, even to recall Hannibal, were rejected and new troops were energetically recruited in the city itself and the surrounding territory; a force of 4,000 Celtiberian mercenaries arrived in Africa and joined Hasdrubal and Syphax in the area called the Great Plains, in the region of Souk El Kremis, seventy-five miles south-west of Carthage. Scipio decided to strike before the Carthaginians could recover further, and leaving part of his force to continue the siege of Utica, marched to the Great Plains with no more than one legion and a substantial cavalry force. Hasdrubal decided to fight, in view of his numerical superiority; he might perhaps have considered Fabian tactics and so forced Scipio to retire to Utica when his supplies ran low, but this would probably have been taken as a sign of weakness by Syphax and his Numidians. In the engagement that followed, Roman cavalry for the first time won a decisive victory; on the left wing Masinissa routed his rival Sphax, and on the right the Italian horse put the Carthaginians to flight. The Celtiberians fought to the last when their flanks were turned. After the battle Scipio sent all his cavalry to restore Masinissa to his tribe and pursue Syphax.

Following the example of Agathocles and Regulus, he then seized Tunis, from which he could cut off Carthage from the interior. In the deliberations of the senate, those who considered asking for terms were still few, and it was decided to put the city in readiness for a siege, make a surprise attack on Scipio's ships at Utica, and recall Mago and Hannibal. The former had been able to break out of Liguria and enter the Po valley earlier in the year; he had been defeated, but had saved most of his army, though he himself died of a wound on his way back to Africa. Before Hannibal could obey the call to return, ships had to be built, and in the meantime other events in Africa had supervened. The attack on the Roman ships at Utica had been moderately successful, but the lack of confidence of the Carthaginian fleet prevented a victory which might have lifted the blockade. Towards the end of the summer came the news that Syphax had been captured at his eastern capital of Cirta, and so Carthage's last ally was out of the field.

The peace party in Carthage now became dominant, as the old enemies of the Barcids pointed to the disasters of the war they had opposed for factional not political or economic motives; even those who were still determined to resist may have supported negotiations to gain time till Hannibal returned. Scipio also was prepared to make peace, since he had defeated two Carthaginian armies, and at this stage no one thought in terms of the destruction of the city itself.

Thirty members of the Carthaginian senate prostrated themselves before the Roman general, casting the entire blame for the war on Hannibal. We are hardly to see in this the triumph of the anti-Barcid faction, but rather the evasive diplomacy of a defeated power before the victor. Scipio will not have believed the accusation, though it was standard in the later Roman tradition. The conditions imposed were the surrender of all prisoners, deserters, and fugitive slaves, the evacuation of Italy and Gaul, the abandonment of Spain and all islands between Italy and Africa, the surrender of the entire navy except twenty ships, and an indemnity of 5,000 talents. In addition Carthage had to pay Scipio's troops and keep them supplied till the treaty was ratified. A peace on these terms would have confined Carthage to Africa and effectively prevented her ever becoming a great power again; without a fleet she could hardly control distant dependencies on the north African coast, while Masinissa would be able to prevent expansion into the interior beyond what was already held by Carthage.

The terms were not ratified by Rome till the end of the year, after Hannibal had in fact left Italy. No doubt there was truth in Livy's sympathetic remark that he left the land of his enemies with as much grief as most men felt on going into exile. With less probability he is said to have blamed the Carthaginian government for not sending him more help because of the influence of his old enemy Hanno. Most of his army was now dispersed, but he landed at Leptis Minor with perhaps 15,000 men, of whom 8,000 were veterans of many years' campaigning in Italy. Whether he expected that his arrival in Africa, shortly followed by Mago's force, would lead to a demand in Carthage that the truce be broken and the war continued cannot be determined, but his place of disembarkation certainly left him well placed for a renewal of hostilities. For over thirteen years he had maintained himself unbeaten in hostile territory at the head of an army of Africans, Spaniards, and Gauls who were bound together by no national loyalties. Only the inspiring leadership of Hannibal himself could have kept their unwavering loyalty in the long years of disillusionment in southern Italy with never the prospect of a major victory to elevate their hopes. His reputation among the great majority of his fellow countrymen stood as high as ever, and this partly led to the incident which broke the truce.

A convoy of supply ships coming from Italy to the Roman camp was wrecked in the Bay of Carthage itself in the sight of the city. Owing to the devastations of the past year and the burden of providing for the Roman army, there was a fear of famine; the senate met in an atmosphere of popular demands that the supply ships be seized, and this was agreed to with little opposition. When Scipio protested against this, particularly as news had just arrived of the ratification of the terms in Rome, his envoys were insulted and sent away without satisfaction. The confidence of the war party was such that an attack was prepared on the envoys as they returned to Scipio.

Much of the summer of 202 was spent by both generals in collecting their forces, until in early autumn Hannibal marched out to meet Scipio in the upper part of the Medjerda valley. He failed to get there before the arrival of Masinissa with a vital reinforcement of 4,000 horsemen for the Romans, so the battle was joined with forces about equal, 40,000 in each army but with Scipio greatly superior in cavalry. The site of the engagement was near the Numidian town of Naraggara (Sakiet Sidi Youseff), though it is more familiarly known as the battle of Zama.

Before the battle took place, Hannibal and Scipio had a personal meeting between the two armies. No doubt curiosity on both sides was at work in such an extraordinary encounter, but Hannibal made a last effort to make peace, in the forlorn hope that his reputation would deter the Romans from fighting; but the terms he suggested were far more favourable to Carthage than those agreed the year before, and Scipio was the last man to give way in such a position, when all Roman practice demanded that Carthage be punished for the breach of the truce. So the generals returned to their armies for the battle, which would decide not the result of the war (since a complete Carthaginian recovery even in the event of a victory by Hannibal was inconceivable) but the terms on which it would end.

Two of the finest generals of antiquity were at the head of armies both of which contained veteran elements. The deciding factor was Scipio's superiority in cavalry, which Hannibal did everything in his power to counteract. The Roman intended to use his cavalry to expose Hannibal's wings and then carry out an outflanking movement, as had been so successful at Ilipa. Hannibal seems to have ordered his weaker cavalry to pretend to flee and so to draw away Scipio's cavalry; meanwhile his infantry superiority might tell.

The Carthaginian attack opened with a charge of elephants; Scipio had drawn up his infantry in their usual three lines, but the companies were placed directly behind each other instead of in echelon, and many of the elephants passed harmlessly down the passages left between them. Hannibal's front line of seasoned mercenaries then engaged with the Roman front, but were driven back and out to the wings, as his second line of Libyans and Carthaginians was ordered not to receive them; this second line in its turn was broken by the advancing Roman infantry, now reinforced by its second line. However, Hannibal had

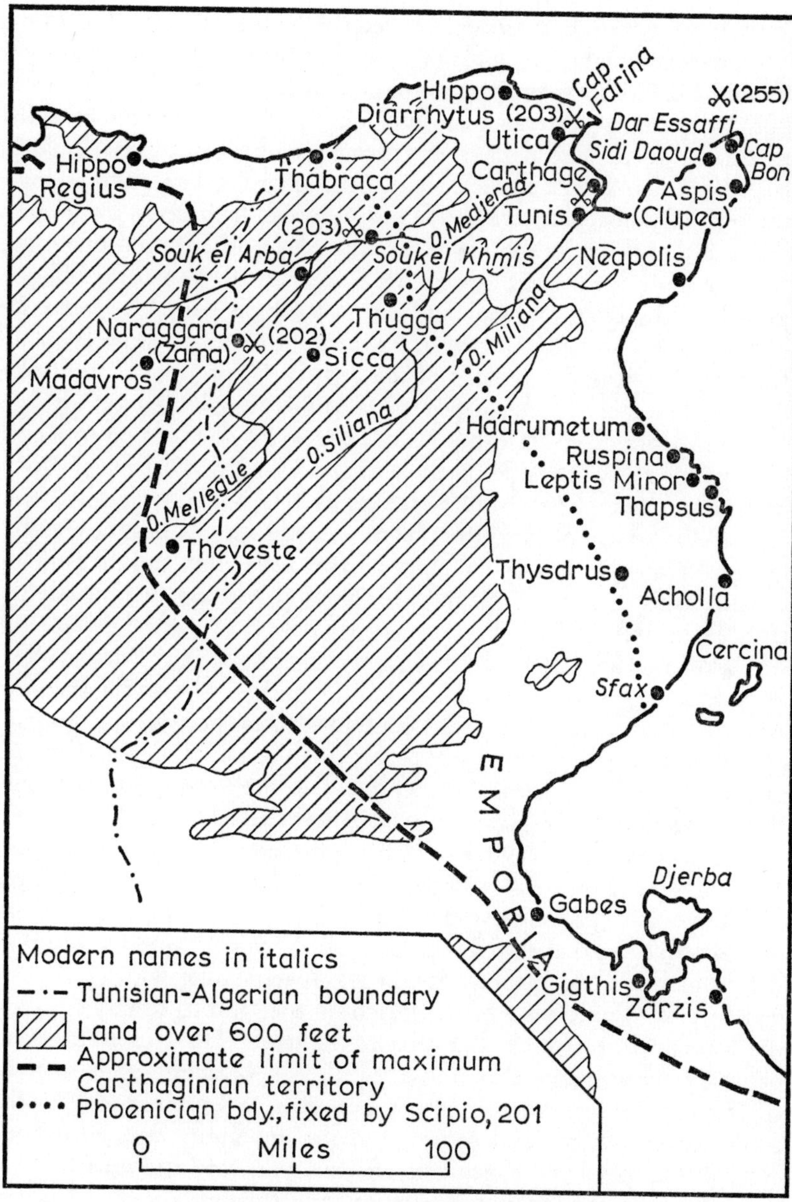

TUNISIA IN THE CARTHAGINIAN ERA

kept in reserve his best troops, his veterans from Italy, and Scipio was consequently unable to outflank or to put his tiring men against this formidable force. He therefore broke off and re-formed, extending his line by putting his two rear lines on the flanks, forcing Hannibal to do the same. The danger was that Hannibal's veterans would be launched on an attack in the centre of the extended line but it seems as though Hannibal's mercenaries and Libyans had been so severely handled that this was impossible, in spite of his urgent need to get in a decisive blow before the Roman cavalry returned. When the infantry joined battle again, a stern and equal struggle continued, and the definitive action was made by the returning cavalry who fell on the Carthaginian rear. In the face of this massive attack, the army broke, though Hannibal himself escaped to Hadrumetum and then to Carthage.

Scipio returned to his camp near Utica and then went on to Tunis, after making a demonstration by land and sea against Carthage. There he received an embassy from Carthage seeking peace, which had been sent on the advice of Hannibal; he of all people knew best how hopeless further struggle would be, with the treasury empty and the Romans in command of the sea and in a dominating position just outside the city. There were some officers with Scipio who urged the destruction of Carthage, and Scipio could certainly have done this. But the effort would have been considerable, and although he had a wider vision of Rome's future than some of his contemporaries, he was not ignorant of the need of Italy for a speedy peace; in any case, his imperialism did not envisage the physical destruction of Rome's enemies but simply their reduction to dependence, which he believed could be achieved by the acceptance of his terms. Lastly, there was his own character; he had been responsible for few ruthless actions in the preceding years, and these had had clearly-defined ends in view; the unnecessary destruction of a great city was an act from which he would hold aloof.

First of all a truce of three months was made, under which Carthage had to pay reparations for the breach of 203, and to supply and pay the Roman forces for the duration of the truce. The final terms were naturally more severe than those which had been agreed in 203. In addition to the surrender of all her elephants, the number of ships she could retain was reduced to ten, and the indemnity was greatly increased; Carthage had to pay 200 talents a year for fifty years.

More serious than these were clauses, unfortunately not entirely clear, referring to her territory in Africa and her status with regard to Rome. Carthage was allowed to retain the territory within the 'Phoenician Boundary' which she had held when Scipio arrived in Africa. This

Boundary, apparently a trench similar to that drawn to demarcate the later Roman province of Africa, seems to have marked off the area of north-east Tunisia under the control of Carthage; she was also allowed to retain such coastal settlements (for instance the Emporia) as were agreed to by Rome. On the other hand, she had to surrender all territory which had ever belonged to Masinissa or his ancestors, even if it was within the Phoenician Boundary. Considering the nomadic existence of many of the tribes and the instability of their government, this clause was likely to be a source of trouble. Carthage was not allowed to make war outside Africa, and within Africa only with Roman consent. Whether this precluded defensive war inside Africa was apparently ambiguous,[21] but it certainly appears that for a long time Carthage acted as though it did, or at least that it precluded her moving troops outside the Phoenician Boundary. She also became an ally of Rome, bound to provide help in Rome's wars when required. Thus she could never again become a Mediterranean power, while in many places her territory was liable to claims by Masinissa whenever he chose to make them.

When these peace terms were discussed at Carthage, a certain Gisgo argued for further resistance, but Hannibal added his voice to those who were for peace. He realized that Carthage could have been destroyed, and that though reduced to a dependent, even a desperate position, the Phoenician community in Africa yet survived. What further thoughts passed through his mind we cannot say. He had been absent from Carthage for thirty-six years, and had brought his city to its highest pinnacle of success only to see all crumble to nothing. Though tendentious in their attribution to him of the responsibility for the war, the Romans rightly saw that it was his genius which had so nearly defeated them. It is his gifts as a leader of men which stand out, rather than his whole personality, partly because of the nature of our sources for his career. He did more, with smaller resources, than almost any other general has ever done, and his achievement in maintaining for so long a completely loyal force of mercenaries testifies to an attractive side to his personality which hardly shows in our sources. He was a professional soldier in a sense that few Roman generals ever were, and had made a thorough study of Hellenistic military history from the time of Alexander. Hannibal's incorporation in the Hellenistic world would be exemplified in a remarkable fashion if a portrait bust found at Volubilis in Morocco represents him. It is a head of a young man in an idealized, even sentimental vein, following the tradition of portraits of young heroes which had developed from representations of Alexander.[22] He was actually accompanied on his campaign by Greek scholars, just as Alexander had been; two of these, Silenus of Caleacte and Sosylus of Lacedaemon, were among those who wrote of the war from a point of view in some degree sympathetic to Carthage. Their works are lost, but were used by Polybius and enable us at times to correct the Roman views expressed in Livy.

The latter does indeed have passages in which the qualities of Hannibal are praised; on one occasion he writes:[23]

It is difficult to decide whether he was more remarkable in success or failure; he waged war far from his home, in enemy territory, for thirteen years of varied fortune, at the head of an army not of his own country, but a mixed force come together from all peoples, differing in law, customs, and language, and having nothing common in their behaviour, dress, arms, and religion; yet he bound them as with a chain, so that there was never any division among them or mutiny against their leader, though money and supplies were often lacking.

His hold over his army may be explained by what Livy writes elsewhere:

He had the greatest audacity in undertaking dangerous enterprises, and intelligence when they were in progress; his body and mind could put up with any amount of activity; he was equally tolerant of heat and cold, and in eating and drinking was governed by what he needed rather than by self-indulgence. As for his sleep, this did not depend on the time of day, but on what could be spared from his work, and he needed no soft bed or absolute quiet; he was often observed covered only with a cloak lying on the ground among soldiers in the outposts. He was distinguished from his fellow soldiers only by his horse and arms, not his clothing. He was the first to set off on foot or on horseback, went first into battle, and was the last to retire from an engagement.

This last remark no doubt testifies to his personal courage rather than his generalship, and is probably exaggerated. Livy then goes on to say that these virtues were equalled by vices:

inhuman cruelty, a more than Punic treachery, no respect for truth; he held nothing sacred, had no fear of the gods, was bound by no oath or religious scruple.

It is significant that Polybius, who also has remarks on Hannibal's personality, does not subscribe to these accusations, which are thoroughly reminiscent of war propaganda. That the Carthaginians in Italy committed atrocities is true: Polybius attributed them to Hannibal's subordinates, or to strategic necessity; in any case there was little to choose between them and those committed by the Romans.

Yet Livy has no comment to make on the general strategy of Hannibal, his wide-ranging diplomacy, and his aim of breaking Rome's Italian confederacy, nor does he show how his objectives changed under the stress of circumstances. Further, the legitimate concentration on the achievement of Hannibal led ancient and modern authors to underestimate the part played by the Carthaginians themselves. Livy sets his 'hero'—the Roman People under the leadership of the senate—over against an individual of infinite cunning and resource, not against another people. Whereas we read in Livy of each year's dispositions and plans of the Romans, with the arguments which went to form them, we have almost nothing of a similar nature from the Carthaginian side. We can thus make no real comparison between the sufferings and sacrifices of the Carthaginians in the war and those of the Romans. Livy put forward the traditional Roman view, derived from Hannibal's political enemies, that the Carthaginian leadership was not enthusiastic for the war, a view which has no solid foundation and which can be contradicted by references in Livy himself to the despatch on numerous occasions of reinforcements and supplies to Italy and other theatres of war. In point of fact it seems clear that the Carthaginians showed a determination to win equal to that of their leader and comparable to that of the Romans.

The basis of Rome's victory is obvious; it was her resources in men which made it possible not only to bear the tremendous losses—300,000 from Italy as a whole—but also to man a fleet sufficient to retain superiority at sea while at the same time sending armies to all the theatres of war. The most admirable decision of the Romans was undoubtedly to persevere with the Spanish war even after the defeat at Cannae, when the temptation to have every man in Italy must have been almost overwhelming. This not only prevented Hannibal from being reinforced from Spain, but also forced Carthage to divide between the two areas the men and materials she had in Africa. It might be said that Carthage should have risked everything in sending help to Hannibal on the largest possible scale; experience showed that it was certainly possible to land large forces in Italy, in spite of Rome's naval superiority. But Hannibal never seems to have demanded this. The difficulties of keeping his army supplied were already considerable enough, and mere increase in numbers, unless of a size beyond the capacity of Carthage to send, would not have greatly affected the position while Rome pursued her Fabian tactics.

Carthage, and by implication Hannibal, has been criticized for neglect of the fleet, which might have made a decisive difference to the result of the war. This criticism has something in it, but would be more convincing if we knew precisely how much strain was placed on Carthaginian resources simply by the effort of keeping large armies in Spain and Italy, and whether at times there were periods of slackness in the direction of the war, as is obviously not impossible. Initially, the decision to concentrate on the army was that of the Barcids, taken from the sound motives already described, including the complete failure of the fleet in the first war and the correct judgement that Rome could only be finally defeated on land. Later in the war, when the prospect of a quick victory receded and a fleet would have been of great service in Sicily, Spain, and Macedonia, it seems that the resources of Carthage were inadequate to build and maintain one large enough to rival that of Rome, and this was certainly true after Scipio's capture of the Spanish mines. If this is not the case, then Hannibal, whose supporters were dominant in the government till the final year of the war, must have decided that a fleet would make no material difference to his prospects. In point of fact the Carthaginians were at times not unenterprising in the use of the ships they had, and were able on a number of occasions to use them for the transport of armies and supplies, but the defeats they suffered merely drove home the lessons of the first war. It is unlikely that Hannibal was at fault in this decision, if we assume that it was open to him to decide, and that Carthage could in fact have made the effort.

It was Hannibal's genius that neutralized for so long Rome's superiority in manpower on land, where alone he could hope for victory; but at last a general arose who refused to be mesmerized by it. Whether Hannibal would have defeated Scipio if he had had with him the army that had won at Cannae is as fruitless a question as one the Romans used to ask about an equal of the two men; would Alexander, if he had lived, have been able to defeat Rome? Hannibal's leadership, personality, and behaviour after the defeat entitle him to be called the noblest failure in antiquity.

9

The Destruction of Carthage[1]

THE last fifty years of the existence of Carthage show both good and bad points in her civilization; the energy, courage, and patriotism of the citizens in times of crisis, and the selfishness and greed of particular sections of the aristocracy.

Two problems in particular faced the city as the effort was made to repair the damage caused by the war in Africa and the loss of overseas possessions: the prompt payment of the yearly instalments of the indemnity, and the preservation of Carthaginian territory from the depredations of Masinissa. We know a certain amount concerning the first of these problems, because of its connexion with the later years of Hannibal. He had remained in command of the remnants of the army for a few months after the conclusion of peace, but in 200 retired to private life. The eclipse of his influence was accompanied by an increase in the corrupt practices of the aristocratic government, which even extended to trying to pay one of the instalments to Rome in debased silver; it sought to place the burden of the extra tax which was said to be needed on the shoulders of the rest of the community, while much of the state's revenue was appropriated by its members and their political supporters.

In 196 popular resentment had grown to such an extent that Hannibal was elected sufet, and at once showed that he was going to use the office to bring in major reforms. He was defied by one of the financial officials, who felt secure because the next year he would become a member of the Hundred and four Judges. By this time membership was certainly for life, and the judges were effectively the rulers of the city. In the conflict which ensued between the official's friends in the senate and the sufet, Hannibal had the opportunity to consult the people, and used it to attack the whole conduct of the Hundred and Four. He proposed a law, which was enthusiastically passed, that in future the judges should be chosen annually and that none should hold office two years running. Such a radical reform put Carthage well on the road to a democratic government of the type of the old Greek city-states, and Hannibal also showed that when the speculations were stopped there was sufficient to pay the indemnity to Rome without extra taxation. But the resentment of the discredited politicians, some of whom had been obliged to repay what they had taken, was such that they wrote to the Roman senate, with which they had personal contacts, and accused Hannibal of being in communication with King Antiochus of Syria and plotting war with Rome.

For some time Scipio, to his credit, used his influence against the acceptance of the complaint, on the ground that it would be unworthy for Rome to intervene in an obvious factional quarrel, but ultimately hatred of the great Carthaginian prevailed. Three commissioners arrived in Carthage in 195, when Hannibal was no longer in office; it was officially stated that they had come to arbitrate in a dispute between Carthage and Masinissa, but Hannibal guessed the truth, that they had come to procure his ruin, perhaps his death. He had made his plans for such an eventuality with the efficiency one would expect, and using relays of horses, slipped away to Thapsus, where he had a ship ready; he then sailed to Tyre and subsequently to Ephesus to join Antiochus.[2]

Such was the departure from Carthage of its greatest citizen, who spent only a few years of his adult life in his home. He was unwilling not only to submit to his fate but also to put Carthage in the position of having to sacrifice him or face Roman punishment for harbouring a 'warmonger'. No doubt there was a substantial section of the aristocracy who would cheerfully have handed him over to Rome, but there was the probability of popular violence in his favour when the people

Views of Monte Sirai. (*below*) North-east tower

Neo-Punic mausoleum, Thugga

saw their leader being ruined at the moment when his reforms had only just begun to work.

It can never be decided whether he had really been in communication with Antiochus. Accustomed to taking the wide view of affairs, he may have hoped when arguing for peace in 201 that Carthage would survive until Rome came into collision with the Hellenistic kingdoms, in which case she would have a chance to recover her power; but such hopes must have suffered a setback in the rapid defeat of Philip of Macedon by Rome in 200–196. On the other hand Antiochus, called the Great for his successful campaigns as far as India, was ruler of a far more powerful kingdom and had immense resources in men and wealth, and it seemed inevitable that he would come into collision with Rome within a very few years.

Whatever the truth of the accusations of his enemies, Hannibal certainly went at once to the court of Antiochus, where he remained for several years. On several occasions he put forward his view as to how a war with Rome ought to be conducted. Reduced to essentials it was his old view that Rome could only be defeated in Italy; either he himself should be entrusted with a fleet and 11,000 men to attack the Romans, while Antiochus fought in Greece, or Antiochus should land in Italy while Hannibal with a fleet prevented the Romans from crossing the Adriatic into Greece. Such a plan might be said to have ignored the fact that Hannibal had fought in Italy for thirteen years and not defeated Rome. However, certain circumstances were in his favour. Antiochus had a very large fleet, while that of the Romans had been allowed to decay; in Italy the terrible losses of the Punic War had hardly begun to be made good, and there was a great deal of unrest owing both to the economic distress and to Rome's increasing arrogance. In Spain a large Roman army was tied down by the Spanish tribes, who viewed a change of masters with no enthusiasm. Hannibal could hope to do better this time in the recruitment of allies in Italy, and if Antiochus could bring sufficient forces with him they could face Rome on more level terms. Carthage itself was to be brought in, and in 193 an agent of Hannibal went there to prepare his friends for his possible return, but was discovered.[3]

Yet even if Hannibal's plan was excessively optimistic and would have had no better result than that of the Punic War, it was at least an attempt to deal with the essential problem, namely that a war with Rome was a war which would only end with the complete defeat of one or other of the parties. If ever any man knew the truth of this it was Hannibal. But the Hellenistic states had played with war rather in the manner of eighteenth-century Europe; compromise and accommodation had been the usual result. Antiochus did not realize that war with Rome was in a different category altogether; and no accommodation short of the admission of defeat would be sufficient in a war with her, unless he himself was prepared for the effort required to win.

So Hannibal failed. He had been fighting at the court of Antiochus not only for his own country—to which his absolute loyalty and devotion, in circumstances when others might have turned to revolutionary action or, in defeat, to a cynical retirement, was one of his most attractive characteristics—but for all the others of the east. Rome's enemies had never combined against her, and so she had gone from strength to strength. If Antiochus' power were destroyed, there would be no other great power left to dispute with Rome the mastery of the world. This was an ironic turn of events, considering the long history of conflict between Carthage and the Siceliots, but in these decades there can be little doubt which power, Rome or Carthage, represented the greater threat to independent Hellenism. Antiochus was easily defeated by the Romans, in a brief war in which Hannibal only had a minor and unsuccessful part at the head of a contingent of Phoenician ships.

There then began a period of 150 years in which the cause of Hellenism suffered ruinous losses at the hands of the Romans, and of others from whom they were unwilling to protect the Greeks they themselves had weakened. What was left of Hellenism was only preserved when the Romans had fallen more completely under its attraction and learnt (or re-learnt) the moral obligations of imperial powers.

Hannibal (whose surrender by Antiochus was demanded) escaped and spent his remaining years in frustrated exile among the powerless minor states of the Aegean; finally in 182 he joined King Prusias of Bithynia. The Romans put pressure on the king to hand over his guest, which he was unable to resist; but Hannibal, who had foreseen such an event, took poison and so deprived his enemies of a final satisfaction.[4]

By their appeal to Rome when attacked by Hannibal, the Carthaginian aristocracy had regained power, but it is possible that Hannibal's revelation of the true state of the finances made it impossible to return entirely to the old ways of corruption; we find that in 191 Carthage could offer to pay all the remaining instalments, undoubtedly a vast sum, and make voluntary contributions of corn on several occasions.[5]

But if a measure of financial prosperity returned with a speed which testified to vigorous trade, probably in foodstuffs, as well as proper administration, it was not so easy to prevent the gradual erosion of

Carthaginian territory by Masinissa. This prince was thirty-seven years of age at the end of the war with Hannibal, and had a remarkably vigorous constitution. When he died he was survived by ten out of forty-four sons who had been born to him, the last when he was eighty-six. In addition he was a man of enormous ambition and diplomatic address, and was no stranger to civilized life, as he had spent much of his youth in Carthage. His aim, by no means an unworthy one, was to change the Numidians from a collection of restless and nomadic tribes to a united nation in which an increasing number of the inhabitants lived a settled agricultural life. He fully realized that this meant the introduction of Carthaginian civilization on a large scale, and it was largely through his agency that a mixed Numidian and Carthaginian culture became dominant over much of the hinterland of North Africa until the period of large scale Italian immigration in the Roman period.[6]

He had been installed by Scipio not only as king of his own tribe but also as ruler of the eastern and more prosperous part of the former kingdom of Syphax. It was at Cirta, in the latter area, that he fixed his new capital and attracted there a substantial number of Carthaginians. As his power increased, he appears to have hoped for the acquisition of Carthage itself and its dependent territory, if not indeed for rule over the whole of North Africa, as Livy (or his source) alleges.[7] His progress was limited only by his estimate of how far the Romans would let him go; he had the patronage of the Scipionic family (until its decline) and had played a major part in the victory in Africa, and could hope that Rome would not be reluctant to see her old enemy weakened still further. But Masinissa was far too intelligent to believe that Rome would always remember him with gratitude, and his long success shows that he had grasped the essential role of a client king in the Roman system; it was to show unconditional obedience to Roman orders, and if possible to anticipate them. A client was not expected to have ambitions of his own, and Masinissa's approach was always cautious, his demands well prepared with allegations of Carthaginian revival, coupled with demonstrations of his own enthusiastic support for Rome.

The Carthaginians themselves, whatever rights of self-defence existed under the peace treaty, felt that they could only defend themselves in practice against Masinissa's demands by appealing to Rome themselves and equalling the Numidian in deference. For this policy the aristocracy who had called in Rome to get rid of Hannibal was obviously suited, and if it had been successful in obtaining Roman protection would to some extent have justified itself. But Rome, though glad to have a government of such a complexion at Carthage, and not disposed to encourage Masinissa, did not lessen her inclination to keep her as weak as possible.

Masinissa's first encroachments were in 193 in an area apparently near the Emporia. He no doubt was taking advantage of Roman alarm at the sufetship of Hannibal in 196, his subsequent flight to the court of Antiochus, and the discovery of his agent Aristo in the city in 193. After both sides had been heard in Rome, the senate sent a commission headed by Scipio himself. Although the latter, of all people, could have settled the dispute by his own authority and his knowledge of the peace settlement, the commission made no decision, which may mean that Masinissa was able to hold what he had seized.[8] However, he made no further move for a decade and it has been supposed that he was privately warned by Scipio.[9] Like Masinissa, Carthage offered help to the Romans for the Syrian war in 191, but the Romans refused the offer to pay the remainder of the indemnity in a lump sum, no doubt in order to maintain in the Carthaginians a sense of their dependence. In 182 there was another dispute, this time over territory in the Bagradas valley, and again no decision was reached; the following year Masinissa was still in armed possession of the territory, but presumably as a sop to Carthage, a hundred hostages were returned by Rome and the terms of the peace treaty were reaffirmed.[10]

In 174, Masinissa alleged that the Carthaginians had secretly received envoys from Perseus, king of Macedon, at a time when another conflict between Rome and Macedon seemed inevitable. It is obviously not impossible that Perseus had in fact sent envoys to see if in some way Carthage might be brought into the conflict, but the improbability that the Carthaginian senate had anything to do with such a proposal is heightened by the fact that Rome did nothing about it although her own commission of inquiry tended to support Masinissa. The latter nevertheless seized some further territory, and in 172 Carthage complained to Rome that seventy towns and forts had been seized, and asked for their restoration and for the return of land seized on the two previous occasions. Rome temporized by asking for a full explanation from Masinissa, but all attention was reserved for the war with Perseus. The king and the Carthaginians seem to have vied with each other in the assistance they offered to Rome; in addition to large amounts of grain, Masinissa sent cavalry and elephants, the Carthaginians ships, which enabled Masinissa to allege that they were building a new fleet in contravention of the peace treaty.[11]

The battle of Pydna in 168, in which Perseus was defeated and Macedon lost her independence, marked a turning point in Roman diplomacy throughout the Mediterranean, as she turned increasingly to domineering and ruthless solutions to diplomatic problems. In Africa this showed itself in growing hostility to Carthage. Whereas previously Masinissa had made his gains through Roman default, from now on she favoured him openly in adjudications. Between 168 and 162 he obtained the whole of the Emporia district round the gulf of Gabes, from which substantial revenues were derived. Masinissa's territory now stretched well into modern Libya, and by this date he must have obtained all the settlements on the North African shore west of Thabraca.[12]

After about 160, feeling at Carthage began to grow increasingly bitter about the circumstances in which the city was placed. In the years immediately preceding the final conflict with Rome, there were three opposing views as to the policy that ought to be adopted. There was the view of those who had been prominent since the end of the Hannibalic war and who still advocated continued deference to Rome in the hope that sooner or later Masinissa would overstep the mark; it was doubtless owing to the continued support given to the king by Rome that this policy had been discredited and the governing class had split. There was a party which our source calls 'democratic', which was no doubt following the policies of the Barcids in obtaining support amongst the mass of the citizens, though the leaders themselves were men of substance; this party had nothing particularly constructive to offer, but gained in popularity as it was loudest in denouncing Rome and Masinissa. A third party advocated reaching an understanding with Masinissa; this was a sensible point of view, because while any solution of this sort would doubtless mean effective subordination to the Numidian, it would be materially profitable because of his known attitude towards the advance of civilization in his kingdom, and could hardly be less dignified than the existing position. But the third party failed to win much support, because its policy meant the end of a history of 500 years of independent existence and a submission to people who had once been subjects; it was the democratic party, which advocated the understandable but dangerous policy of resistance to Masinissa's encroachments, which became dominant.[13]

Between about 160 and 155 one of its leaders named Carthalo made a raid into territory which had been usurped, and there followed several years of minor raids by both sides, until the Romans decided as usual in favour of the king. The latter then went on to occupy the Great

Plains (around Souk el Kremis) and the territory of Thugga. A Roman commission, headed by one of the oldest and most distinguished politicians, Marcus Porcius Cato, came to Africa in 153 in response to a Carthaginian appeal. It insisted that both sides agree to its decision in advance; Masinissa naturally assented, but Carthage refused, remembering the succession of unfavourable decisions by Rome, and the commission returned to Rome leaving the dispute unsettled.

Yet this incident had momentous consequences, for the trivial show of independence which Carthage had at last made aroused the strongest emotions in the eighty-one-year-old Cato. He had served in the Hannibalic war; the memory of those fearful years, and the hatred of Carthage which they had evoked, returned. He set himself to the task of persuading the Roman senate of the danger of a reviving Carthage and the proximity (not the distance) of Africa, which he is said to have illustrated by showing the senators a fig, still fresh, which had been picked in Africa only three days before. He ended all his speeches in the senate on whatever subject, with the famous words 'ceterum censeo Carthaginem esse delendam'—'for the rest, it is my opinion that Carthage must be destroyed'.

He was opposed by Publius Scipio Nasica, who had married a daughter of the great Africanus, to whom he was closely related, and a compromise was reached whereby another commission, headed by Nasica, went to Africa in 152 and induced Masinissa to yield some of the territory. But the next year Rome strongly protested against the rebuilding of the Carthaginian fleet and army and threatened to discuss a proposal for war if they were not disbanded. It certainly appears that by now Carthage had an army of some size, though it seems doubtful whether she would have risked such an obvious breach of treaty as building a really large fleet. But the damage was done; Cato worked up sufficient support to bring about drastic action against Carthage if a reasonable excuse should present itself, though it is too much to say, as one tradition had it, that a secret resolution of the senate to go to war was taken as early as 153, pending a proper *casus belli*; if this had been so, there would have been no need for Cato's campaign.[14]

The real motives behind the ultimate support of Cato's policy are hardly so difficult to disentangle as those of the first and second Punic Wars. There is no real evidence of an economic motive; Italian exports to Carthage had been considerable in the last decades, while there is no sign that Carthaginian goods competed with Italian to any degree in other markets; and it was some time before there was any exploitation of the fertile lands of Africa available after the conquest, so it does not seem that greed for land on the part of some senators was a leading motive.

It has been argued that Carthage was destroyed to prevent her falling willingly or unwillingly into the hands of Masinissa, now grown too powerful for Rome; but the consistency of our sources in asserting Rome's continued support for Masinissa cannot be overlooked, and there were other ways of achieving such a result. The fact is, as one Roman author saw, that the Romans were willing to believe anything that was said against the Carthaginians, and it is significant that Scipio Nasica agreed with Cato about the strength of Carthage. His argument[15] for not proceeding against her was that Rome would only retain her inner strength, her virile way of life, so long as a potential enemy was in existence, particularly as there were already ominous signs of a degeneration in Roman society. This remarkable viewpoint was not confined to Scipio, and was indeed already a commonplace in his day. It seems at this distance incredible that an experienced Roman senator could possibly have considered Carthage to be a possible threat to Rome. It is true that in 151 the final instalment of the indemnity from Carthage would be paid and Carthage thus freed from a severe burden, that vast quantities of arms were surrendered in 149, and that in spite of this sufficient new arms could be manufactured with great speed and resistance kept up for three years; but the Carthaginians themselves knew that they could not resist Rome, and the last struggle was a mass suicide.

The fact is that Rome had entered a period when ruthlessness was increasingly used not so much from policy so as to secure her supremacy, as from lack of any policy at all; it was a substitute for the thought and consistency required when dealing with the complicated pattern of states of different races, cultures, and institutions—far more than at present inhabit the Mediterranean coasts—when they refused to recognize the plain fact of Rome's dominance and insisted with intransigence on the old traditions of independence; the destruction of a city was a thing understood everywhere.[16]

The breach of the peace treaty of 201, which gave the legal justification so much desired by the Romans before they went to war, came in 151–150.[17] The leaders of the pro-Numidian party in Carthage were exiled at the instigation of the popular party, which was now in a dominant position. They went to Masinissa, who sent two of his sons to demand their recall. Carthalo prevented their entry into the city, and another leader of the popular party, Hamilcar, attacked them on their way home. The Numidian then laid siege to a town called Oroscopa, and a Carthaginian army of 25,000 was sent against him under a commander named Hasdrubal. Masinissa was forced by desertions to retreat. It happened that an adopted member of the Scipionic family, Scipio Aemilianus, was in Africa at the time, and the Carthaginians sent to him and offered to surrender all claim to the Emporia, into which they had followed Masinissa, but they refused to hand over the deserters, who included two sons of Masinissa. The retention of these would be a good diplomatic card in their hand, in view of the advanced age of Masinissa and the likelihood of a break-up of his empire on his death, through dynastic quarrels. The struggle continued, and Masinissa was able to surround the Carthaginian camp; an epidemic broke out, accompanied by increasing shortage of food, and in the end the Carthaginians were forced to surrender. A promise was made to pay an indemnity, but the survivors were attacked as they left the camp.

Even before the defeat of the Carthaginian force, Rome had begun to raise troops in Italy. It was not said what these were for, but the Carthaginians were not deceived.[18] After the disaster they had suffered they were in the weakest possible position from which to negotiate, but they did their best. Those responsible for the war against Masinissa were sentenced to death, though Hasdrubal escaped and raised a force of 20,000 men in the country districts. Envoys to Rome asking how they could obtain pardon received obscure but threatening replies, and the preparations for war continued. During this period Utica deserted the Carthaginian cause and surrendered to Rome, following which there seemed no other alternative for Carthage but to give up hope of getting off with a further indemnity or surrender of territory and to make a formal surrender. Five envoys were sent to Rome with this offer, only to be told that war had been declared and that the fleet and army were on their way. However, the surrender was accepted and the Carthaginians were told they would be allowed to retain their freedom, the enjoyment of their own laws, and the possession of their territory and public and private property. On the other hand, the Carthaginians were to send as hostages 300 children of members of the senate and to obey any further commands of the consuls.

The hostages were handed over, and the consuls crossed to Utica with their army. There they demanded that the Carthaginians surrender all the arms that were in the city. This too was agreed to, and no less than 200,000 sets of arms and 2,000 catapults were handed over. When this had been done, the consuls demanded the presence of another embassy to receive their final instructions; these were that the Carthaginians were to leave their city, which the Romans were determined to destroy: they could settle anywhere they liked, so long as it was at least ten miles from the sea.[19]

So the final intentions of the Romans were revealed; and the stages of the revelation over the preceding months show a ruthless cunning which would have fitted better with the Roman view of Carthaginian morality. Carthage had been kept in suspense about her fate until she was disarmed, so that the chance of resistance was minimized. Popular opinion in Italy gave her very little chance even before this demand (which had naturally been kept secret); 80,000 had quickly volunteered for the campaign, which offered easy prospects, though only a few years before it had been found very difficult to raise men to go to fight the warlike Celtiberians in Spain. It should be noted that none of their demands went beyond strict legality as the Romans understood it; the surrender made by Carthage had the same effect as unconditional surrender in modern usage. Assurances were sometimes given before a surrender was made, and though this had not been done in the case of Carthage there was a presumption that the city would not be sacked nor the people enslaved. It was the Carthaginians' refusal of the order to leave their city which brought about the final sack and enslavement; the order to leave was not verbally inconsistent with the assurances given after the surrender, which had not mentioned the fate of the city itself, since the people could still exist somewhere else.

This was not the view of the Carthaginians. Quite apart from the destruction of their homes and sacred places, which were dear enough to them, vast numbers were in effect condemned to death by starvation when they were cut off from the sea or had their workshops destroyed; in any case, once separated from their defences they would fall directly into the hands of Masinissa.

A final appeal was made by one of the envoys but rejected; some, knowing the fierce and stubborn attitude of their fellow citizens when driven too far, took to flight or stayed with the consuls. The rest returned to the city and passed through the waiting crowds to the senate house with expressions which gave away the disastrous nature of their message. When cries of dismay were heard from the senate house, it was invaded by the people, who on learning of the Romans' order stoned to death the unfortunate envoys and others who had advised submission to Rome, and massacred any Italians who could be found. The whole city was gripped with a sense of despairing anger and hatred towards the Romans; if any paused to consider that resistance was bound to be in vain, it must have seemed that to be killed in defence of the city against a vindictive enemy was better than to starve to death in ignominious exile. Since all their arms had been handed over, the temples and public places were turned into workshops, in which the citizens worked night and day to manufacture new ones out of the raw material which was to hand; 100 shields, 300 swords, 500 javelins were made every day, besides numerous catapults, for the cords of which the women offered their hair. Two generals were chosen, of whom one was the Hasdrubal who had shortly before been condemned to death but who now commanded 20,000 men in the interior. Although six important cities including the ancient foundations of Hadrumetum, Leptis Minor, Thapsus, and Acholla went over to the Romans, Hasdrubal ensured the loyalty of some of the Libyans and got food into the city.[20]

The consuls were slow to advance to the attack, as they believed it would be an easy matter to take it once the initial sense of desperation had worn off; but they underestimated the Carthaginians. An assault was made on a section of the wall bordering the Lake of Tunis, and though a breach was made, the Romans were driven out again. When the blockade was begun, one of the two Roman divisions, camped on the edge of the lake, suffered during the heat of the summer from sickness caused by the unhealthy position, and its commander Censorinus had to move it to the tongue of land separating the lake from the sea, where it got the benefit of the sea breezes.

During the winter the other consul, Manilius, whose camp was on the isthmus, suffered heavy losses in a sally made by the defenders, and disaster was only averted by the courage of Scipio Aemilianus, who was serving in the army with the rank of military tribune. Scipio was also responsible for actions during the winter, in which by his resourcefulness he prevented Manilius' incapacity, when leading expeditions against Hasdrubal in the interior of the country, from having serious results for the Romans. The only success they had was in persuading Hasdrubal's cavalry commander, Himilco Phameas, to desert; this too was Scipio's doing. In the meantime Masinissa had died, apparently full of resentment that his hopes of adding Carthage itself to his empire had been frustrated by his friends. Scipio was responsible for the division of the powerful kingdom between three of Masinissa's sons.

The next year, 148, the courage of the Carthaginians was still further rewarded; some Numidian cavalry deserted to them, and the sons of Masinissa manifested reluctance to provide help for the Romans. In spite of the Roman fleet blockading the harbour, they had been able to get into touch with the Mauretanians and with Andriscus, who was leading a revolt against Rome in Macedonia, though these contacts did more to maintain the morale of the citizens than to bring any practical help. The town of Hippo Acra also fiercely resisted an assault, after the Romans had ruthlessly sacked Neapolis although it had made a surrender, and Hasdrubal was able to maintain himself in the country and get supplies into the city. There was, however, some division in the city; the general in charge of the defence was another Hasdrubal, through his mother a grandson of Masinissa; for this reason he was apparently suspected of being lukewarm, and one day was attacked and killed in the senate house itself. But dissatisfaction in Rome was growing, and it appeared that only Scipio could carry through the siege with the necessary vigour. He was still below the minimum age at which the consulship could be held, but the constitutional requirements were waived for his benefit. He enrolled some fresh troops, and took with him in his entourage two famous Greeks, Panaetius the Stoic philosopher and the historian Polybius; both of these had been his friends for some time, for he was one of those Romans who had an intense admiration for Greek civilization.

His dispatch to Africa meant the arrival of a decisive moment for Carthage. It was not only the incompetence of the commanders but also the indiscipline of the Roman soldiers, who had enlisted thinking the campaign would be a promenade, that had delayed action for so long. While Scipio employed himself with the restoration of discipline, the Carthaginians recalled Hasdrubal from the country in case he should be cut off, and he established himself in a fortified post on the isthmus outside but close to the walls; from here he was well placed to threaten any assault which might be made on the formidable defences. This was carried out on a sector apparently on the Sebka er Riana; the Romans broke in through a gate and 4,000 entered; but the ground was favourable to the defenders, and they were forced back.

Hasdrubal had meanwhile withdrawn within the walls, in the belief that the assault would be decisive, and had thus lost his valuable strongpoint. This general was a man of some military talent, as his success with limited forces in the country had shown, but was of a cruel and domineering disposition. He adopted the savage tactics used by the mercenary leaders in the Mercenary War, in order to prevent any weakening of the will of the citizens to resist; Roman prisoners were taken on to the walls, mutilated and tortured in the full view of their comrades, and thrown down outside. Those Carthaginians who protested against this needless savagery were killed.

Scipio now devoted his attention to a complete blockade. Elaborate earthworks were built across the isthmus, parallel to the Carthaginian defences, and carried right round the Roman position. This prevented any possibility of food reaching the city from the remaining Libyan allies. Transport ships still ventured at times to run the blockade of the Roman fleet, so here, after establishing a camp to the south of the city near Le Kram, Scipio undertook the enormous task of building a mole right across the harbour mouth.

As the work proceeded, the defenders planned a counter-stroke. The inner harbour was out of sight of the attackers, and in it a fleet of fifty ships was built out of old materials. Meanwhile an alternative exit from the harbour was dug, in an easterly direction; it probably was roughly where the modern exit from the inner lagoon has been made. When the fleet was ready, a breach was made in the wall and the fleet sailed out. If it had attacked at once, with the advantage of surprise, it might have destroyed all the Roman ships which were beached on the seaward side of the tongue; but the sailors had not the confidence in their ships and rowing. Next day the Romans were ready, and a naval battle took place more or less under the walls. The Carthaginians resisted desperately, but were outnumbered by the Romans, whose ships were in any case much larger, and the survivors were forced back within the harbour. Scipio was able to seize the large quay outside the walls to the east of the original harbour mouth, although his siege engines were more than once burnt by courageous sallies of defenders now made desperate by growing hunger.

During the winter of 147–146 the Libyans all submitted to Scipio and in the spring he judged that the defenders had reached the limit of their endurance, as many died from hunger and others gave themselves up. The attack was to be launched from the quay in the direction of the harbours, and to hinder it Hasdrubal fired all the buildings of the outer port. The Romans got on to the wall, however, and Scipio's lieutenant Laelius followed it to the region of the inner harbour, which fell into his hands with little resistance, as did the market place.

It now remained to assault the defences of the Byrsa, which were on nothing like the same scale as the outer defences of the city; but the Carthaginians turned every house into a fortress, and for six days a bitter struggle went on. The description of this scene in Appian (undoubtedly taken from the account of Polybius, who was an eye-witness), though rhetorical in parts, has the ring of reality about it.

The streets leading from the market square to the Byrsa were flanked by houses of six storeys, from which the defenders poured a shower of missiles on to the Romans; when the attackers got inside the buildings, the struggle continued on the roofs and on planks crossing the empty spaces; many were hurled to the ground or on to the weapons of those fighting in the streets. Scipio ordered all this sector to be fired and the ruins cleared away, to give a better passage to his troops, and as this was done there fell with the walls many bodies of those who had hidden in the upper storeys and been burnt to death, and others who were still alive, wounded and badly burnt. Scipio had squadrons of soldiers ready to keep the streets clear for the rapid movement of his men, and dead or living were thrown together into pits; and it often happened that those who were not yet dead were crushed by the cavalry horses as they passed, not deliberately but in the heat of the battle.

On the seventh day, some men came out of the Byrsa asking for the lives of those who surrendered. Scipio agreed, and 50,000 men, women, and children, half starved, filed out of the citadel. Nine hundred deserters from the Romans, who could expect crucifixion as a punishment, continued to resist with Hasdrubal in the enclosure of the temple of Eshmoun, until forced to retreat into the building, on the roof of which they took up their final position. At this point the courage of Hasdrubal—who had often proclaimed his determination to fight till death—collapsed: he came out with his wife and two children to ask for Scipio's mercy. The deserters who saw this asked Scipio for a few moments' respite, during which they hurled insults at the Carthaginian general; after which they fired the temple and died in the flames. Hasdrubal's wife also turned on her husband, after thanking Scipio for granting their lives, and calling Hasdrubal a coward and traitor, threw herself and her children into the burning temple.

For ten days or more the fires raged in the city. Reserving the gold and silver and sacred objects for the state, Scipio allowed his troops to plunder. Those who had surrendered were sold into slavery, and all the arms captured were ceremonially dedicated to Mars and Minerva and burned. Finally, everything that was still standing was levelled; Scipio pronounced a curse over the remains, a plough was drawn over the site and salt sown in the furrow, to signify that it was to remain uninhabited and barren for ever.

Such was the end of the city of Carthage, after an existence of about six centuries; it remains to be seen what was left of her civilization in Africa in subsequent centuries. There still survived many thousands of people of Phoenician race in North Africa; quite apart from the cities which had made a timely surrender to Rome and were given a privileged status when the Roman province was established, there were the numerous inhabitants of the coastal cities which had been taken over by Masinissa and now formed part of the kingdoms of his sons, and many who had migrated to Numidian territory in the previous fifty years. For over a century these provided what there was of civilization over most of North Africa, since Roman immigration to the new province was slight and restricted to the immediate hinterland of Carthage. In any case, under the Roman provincial system, both at this early stage and later when it extended over the whole of North Africa, local authorities continued to function with the minimum of interference from Roman provincial governors.

The Romans, like most people in antiquity, attached little importance to the idea of race, and the destruction of Carthage did not mean that there was any attempt to root out Carthaginian civilization. The most important known change introduced by them as a deliberate reform of some previously existing custom was the prohibition of human sacrifice; apart from this, religious, social, and political institutions continued as before. The position of the Carthaginians in Numidian territory continued to be privileged even after the destruction of the city and the death of Masinissa, and his successors continued to encourage the arts and techniques which had been introduced by Carthage. A remarkable instance of this was the fact that the Romans handed over to the Numidian kings the contents of the libraries of Carthage, which fell into their hands at the sack; it is to be presumed that there were many books, like that of Mago, of immediate practical use in the backward territories. The language of Carthage became the official language throughout North Africa, and there can be no doubt that a large number of Numidians came to learn it.[21]

The religion of the native peoples was greatly influenced by the immigrants and no doubt also by what had been learnt by the numbers of Numidians who served with the armies of Carthage. In the reign of Masinissa there was a tophet at Cirta at which human sacrifices were performed with the same rites as at Carthage itself, though the practice died out fairly quickly.

During the century following the destruction of Carthage, many of the more fertile parts of Numidia, particularly those corresponding to eastern Algeria, came to be cultivated by sedentary tribesmen, but at the end of this period, in 46 B.C., two events put a term to the mixed Numidian and Carthaginian civilization: Julius Caesar came to North Africa to complete the destruction of his political enemies, led ironically enough by Cato the Younger, descendant of the man who had brought about the destruction of Carthage; while there, he annexed the eastern part of Numidia to the Roman empire and began the rebuilding of Carthage as a colony of Roman citizens, a venture which had been tried once before, in spite of the solemn curses on the site, but which had not been successful.[22]

Thus a new civilization was planted in North Africa with all the resources and prestige of the greatest empire that had yet existed. Already the descendants of the original Carthaginian population in all parts of Africa had become considerably intermingled with the native populations, and their speech was undergoing a rapid change to form the distinct language called Neo-Punic, though for official purposes and in religious rites the original forms were still adhered to.

But although Carthaginian civilization was diluted, it showed that obstinacy and persistence that had marked it in its great days, and by no means gave way at once to the new and socially more useful Latin importation. The Romans found it useful to recognize its strength; in over thirty communities, as far apart as Volubilis near Fez in Morocco and Lepcis Magna in Tripolitania, the highest local officials were still called sufetes even in the first century A.D. The Carthaginian nomenclature lasted as long in many small towns. The stepson of the writer Apuleius in the middle of the second century neither knew nor wanted to know Latin, and later in the century a relative of the emperor Septimius Severus, who was himself born at Lepcis Magna, spoke it very badly.[23] But the advantages to be gained from the adoption of the Latin language, and from participation in the imperial administration, which was open to all men of substance and education who acquired Roman citizenship, were too great to be ignored. An emperor born in a former colony of Carthage was the culmination of a process begun a hundred years before when the first men of African origin entered the Roman senate.[24]

At the same time the old religion underwent important changes, the temples and liturgies now being modelled on the Roman practice. Only among the country people, who felt the influence of the new civilization much less, did the old ways linger on; but even there the language of Carthage rapidly disappeared, though in some parts it left sufficient mark on Libyan dialects for St Augustine to record the use of the 'Punic language' in the early fifth century and to realize its close connexion with Hebrew.[25]

Lastly, it is not far-fetched to see in the intensity of Carthaginian religion, which affected the native peoples also, and the tendency towards henotheism in it, a reason for the spread of Christianity in North Africa far more rapidly than elsewhere in the West, and also for the great vigour of its expression there. We even find personal names of the old Carthaginian type, now in Latin form, such as Deusdedit—Baalyaton—'God has given him', or Donatus—Muttumbaal—'Gift of God', used amongst the Christian population.

The civilization of Carthage must therefore be numbered with those, chiefly in the early history of the near East, which have left neither descendants in an existing people nor a literature or religion of formative influence in the later development of the civilizations of the Mediterranean. Historically speaking, it was an extension into the western Mediterranean of the old civilizations of the East, all of which it outlived. For all its acquisition of a substantial colouring of Hellenism in its later stages, it remained curiously archaic, particularly in its religion, and appeared unable to develop in new directions as did its Greek and Roman counterparts.

The history of western Europe would have been very different if Rome had been defeated by Hannibal, but it is clear there would have been no Carthaginian Empire of anything like the extent or quality of the Roman; we could not substitute a Carthaginian reference in Gibbon's ingenious fancy of the consequences of a victory of another Semitic power in the west, the Arabs: 'Perhaps the interpretation of the Koran would now be taught in the schools of Oxford, and her pulpits might demonstrate to a circumcised people the sanctity and truth of the revelation of Mohammed.' In a more general sense, the Phoenician settlement in North Africa was part of the movement which brought the western Mediterranean, till then inhabited by backward tribes of infinite variety, within the sphere of the more advanced civilizations of the Aegean and Levantine coasts. The geographical conditions which made this area part of the Mediterranean rather than the African world were emphasized. All except one of the invaders who in later times dominated its coast came by sea—Romans, Vandals, Byzantines, Turks, Spaniards, and French. Only the Arabs came by land, a triumph of man over geographical circumstances, and imposed the dominant culture on an area which yet is associated with the West by so many historical events.

The total destruction of Carthage was an action ever remembered in antiquity. It gained point from the sack of Corinth in the same year, when Rome once for all established her rule in Greece. Yet it was not only because of the ruthlessness of the action in itself, as an impressive demonstration of Rome's temper at this period, that it was regarded as a critical point in the development of Rome. Certainly, when the great wealth and power of Carthage and her remarkable resistance to

Rome were considered, it was inevitable that the two powers should be portrayed as contending for the mastery of the world. Already, in the period between the Hannibalic war and the destruction of Carthage, Rome had easily defeated the Hellenistic powers of Macedon and Syria and there were no further serious rivals left; the destruction of the city that had resisted Rome longest demonstrated that the entire Mediterranean was in her grasp whenever she chose to take the opportunity of formally reducing to subjection those states who were already dependent.

The Romans, however, for all the pride they naturally felt in their great achievements, came to feel that in some sense the victory over Carthage marked a turning-point in Rome's internal history as well as in the growth of her empire. From the surviving books of Livy it is clear that he regarded the Roman victory against Hannibal as the high point of her history. The hero of his whole work, the Roman People, then reached full maturity, in the bitter struggle against the man who in his own person not only brought the war on Rome but was the directing genius of all the Carthaginian successes. Livy's talent was equal to the task of doing full justice to Hannibal's enormous achievement (thus enhancing Rome's ultimate victory) while at the same time preserving intact the Romans' reputation for invincibility, by showing that none of her defeats was due to a deficiency in fighting quality but to extraneous or unforeseeable circumstances. Above all, he sought to show that the discipline and courage of the Roman citizens, and the honest and unselfish leadership of the senate, reached heights from which in the succeeding decades they began to decline.

Livy's account of the destruction of Carthage and his judgement on it are lost, but he must have taken into account a viewpoint found particularly in Sallust but also in other historians. This was connected with the arguments of Scipio Nasica against the decision to destroy Carthage, to the effect that the continued existence of the city was a necessity for the preservation of a healthy society at Rome. Sallust, following a Greek commentator Poseidonius, saw in the destruction of Carthage the opening of the floodgates to a river of vices in the Roman state. No longer having the need to preserve the good old ways, the Romans became idle and luxury-loving, filled with a lust for power and riches. It was indeed the case that at this moment in Roman history a number of political, economic, and social problems urgently needed solutions; and these solutions were not forthcoming, owing to defects in the Roman constitution and a real deterioration in the standards of political behaviour among all classes in the state. These problems
16

and political failures were connected with the acquisition of the empire, but it was a naïve piece of over-simplification which attributed them to the events of 146. It was the greatness of the catastrophe, the blotting out of a city which had been so rich and powerful, that impressed itself on the imagination; and the greater Rome grew, the greater was the importance attributed to Carthage as the chief antagonist.

The fate of Carthage was a truly tragic event, the type of greatness laid low, whether of individual or people. Scipio Aemilianus, only a Scipio by adoption but endowed with some of that family's sensibility saw in his moment of triumph the ultimate fate of Rome.[26]

Scipio looked over the city which had flourished for over seven hundred years since its foundation, which had ruled over such extensive territories, islands, and seas, and been as rich in arms, fleets, elephants, and money as the greatest empires, but which had surpassed them in daring and high courage, since though deprived of all its arms and ships it had yet withstood a great siege and famine for three years, and was now coming to an end in total destruction; and he is said to have wept and openly lamented the fate of his enemy. After meditating a long time on the fact that not only individuals but cities, nations, and empires must all inevitably come to an end, and on the fate of Troy, that once glorious city, on the fall of the Assyrian, Median, and Persian empires, and on the more recent destruction of the brilliant empire of the Macedonians, deliberately or subconsciously he quoted the words of Hector from Homer—'The day shall come when sacred Troy shall fall, and King Priam and all his warrior people with him.' And when Polybius, who was with him, asked him what he meant, he turned and took him by the hand, saying: 'This is a glorious moment, Polybius; and yet I am seized with fear and foreboding that some day the same fate will befall my own country.'

Bibliography

This bibliography contains a selection of books and articles which are important for the study of Carthage, and includes some other works which are not primarily concerned with Carthage but which have material on some particular aspect of Carthaginian history or civilization. Much information is contained in periodicals which are difficult to obtain because of their limited range or their date; I have listed only the more recent and important items. Complete references to earlier works, in particular to the archaeology of North Africa, may be found in Gsell, *Histoire ancienne de l'Afrique du nord*, and to works on Phoenician archaeology in Harden, *The Phoenicians*, and Moscati, *The World of the Phoenicians*.

W. F. Albright, *The Archaeology of Palestine*, rev. ed., Harmondsworth, 1949.

J. G. Baldacchino, 'Punic Rock Tombs near Pawla', *Papers of the British School at Rome*, XIX, 1951, 1 ff.

J. Beloch, *Griechische Geschichte*, I–IV, Berlin, 1924–31.

A. Berthier, *Le sanctuaire punique d'El Hofra à Constantine*, Paris, 1955.

E. Boucher-Colozier, 'Les Étrusques et Carthage', *Mél. d'Archéol. et d'Histoire de Él'cole Fr. de Rome*, LXV, 1953, 63 ff.

Cambridge Ancient History, IV, VI–VIII.

J. Carcopino, *Le Maroc antique*, Paris, 1944.

M. Cary and E. H. Warmington, *The Ancient Explorers*, London, 1929.

P. Cintas, *Céramique punique*, Tunis, 1950.

'Dar Essafi', *Comptes Rendus de l'Académie des Inscriptions*, 1953, 256 ff.

'Deux campagnes de recherches à Utique', *Karthago*, II, 1951, 5 ff.

'Le sanctuaire punique de Sousse', *Revue Africaine*, XC, 1947, 1 ff.

'Nouvelles recherches à Utique', *Karthago*, V, 1954, 89 ff.

G. Contenau, *La Civilisation phénicienne*, Paris, 1926.

T. J. Dunbabin, *The Western Greeks*, Oxford, 1948.

R. Dussaud, *Les découvertes de Ras Shamra*, Paris, 1941.

V. Ehrenberg, *Karthago*, Leipzig, 1927.

T. Frank, *Roman Imperialism*, New York, 1914.

E. A. Freeman, *History of Sicily*, Oxford, 1891–4.

W. H. C. Frend, *The Donatist Church*, Oxford, 1952.

A. Garcia y Bellido, *Fenicios y Cartagineses en Occidente*, Madrid, 1942.

P. Gauckler, *Nécropoles puniques de Carthage*, Paris, 1925.

E. F. Gautier, *Le passé de l'Afrique du nord*.

G. Griffiths, *Mercenaries of the Hellenistic World*, Cambridge, 1935.

E. Groag, *Hannibal als Politiker*, Vienna, 1929.

S. Gsell, *Histoire ancienne de l'Afrique du nord*, I–IV, Paris, 1912–20.

N. G. L. Hammond, *A History of Greece*, Oxford, 1959.

D. B. Harden, *The Phoenicians*, London, 1962.
  'The Topography of Punic Carthage', *Greece and Rome*, IX, 1938, 1 ff.
  'The Phoenicians on the West Coast of Africa', *Antiquity*, XXII, 1948, 141 ff.

B. V. Head, *Historia Nummorum*, 2nd ed., Oxford, 1911.

A. Heuss, 'Der Erste Punische Krieg und das Problem des Römischen Imperialismus', *Historische Zeitschrift*, CLXIX, 1949, 457 ff.

G. F. Hill, *Coins of Ancient Sicily*, London, 1903.

B. S. J. Isserlin, 'Motya 1955', *Papers of the British School at Rome*, XXVI, 1958, 1 ff.

J. Kromayer and G. Veith, *Antike Schlachtfelde*, I–IV, Berlin, 1903–31.

G. G. Lapeyre and A. Pellegrin, *Carthage punique*, Paris, 1942.

G. Lilliu, 'Rapporti fra la civilizzazione nuragica e la civilizzazione fenicio-punica in Sardegna', *Studi Etruschi*, XVIII, 1944, 323 ff.

O. Meltzer and U. Kahrstedt, *Geschichte der Karthager*, I–III, Berlin, 1879–1913.

Ed. Meyer, *Geschichte des Altertums*, Stuttgart, 1907–34.
  Hannibal und Scipio, Stuttgart, 1923.

G. Picard, *Les religions de l'Afrique antique*, Paris, 1954.
  Le Monde de Carthage, Paris, 1956.

G. and C. Picard, *La vie quotidienne à Carthage au temps d'Hannibal*, Paris, 1958.

L. Poinssot and R. Lantier, 'Un sanctuaire de Tanit à Carthage', *Rev. de l'Histoire des Religions*, LXXXVII, 1923, 32 ff.

J. Reynolds and J. B. Ward Perkins, *Inscriptions of Roman Tripolitania*, British School at Rome, 1952.

Rhys Carpenter, 'The Phoenicians in the West', *American Journal of Archaeology*, LXVII, 1958, 35 ff.

E. S. G. Robinson, 'Punic Coins in Spain', *Essays in Roman Coinage presented to H. Mattingly*, Oxford, 1956, 34 ff.
  'The Libyan Hoard (1952)', *Numismatic Chronicle*, LVI, 1956, 9 ff.

H. H. Scullard, *Roman Politics, 220–150 B.C.*, Oxford, 1951.
Scipio Africanus and the Second Punic War, Cambridge, 1930.
W. W. Tarn, 'The Fleets of the First Punic War', *Journal of Hellenic Studies*, XXVII, 1907, 48 ff.
Hellenistic Military and Naval Developments, Cambridge, 1930.
J. Thiel, *A History of Roman Sea Power before the Second Punic War*, Amsterdam, 1954.
Studies on the Growth of Roman Sea Power in Republican Times, Amsterdam, 1946.
J. Vercoutter, *Les objets égyptiens et égyptisants du mobilier funéraire carthaginois*, Paris, 1945.
J. Vogt (ed.), *Rom und Karthago*, Leipzig, 1942.
F. W. Walbank, *A Commentary on Polybius*, I, Oxford, 1958.
E. H. Warmington, *Greek Geography*, London, 1934.
H. D. Westlake, *Timoleon and his Relations with the Tyrants*, Manchester, 1952.
J. I. S. Whitaker, *Motya*, London, 1921.

SELECT ADDITIONAL BIBLIOGRAPHY

A. Astin, *Scipio Aemilianus*, Oxford, 1967.
J. Baradez, 'Nouvelles recherches sur les ports de Carthage', *Karthago*, IX, 1958, 45 ff.
F. Barreca and others, *Monte Sirai*, I–IV, Rome, 1964–7.
L. Foucher, *Hadrumetum*, Paris, 1964.
G. Garbini, 'I Fenici in Occidente', *Studi Etruschi*, XXXIV, 1966, 111 ff.
G. Halff, 'L'onomastique punique de Carthage', *Karthago*, XII, 1963–4, 61 ff.
J. Heurgon, 'The Inscriptions of Pyrgi', *Journal of Roman Studies*, LVI, 1966, 1 ff.
B. S. J. Isserlin and others, 'Motya, a Phoenician-Punic site near Marsala', *Annual of the Leeds Oriental Society*, IV, 1962–3, 84–131.
G. K. Jenkins and R. B. Lewis, *Carthaginian Gold and Electrum Coins*, London, 1963.
A. Jodin, *Mogador*, Tangier, 1966.
A. Lézine, *Architecture punique*, Tunis, 1961.
S. Moscati, *The World of the Phoenicians*, London, 1968.
'La penetrazione fenicia e punica in Sardegna', *Memorie dell' Academia Nazionale dei Lincei*, ser. 8, 12, 1966.
M. Pellicer Catalan, *Excavaciones en la necropolis punica 'Laurita' del Carro de San Cristobal*, Madrid, 1962.
G. Pesce, *Sardegna Punica*, Cagliari, 1961.
C. Picard, 'Notes de chronologie punique: le problème du cinquième siècle', *Karthago*, XII, 1963–4, 15 ff.
'Sacra Punica', *Karthago*, XIII, 1965–6, 1 ff.

G. Picard, 'Les sufètes de Carthage dans Tite Live et Cornelius Nepos', *Revue des Études Latines*, XLI, 1963, 269 ff.

'Le problème du portrait d'Hannibal', *Karthago*, XII, 163–4, 29 ff.

Ch. Saumagne, 'Le lungomare de la Carthage romaine', *Karthago*, X, 1959–60, 157 ff.

V. Tusa and others, *Mozia*, I–IV, Rome, 1964–7.

G. Vuillemot, 'La nécropole punique du phare dans l'île de Rachgoun (Oran),' *Lybica*, III, 1955, 7–76.

P. Walsh, 'Masinissa', *Journal of Roman Studies*, LV, 1965, 149 ff.

Notes

ALL dates, except publication dates, are B.C. unless otherwise specified. The following abbreviations are used in the notes:

Beloch = J. Beloch, *Griechische Geschichte*, Berlin, 1924-31.

C.A.H. = *Cambridge Ancient History*.

Carcopino = J. Carcopino, *Le Maroc antique*, Paris, 1944.

Cintas, *Céramique* = P. Cintas, *Céramique punique*, Tunis, 1950.

Cintas, *Dar Essafi* = P. Cintas, *Comptes Rendus de l'Académie des Inscriptions*, 1953, 256 ff.

Cintas, *Nouvelles recherches* = P. Cintas, 'Nouvelles recherches à Utique', *Karthago*, V, 1954, 89 ff.

Cintas, *Sousse* = P. Cintas, 'Le Sanctuaire punique de Sousse', *Revue Africaine*, XC, 1947, 1 ff.

Cintas, *Utique* = P. Cintas, 'Deux campagnes de recherches à Utique', *Karthago*, II, 1951, 5 ff.

Dunbabin = T. J. Dunbabin, *The Western Greeks*, Oxford, 1948.

Frend = W. H. C. Frend, *The Donatist Church*, Oxford, 1952.

Gsell = S. Gsell, *Histoire ancienne de l'Afrique du nord*, Paris, 1912 ff.

Hammond = N. G. L. Hammond, *A History of Greece*, Oxford, 1959.

Harden = D. B. Harden, *The Phoenicians*, London, 1962.

Isserlin = B. S. J. Isserlin, 'Motya 1955', *Papers of the British School at Rome*, XXVI, 1958, 1 ff.

Jenkins = G. K. Jenkins and R. B. Lewis, *Carthaginian Gold and Electrum Coins*, London, 1963.

Meyer = Ed. Meyer, *Geschichte des Altertums*, Stuttgart, 1931.

Moscati = S. Moscati, *The World of the Phoenicians*, London, 1968.

G. Picard (1954) = G. Picard, *Les religions de l'Afrique antique*, Paris, 1954.

G. Picard (1956) = G. Picard, *Le monde de Carthage*, Paris, 1956.

G. and C. Picard = G. and C. Picard, *La vie quotidienne à Carthage au temps d'Hannibal*, Paris, 1958.

247

Reynolds = J. Reynolds and J. B. Ward-Perkins, *Inscriptions of Roman Tripolitania*, British School at Rome, 1952.

Rhys Carpenter = Rhys Carpenter, 'The Phoenicians in the West', *American Journal of Archaeology*, LXVII, 1958.

Scullard = H. H. Scullard, *Scipio Africanus and the Second Punic War*, Cambridge, 1930.

Walbank F. W. Walbank, *A Commentary on Polybius*, I, Oxford ,1958.

Walsh = P. Walsh, 'Masinissa', *Journal of Roman Studies*, LV, 1965, 149 ff.

Whitaker = J. I. S. Whitaker, *Motya*, London, 1921.

CHAPTER 1

1. On the Phoenicians generally, see Harden, Moscati.
2. Meyer, II: 2: 62–4; 1 Kings 16: 31; Homer, *Iliad*, VI: 290; *Odyssey*, IV: 84.
3. cp. C.A.H., II: 172 ff.
4. Meyer, II: 2: 12 ff.
5. Meyer, II: 2: 78 ff.; Harden, 51.
6. Meyer, II: 2: 124 ff.
7. Isaiah 23: 8.
8. Ezekiel 26; cp. Meyer, III: 177 ff.
9. Justin., XVIII: 4; Pliny, *N.H.*, V: 76; Gsell, I: 397.
10. Sallust, *Jug.*, 19.
11. Rhys Carpenter, 51
12. V: 35
13. Strabo, I: 3: 2, II: 2: 14; Festus Avienus, 268–9; Pliny, *N.H.*, IV: 120.
14. 1 Kings 9: 26 ff., 10: 22; Isaiah 23: 1; Meyer, II: 2: 102.
15. Gsell, I: 103 ff.
16. Gsell, I: 309 ff.
17. D. B. Harden, *Greece and Rome*, IX, 1939, 1 ff.
18. Dion. Hal., I: 74 (after Timaeus); others, Gsell, I: 397.
19. Vell. Pat., I: 2, 4; Pliny, *N.H.*, XVI: 216.
20. See Pauly-Wissowa, *R.E.*, s.v.
21. Dunbabin, 330.
22. On the pottery from the Sanctuary of Tanit, see Cintas, *Céramique*, passim.
23. Thuc., VI: 2, 6.
24. B. S. J. Isserlin, *Annual of the Leeds Oriental Society*, IV, 1962–3, 84–131; V. Tusa, *Mozia*, I–IV, Rome, 1964–7.
25. Diod. Sic., V: 12.
26. F. Barreca, *Monte Sirai*, I–IV, 1964–7.
27. Strabo, III: 5: 6.
28. M. Pellicer Catalan, *Excavaçiones en la necropolis punica 'Laurita' del Cerro de San Cristobal* (*Almunecar, Granada*), Madrid, 1962.
29. G. Vuillemot, 'La nécropole punique du phare dans l'ile du Rachgoun (Oran)', *Lybica*, III, 1955, 7–76.
30. M. Jodin, Mogador, Rabat, 1966.

CHAPTER 2

1. Thuc., I: 2: 2.
2. On Greek colonization in the West, see especially Dunbabin, 1–47.
3. *Od.*, XIV: 288–9; XV: 299, 415; cp. M. I. Finley, *The World of Odysseus*.

4. Herod, IV: 152.
5. Dunbabin, 303, 326.
6. Thuc., VI: 2: 6; Diod. Sic. V: 9; Pausan. X: 11: 3; cp. Dunbabin, 328 ff.
7. Diod. Sic., loc. cit.; Thuc., III: 88.
8. Meyer, III: 177 f.
9. Justin, XVIII: 7.
10. Whitaker, 142, 208.
11. Thuc., VI: 6: 2.
12. F. Barreca, *Monte Sirai*, IV.
13. Herod., I: 165–6; Thuc., I: 113.
14. Herod., I: 170.
15. Thuc., I: 13; Herod., I: 167.
16. J. Heurgon, 'The Inscriptions of Pyrgi', *J.R.S.*, LVI, 1966, 1–15.
17. Justin., XVIII: 7.
18. Justin., XIX: 1: 1; first directly attested in 480, Herod., VII: 165; Diod. Sic., XI: 1.
19. e.g. Diod. Sic., XIII: 44: 6, XIV: 2: 4.
20. Plut., *Timoleon*, 28.
21. Diod. Sic., XVI: 81.
22. Herod., VII: 165.
23. Polyb., I: 67.
24. Livy, XXVIII: 20; Polyb., III: 72, 113–15.
25. Livy, XXIX: 34; Polyb., I: 19, 78, III: 56, 71.
26. Herod., VII: 165; Diod. Sic., XIII: 44; Polyb., I: 17; Livy, XXI: 11, XXIV: 42: 6.
27. Polyb., VI: 23; Livy, XXXI: 34.
28. Diod. Sic., XIII: 80, XIX: 106; Polyb., I: 67; Diod. Sic., V: 17.
29. Diod. Sic., XVI: 73; Polyb., II: 5–7. On their use by Hannibal, see below, 199 ff.
30. Diod. Sic., XIII: 44, XIV: 9.
31. Diod. Sic., XIII: 58; Plut., *Timoleon*, 20; Polyb., I: 32, 43.
32. See below, 186 ff.
33. See below, 159 ff.
34. Justin., XIX, 1.
35. Justin., ibid.; Herod., V: 43, 46–8, VII: 158, 205; Diod. Sic., IV: 23.
36. Herod., III: 17, 19.
37. See A. Andrewes, *The Greek Tyrants*, 1956.
38. Herod., VII: 158.
39. Herod., IV: 165; Diod Sic., XI: 21, XIII: 55.
40. Herod., VII: 145, 153, 157–62.
41. Herod., VII: 166.
42. *Poetics*, XXIII: 3.
43. Diod. Sic., XI: 1.
44. Herod., VII: 165; Diod. Sic., XI: 1 and 20.
45. Diod. Sic., XI: 20–6.

CHAPTER 3
1. Pindar, *Nem.*, IX: 28; *Pyth.*, I: 72.
2. Hammond, 250.
3. *I.G.* I(2), 929.
4. G. Picard (1956), 39 ff. and 191; C. Picard, *Karthago*, XII, 1963–4, 15 ff.
5. Jenkins, 1 ff.

6. Rostovzeff, *Social and Economic History of the Hellenistic World*, 1: 85 f.
7. See below.
8. Against this, Moscati, 241–2; but no tophet is yet known from Spain.
9. See below, 137 ff.
10. XXV: 7.
11. Diod. Sic., XX: 57.
12. Polyb., 1: 73; Diod. Sic., XXIV: 10; Jerome, *P.L.*, XXVI: 353.
13. Polyb., 1: 66.
14. Apuleius, *Apol.*, 24.
15. Diod. Sic., XX: 8.
16. Herod., II: 32, IV: 37; Diod. Sic., XX: 55; Polyb., III: 33.
17. Diod. Sic., XX: 55; Polyb., III: 33.
18. e.g. Diod. Sic., XX: 17; Appian, *Lib.*, 3, 68.
19. Gsell, II: 105 ff.
20. See the indications in pseudo-Scylax, 111 (*Geog. Graeci Min.*, ed Müller) of mid fourth century B.C. date.
21. Pseudo-Scylax, ibid.
22. See below, 134.
23. Gsell, I: 342 and 477, II: 94.
24. R. G. Goodchild, *Papers Brit. Sch. Rome*, 1952, 94 ff.
25. Strabo, XVII: 3.
26. Polyb., 1: 82; Livy, XXIX: 25, XXXIV: 62, Reynolds, 73 ff.
27. Reynolds, 80.
28. Silius Italicus, III: 256 ff; pseudo-Scylax, 110; Reynolds, 63 ff.
29. Reynolds, 20 ff.
30. Strabo, XVII: 3: 18.
31. Polyb., 1: 39; Pliny, *N.H.*, V: 41; pseudo-Scylax, 110.
32. Gsell, II: 125–6.
33. Strabo, XVII: 16: 3; Caesar, *Bell. Afr.*, XLII; Pliny, *N.H.*, V: 25.
34. Appian, *Lib.*, 94; Steph. Byz., s.v. Acholla.
35. Appian, loc. cit.; Diod. Sic., XX: 17.
36. Polyb., 1: 86; Caesar, *Bell. Afr.*, XXIX; Appian, loc. cit.
37. Cintas, *Sousse*.
38. Thuc., VII: 50.
39. Cintas, *Dar Essafi*.
40. See below, 79.
41. Also called Hippo Acra; Pliny, *N.H.*, V: 23; pseudo-Scylax, 111; Diod Sic., XX: 55; Polyb., 1: 70, 73.
42. Pliny, *N.H.*, V: 22; cp. Gsell, II: 155 ff.
43. Pseudo-Scylax, 111.
44. Gsell, II: 151 ff.
45. Gsell, II: 157 ff.
46. R. Cintas, 'Fouilles puniques à Tipasa', *Rev. Africaine*, XCII, 1949, 1 ff.
47. Gsell, II: 161 ff.
48. Hecataeus, F. H. G., 1: 25.
49. See E. H. Warmington, *Greek Geography*, xxiv, f.
50. e.g. Herod., IV: 42; Pliny, *N.H.*, II: 160.
51. E. H. Warmington, loc. cit.
52. Meyer, II (2): 102 f.

53. IV: 42.
54. Herod., ibid.
55. Herod., IV: 43.
56. *N.H.*, II: 169; cp. Justin, XIX: 2.
57. Herod., IV: 196.
58. E. W. Bovill, *The Golden Trade of the Moors*, London, 1958.
59. Müller, *Geog. Graeci Min.*, I: 1–14. For commentaries, see especially Carcopino, 73–163; Gsell, II: 472 ff.; M. Cary and E. H. Warmington, *The Ancient Explorers* (London, 1929).
60. *N.H.*, V: 2 ff.
61. See above, 34.
62. Pseudo-Scylax, 112.
63. Carcopino, 152.
64. Pliny, *N.H.*, VI: 200.
65. Pliny, *N.H.*, V: 9–10, VI: 199.
66. Pindar, *Nem.*, IV: 69.
67. *N.H.*, V: 2 ff.
68. Pliny, *N.H.*, II: 169; Festus Avienus, *Ora Martima*.
69. See above, 24.
70. cp. Rhys Carpenter, 51.
71. M. V. Taylor, *Victoria County History of Cornwall*, part V: 15 ff.; Pauly-Wissowa, *R.E.*, s. v. Kassiterides.
72. Strabo, 175.
73. Pauly-Wissowa, *R.E.*, s. v. Gades, 452.
74. Plut., *Moralia*, 799D.
75. Livy, XXVIII: 37; *C.I.S.*, I: 143; *I.G.*, XIV9: 953; *C.R.A.I.*, 1901, 578.
76. Diod. Sic., XX: 55; Polyb., VII: 9.
77. Diod. Sic., XIII: 80; Polyb., III: 33; Gsell, II: 296 f.
78. See below, 160.
79. See below, 85.
80. *C.I.S.*, I: 135; Gsell, II: 309.
81. B. V. Head, *Historia Nummorum*, 138, 165 f., 161, 170, 158, 161.
82. Head, *op. cit.*, 139, 170, 136.
83. Polyb., III: 22, 24.
84. Diod. Sic., XIII: 59, 114, XIV: 65; Cicero, *Verr.*, II: 3, 6.
85. Diod. Sic., XIII: 62, XIV: 8, XVI: 9.
86. See below, 160.
87. See below, 149.
88. Polyb., I: 72.
89. See below, 187 ff.

CHAPTER 4

1. For the chronology of events in Sicily, see Beloch, II, 2: 162 ff., 254 ff., III, 2: 366 ff.
2. For these events, see Freeman, II.
3. Thuc., VI: 6; Diod. Sic., XII: 82 f.
4. Thuc., VI: 15: 2; Plut., *Alcibiades*, 17; M. Treu, *Historia*, III, 1944–5, 41 ff.
5. Diod. Sic., XIII: 43.
6. e.g. Diod. Sic., XIII: 81, 109, etc.

7. On the genealogy, see Beloch, III, 2: 120.
8. Diod. Sic., XIII: 36.
9. See above, 60.
10. Diod. Sic., XIII: 43.
11. On the campaign of Selinus, Diod. Sic., XII: 43 ff.
12. Head, op. cit., 166.
13. Diod. Sic., XIII: 59 ff.; Xen., *Hell.*, 1: 1: 37.
14. Diod. Sic., XIII: 63, 75.
15. K. F. Stroheker, *Historia*, III, 1944–5, 163 ff.
16. Diod. Sic., XIII: 79.
17. Diod. Sic., XIII: 81.
18. Diod. Sic., XIII: 80 ff.; Polyaenus, V: 7–10.
19. cp. G. Picard (1956), 51.
20. On the rise of Dionysius, see Diod. Sic., XIII: 91 ff.
21. Diod. Sic., XIII: 93, 108 ff.
22. Diod. Sic., XIII: 113.
23. Diod. Sic., XIII: 114.
24. Beloch, III, 2: 194 ff.
25. Diod. Sic., XIV: 7.
26. Diod. Sic., XIV: 7, 14–15; Polyaenus, V: 2.
27. Diod. Sic., XIV: 18, 41–4.
28. Diod Sic., XIV: 41, 45–7.
29. Diod. Sic., XIV: 48–53; Polyaenus, V: 2.
30. Arrian, *Anab.*, II: 17; Diod. Sic., XVII: 40–5; Q. Curtius, IV: 4–27.
31. Diod Sic., XIV: 54–5, XXII: 10, XIII: 54; Polyaenus, V: 10.
32. Diod. Sic., XIV: 56–60.
33. Diod. Sic., XIV: 61–76; Polyaenus, II: 11; Justin., XIX: 2.
34. Diod. Sic., XIV: 77.
35. Jenkins, 11.
36. Beloch, III, 2: 116.
37. Diod. Sic., XIV: 90, 95–6.
38. Hammond, 478 ff.
39. Lysias, *Or.*, 33.
40. Diod. Sic., XV: 14; Strabo, V: 226.
41. Diod. Sic., XV: 15–17.
42. Diod Sic., XV: 73; Polyaenus, V: 9.
43. P. Gauckler, *Nécropoles puniques*, Paris, 1915, 520–1; G. C. Picard, 80 ff.

CHAPTER 5

1. For the chronology of this period see Beloch, III, 2: 378 ff., IV, 2: 249 ff.
2. Diod. Sic., XVI: 5; Plut., *Dion*, 6.
3. Justin., XX: 5.
4. On Dion, see Plutarch, *Dion, passim*; Diod. Sic., XVI: 9–20; H. Berve, *Dion*.
5. Plato, *Ep.*, VIII: 353 f.
6. Beloch, III, 1: 580.
7. Beloch, III, 2: 117.
8. Justin., XXI: 4.
9. Plut., *Timoleon*, 1 ff.

10. On Timoleon, see Plutarch, *Timoleon, passim*; Diod Sic., XVI: 66 ff.; H. D. Westlake, *Timoleon and his Relations with the Tyrants*, Manchester, 1952.
11. Diod. Sic., XIX: 3–5.
12. Below, 166.
13. W. W. Tarn, *Alexander the Great*, II: 378 ff.
14. But see Beloch, IV, 1: 268 ff.
15. Diod. Sic., XIX: 2–4; Justin., XXII: 1.
16. Diod. Sic., XIX: 5 ff.; Justin., XIX: 2.
17. Beloch, IV, 1: 181, note 3.
18. Diod. Sic., XIX: 65.
19. Diod. Sic., XIX: 70–1.
20. Justin., XXII: 2.
21. Diod. Sic., XIX: 71, 72.
22. Beloch, III, 2: 119.
23. Diod. Sic., XIX: 72, 102 ff.
24. Diod. Sic., XIX: 106–10.
25. Diod. Sic., XX: 1–7; Justin., XXII: 4, 5.
26. Diod. Sic., XX: 8.
27. Diod. Sic., XX: 9–13.
28. Diod. Sic., XX: 14; Justin., XVIII: 6; Lactant., *Div. Inst.*, I: 21.
29. Diod. Sic., XX: 15–18.
30. Diod. Sic., XX: 29–30.
31. Diod. Sic., XX: 31–3.
32. Diod. Sic., XXI: 40–2; Justin., XXII: 7; Polyaenus, V: 3; Strabo, XVIII: 3: 3.
33. Diod. Sic., XX: 43–4.
34. Diod. Sic., XX: 54–5; Appian, *Lib.*, 110.
35. Diod. Sic., XX: 57–61.
36. Diod. Sic., XX: 61–9, 79; Justin., XXII: 8.

CHAPTER 6

1. Extensive bibliography up to 1920, Gsell, II: 38 ff. For later discussions, G. and C. Picard, 26 ff., 258–9; Harden, 30 ff.; Harden, *Greece and Rome*, IX: 1 ff.; Saumagne, *Karthago*, X, 1959, 157 ff.
2. Appian, *Lib.*, 96 ff.; Strabo, XVII: 3: 14; Diod. Sic., III: 44.
3. Appian, *Lib.*, 95; Strabo, loc. cit.; Diod. Sic., XIX: 106, XX: 9, 13; Polyb., I: 73; Gsell, II: 21 ff.,; General A. Duval, *C.R.A.I.*, 1950, 53.
4. See below, 236 f.
5. G. and C, Picard, 35.
6. Diod. Sic., XX: 44: 5; Appian, *Lib.*, 128.
7. G. and C. Picard, 48.
8. Diod. Sic., XIX: 202.
9. Diod. Sic., XX: 44, XIV: 51; Strabo, XVI: 2: 23.
10. G. and C. Picard, 48.
11. Cintas, *Dar Essafi*.
12. Appian, *Lib.*, 95.
13. G. Picard (1954), 74 ff.
14. Appian, *Lib.*, 130; Strabo, XVII: 3: 14.
15. Appian, loc. cit.
16. Strabo, XVII: 3: 15.

17. Beloch, *Bevölkerung der griechisch-römischen Welt*, 467.
18. Jenkins, 25.
19. Gsell, IV: 113.
20. Harden, 144.
21. E. Bouchier-Colozier, *Cahiers du Byrsa*, III, 1953, 11 ff.
22. See above, 43.
23. Diod. Sic., XIII: 81.
24. Gsell, III: 7.
25. Harden, 160.
26. See below, 234.
27. See below, 226.
28. Seltman, *Greek Coins*, 249.
29. e.g. C.A.H., VII: 665–6, 689; Walbank, 118.
30. For differing modern views, see Beloch, III, 2: 107 ff .; Gsell, II: 193 ff.; G. Picard (1956), 39 ff.
31. W. Jaeger, *Aristotle* (Oxford Paperbacks ed.), 265 ff.
32. Strabo, I: 4.
33. e.g. Cicero, *De Rep.*, I: 3; Gsell, II: 233 ff.
34. Athenaeus, XIV: 27.
35. Aristotle, *Politics*, 1272b24–1273b24; Polyb., VI: 51–6; Isoc., *Nicocles*, 24.
36. cp. also the general admiration for the Spartan constitution.
37. Gsell, II: 184.
38. Herod., VII: 166.
39. Livy, XXX: 7, XXXIV: 6.
40. Diod. Laert., III: 82; Aristotle, *loc. cit.*; Diod. Sic., XIII: 43, XIV: 54; Nepos, *Hannibal*, 26.
41. Diod. Sic., XXV: 16; Polyb., III: 33.
42. Nepos, *Hannibal*, 26; see G. Picard, *Rev. Et. Lat.*, XLI, 1963, 269 ff.
43. Livy, XXXIII: 46; Nepos, *Hamilcar*, III: 2.
44. XIX: 2.
45. Aristotle, *Politics*, 1272b.
46. Aristotle, *Politics*, 1273a.
47. Aristotle, *Politics*, 1273a; Diod. Sic., XIII: 43, XIV: 47; Justin., XX: 5, XXI: 4; Gsell, II: 202 ff.
48. Livy, XXX: 16; Polyb., XV: 1, 6–8; X: 18.
49. *Politics*, 1273a.
50. Aristotle, *Politics*, 1272b.
51. See above, 125.
52. See below, 170.
53. Aristotle, *Politics*, 1273a; 1293b.
54. Plutarch, *Moralia*, 799d; Aristotle, *Politics*, 1273b, 1320b.
55. Aristotle, *Politics*, 1272b, better evidence than Diod. Sic., XX: 10.
56. See below, 224.
57. Harden, 82 ff.
58. Diod. Sic., XX: 14: 4; Dracontius, V: 148; Justin., XVIII: 6.
59. Harden, 87; G. Picard (1956), 34 and 41; G. and C. Picard, 60 ff.
60. Tertullian, *Apol.*, 9: 2; Frend, 79.
61. *Liber de promissionibus Dei*, III: 44.
62. G. and C. Picard, 72 ff.

63. Pomponius Mela, III: 46; Silius Italicus, III: 17 ff.; Strabo, III: 5: 5; Harden, 85 ff.
64. Polyb., VII: 9, 2–3. See this text for other deities.
65. 2 Kings 23: 10; Cintas, *Céramique*, 490; D. B. Harden, *Iraq*, IV, 1937, 59 ff.
66. G. and C. Picard, 260 ff.; R. Dussaud, *C.R.A.I.*, 1946, 371 ff.
67. Diod. Sic., XX: 14.
68. Livy, XXII: 57.
69. Gsell, I: 438; Justin., XIX: 1, 10–12.
70. Cintas, *Sousse*.
71. G. Halff, 'L'onomastique punique de Carthage', *Karthago*, XII, 163, 61 ff.
72. III: 23–7.
73. Gsell, IV: 396 ff.
74. Gsell, IV: 410 ff.
75. Gsell, IV: 442 ff.
76. G. Picard, 'Sacra Punica', *Karthago*, XIII, 1965, 7 ff.
77. Pliny, *N.H.*, XVIII: 22; Varro, I: 1, 10; Columella, I: 1, 13; Gsell, IV: 4 ff.
78. Iamblichus, *De Pythagorica Vita*, XXVII: 128, XXXVI: 267.
79. Diog. Laert., IV: 67; Cicero, *Tusc.*, III: 22, 54; Gsell, III: 405.
80. *Moralia*, 799D.

CHAPTER 7

1. In view of the substantial modern literature about the Punic Wars, and the nature of our surviving sources, references for the various incidents in the conflict are not given here. All the ancient authorities are listed in the *Cambridge Ancient History*, VII: 925. The basic source is Polybius, I: 13–64, who had good material at his disposal including some from the Carthaginian side in a work by the Greek of Agrigentum, Philinus; see Walbank, 26 ff. Livy survives only in epitome (16–19). Items from the annalistic tradition, often of inferior value, are to be found in isolated later writers, e.g. Diodorus Siculus, XXII–XXIV; Florus, I; Nepos, *Hamilcar*; Eutropius, II; Orosius, IV; Zonaras, VIII.
2. See especially A. N. Sherwin White, *The Roman Citizenship*, 1939.
3. Polyb., III: 22: 4–13.
4. Walbank, 344.
5. Polyb., III: 24: 1–16.
6. On Pyrrhus and the earlier Greek, venture in Italy, see *C.A.H.*
7. Diod. Sic., XXI: 16, 18; Beloch, IV. 1541.
8. Diod. Sic., XXII: 7.
9. Diod. Sic., XXII: 8.
10. Polyb., III: 25: 1–9; Diod. Sic., XXIII: 7.
11. Justin., XVIII: 2, 11; Appian, *Samn.*, 11; Plutarch, *Pyrrhus*, 22.
12. Polyb., I: 7; Diod Sic., XXI: 18.
13. Plut., *Pyrrhus*, 24.
14. Polyb., III: 6–33; see Walbank, 305 ff.
15. Polyb., I: 7: 2 ff.
16. Polyb., I: 8–10; Diod. Sic., XXII: 13.
17. Jacoby, *F.G.H.*, II: D: 598.
18. Polyb., III: 26.
19. Livy, *Epit.*, XIV: cp. XXI: 10: 5–8; Dio Cassius, XLIII: 1.
20. IX: 43: 26.
21. Polyb., I: 7: 6–13; Livy, XXXI: 29–31.

22. Diod. Sic., XXIII, 14.
23. Polyb., I: 11, III: 26; Livy, *Epit.*, XVI; XXX: 31: 4.
24. *I.L.S.*, 65.
25. W. W. Tarn, *J.H.S.*, 1907, 52 ff.
26. Pauly-Wissowa, *R.E.*, s. v. Atilius, No. 51.

CHAPTER 8

1. Modern literature and ancient authorities on the subject of this chapter are even more voluminous than on the preceding one. Hence no attempt is made to provide detailed references to the Second Punic War. All sources are listed in the *Cambridge Ancient History*, VIII: 721, ff. The following are the most important. Polybius III is the best source up to the battle of Cannae; fragments of VII–XI, XIV–XV which survive are relevant. Our main source for the whole way is Livy, XXI–XXX, who used Polybius directly and also a number of later and inferior authors such as Valerius Antias. Further material from the annalistic tradition figures in, *inter alia*, Appian, *Libyca*; Nepos, *Hannibal*; Diodorus Siculus, XXV, XXVI; Justinus, XXIX; Eutropius, III; Orosius, IV; Zonaras, VIII, IX.
2. Polyb., I: 65–88; Diod. Sic., XXV.
3. E. S. G. Robinson, 'The Libyan Hoard (1952)', *Numismatic Chronicle*, XVI, 1956, 9 ff.
4. I: 88, III: 27–8; Livy, XXII: 54.
5. Polyb., III: 10.
6. Polyb., III, 8–9.
7. Appian, *Hisp.*, 5; Nepos, *Hannibal*, 2; Polyb., II: 1, 5.
8. Nepos, *Hamilcar*, III: 3; Livy, XXI: 2, 4.
9. Polyb., II: 1 on Hannibal in Spain.
10. Polyb., II: 1; Livy, XXI: 2. E. S. G. Robinson, 'Punic Coins of Spain' in *Essays in Roman Coinage Presented to Harold Mattingly*, Oxford, 1956.
11. Polyb., II: 13–36, III: 13–15; Diod. Sic., XXV: 10 ff.
12. Polyb., II: 13–14; Livy, XXI: 5. For bibliography and discussion of the preliminaries to the war, see Walbank, 167–72, 214–15, 310–24, 237–9, 331–6.
13. Polyb., III: 30.
14. Polyb., III: 15.
15. Polyb., III: 15; Livy, XXI: 10–11.
16. Polyb., III: 29–30; Appian, *Hisp.*, 7, *Lib.*, 6; Livy, XXI: 2; Zon., VIII: 21.
17. Polyb., III: 8–9; Diod. Sic., XXV: 12.
18. Polyb., III: 9; Livy, XXI: 1.
19. Polyb., III: 17, 20–1; Livy, XXI: 6–18.
20. On the various interpretations of Scipio's character in our authorities, see Scullard, 2–31.
21. Walsh, 156.
22. See plate. G. Picard, 'Le problème du portrait ·d'Hannibal', *Karthago*, XII, 1963, 29 ff.

CHAPTER 9

1. Polybius was present in the company of Scipio Aemilianus at the destruction of Carthage, and also obtained information from other participants. Only fragments of his account survive, but it was the source of Appian's fairly full account

(*Libyca*), and of most others, including that of Livy, which now survive only as epitomes.

2. Livy, XXXIII: 45 ff.; Nepos, *Hannibal*; Justin., XXXI: 2.
3. Livy, XXXIV: 60; Justin., XXXI: 3.
4. *C.A.H.*, VIII: 282.
5. Livy, XXXVI: 4, 7.
6. Gsell, III: 310 ff.; Walsh, 149–155.
7. Livy, XLII: 29.
8. Livy, XXXIV: 62.
9. Walsh, 158. This scholar is in general inclined to minimize the ambitions of Masinissa.
10. Livy, XL: 17 and 34.
11. Livy, XLI: 22; XLII: 23, 24; XLIII: 3.
12. Polybius, XXXI: 21; Appian, *Lib.*, 68.
13. Appian, *Lib.*, 68.
14. Livy, XLVIII; Zon., IX: 26.
15. Plut., *Cato*, 27 ff.
16. The view taken here is substantially that of F. E. Adcock, *Cambridge Historical Journal*, VIII, 1946; for others, see Gsell, III: 329 ff.
17. Appian, *Lib.*, 70 ff.; Polyb., XXXVI: 16; Livy, XLVIII.
18. Appian, *Lib.*, 74.
19. Appian, *Lib.*, loc. cit.; 80 and 93; Polyb., XXXVI: 3 f.
20. Appian, *Lib.*, 93 ff.
21. Pliny, *N.H.*, XVIII: 22.
22. Appian, *Lib.*, 136; Plut., *C. Gracchus*, 10 ff.
23. Frend, 37.
24. In the reign of Vespasian.
25. Migne, *P.L.* XXXV: 2096; cp. Saumagne, *Karthago*, IV, 1953, 169 ff.
26. *Lib.*, 132.

Index